AMERICAN CONGO

AMERICAN CONGO

The African American
Freedom Struggle in the Delta

Nan Elizabeth Woodruff

HARVARD UNIVERSITY PRESS

Cambridge, Massachusetts, and London, England | 2003

For Irene Silverblatt

Library of Congress Cataloging-in-Publication Data

Woodruff, Nan Elizabeth, 1949–
    American Congo : the African American freedom struggle in the Delta /
Nan Elizabeth Woodruff.
        p. cm.
    Includes bibliographical references and index.
    ISBN 0-674-01047-7
    1. African Americans—Civil rights—Mississippi—Delta (Region)—
History—20th century.   2. African Americans—Civil rights—Arkansas—
Arkansas Delta—History—20th century.   3. Sharecroppers—Mississippi—
Delta (Region)—Social conditions—20th century.   4. Sharecroppers—
Arkansas—Arkansas Delta—Social conditions—20th century.   5. Civil
rights movements—Mississippi—Delta (Region)—History—20th century.
6. Civil rights movements—Arkansas—Arkansas Delta—History—20th
century.   7. Plantation life—Mississippi—Delta (Region)—History—20th
century.   8. Plantation life—Arkansas—Arkansas Delta—History—20th
century.   9. Delta (Miss. : Region)—Race relations.   10. Arkansas
Delta (Ark.)—Race relations.   I. Title.

F347.M6W667 2003
976.2'400496073—dc21   2002191341

Contents

Introduction

In 1921, freedom fighter William Pickens, a native Arkansan, described the Mississippi River Valley as the "American Congo." As field secretary for the National Association for the Advancement of Colored People, Pickens and his organization had recently investigated in the region numerous lynchings, cases of coerced labor, and a major massacre that had followed World War I. It is not surprising that he chose the Congo as his metaphor for the Arkansas and Mississippi Delta. Planters in the region had forged an "alluvial empire" in the early twentieth century that, like Belgian King Leopold II's African Congo in the late nineteenth and early twentieth centuries, wore the face of science and progressivism, yet was underwritten by labor conditions that were anything but progressive. King Leopold used the rhetoric of uplift and benevolence to mask his relentless search for ivory and rubber in the Congo. Leopold's men burned villages and their inhabitants, raped the women, cut off the hands and heads of thousands of Congolese, and worked them in chain gains until they dropped from hunger and exhaustion. The horrors of Leopold's Congo were so great that leading African Americans in the late nineteenth and early twentieth centuries demanded an end to such practices. The historian George Washington Williams and the leading black political figure of the day, Booker T. Washington, joined with leaders of the Black Baptist Church to lobby President Theodore Roosevelt on behalf of the Congolese people.[1]

Atlantic world slavery had been abolished in the late nineteenth century, but all of the western powers engaged, in the following century, in various forms of coerced labor as they sought to extract the natural riches from their colonies. Delta planters were no different in their corner of the world. They may not have cut off the heads and hands of their African American workers, but they engaged in peonage, murder, theft, and other

1

forms of terror to retain their labor. Some of the meanest corners of the "heart of darkness" were found in the Delta during the first half of the twentieth century. And yet the imperialism and the human carnage it wrought did not go unchallenged by those whose lives were being transformed or destroyed. Slaves, peasants, plantation workers, and those who labored in other extractive industries, such as mining, timber, and rubber, fought their oppression in numerous ways, seeking to protect their land and families against the intrusion of capitalism and white racism.[2]

The Delta plantation economy emerged when U.S. and European capitalists were establishing themselves throughout the world. On some level, the Delta was part of this larger expansion of capitalism in the late nineteenth and early twentieth centuries as U.S. capitalists joined with the Dutch, British, and French in diversifying their holdings, looking for new markets and sources for raw materials in the colonial world.[3] Within the context of United States and southern history, the Delta represented a "New South" plantation economy and society that grew out of the claiming and clearing of the vast swamp lands of the Mississippi River. Lumbermen from the Northeast, Midwest, and England invaded these rich forests in the late nineteenth and early twentieth centuries, clearing the land and paving the way for what Harold Woodman has called the rise of the "business plantations." Delta plantations in the twentieth century were organized along corporate lines and they operated according to the principles of scientific management, which required the close supervision of a routinized and disciplined labor force—in this case, African American sharecroppers and day laborers.[4]

Promoters of the region sold the Delta as an "alluvial empire" of untold riches, a land of progressive farmers who had left behind the Old South past of slavery, racism, ignorance, poverty, and defeat. A wealthy planter class soon emerged in the Delta, many of whose members came from other parts of the country and just as many others claiming southern roots. Like imperialists at the time, the progressive empire these planters created rested on the sweat and labor of a largely "coloured" labor force. America had its Congo.[5]

Underneath the declared progressivism of the new Delta economy lay a labor system underwritten by segregation and disfranchisement that kept black people poor and stripped of the basic civil and human rights accorded to other Americans in the twentieth century. A web of peonage and vagrancy laws sent to convict labor camps on the New South plantations untold numbers of men, women, and children—many of whom disappeared forever, while others managed to survive the harsh conditions and eventually return to their families. County sheriffs, judges, and justices of the peace, often landowners themselves, worked with planters to ensure that no idle black people existed.[6]

Those who escaped the labor camps and worked as sharecroppers found a world completely defined by the planters' need for cheap labor. As sharecroppers, they sold their labor for wages paid in the form of a portion of the cotton crop. They brought only their labor to the contract, receiving from the landlord their housing, food, clothing, tools of production, livestock, seed, and feed—all charged to a credit system that kept them in debt. Planters also built the schools and churches of their workers, often paying the preachers and the teachers, and they controlled the mail, seeking to supervise what croppers read and with whom they corresponded.[7]

In the alluvial empire, planters controlled all levels of government: federal, state, and local. This modern empire was characterized by a polity that defined citizenship in terms of race and that drew a weak distinction between the functions of the various levels of government and those of civil society.[8] What is worse, this was not all a matter of local or regional state jurisdiction—legal disfranchisement of black people was sanctioned by the U.S. Supreme Court, forcing African Americans to enter into an unequal bargain with employers for whatever social space they could obtain in civil society. In the political arena, planters controlled the political offices that had a direct bearing on black peoples' interests. Wherever African Americans turned, they encountered a world circumscribed by constables and justices of the peace who harassed them by arbitrarily enforcing vagrancy laws, by sheriffs who either ignored or engaged in peonage, by planters who had the power to protect their workers from arrests or to send them to the state penitentiary, and, as if that were not enough, by white mobs who resorted to the extralegal terror of lynching to remind them of the costs involved in defying planter authority. Planters may not have posted the heads of their laborers atop spikes in front of their dwellings as did Leopold's soldiers in the Congo, but they did rape, burn, and torture them. Some even took photographs of the lynchings and sent them as postcards to their friends and relatives, and others cut off their victim's remaining parts and saved them as souvenirs, to be passed down as family relics along with the silver or Confederate memorabilia.[9]

As horrible as this world seemed, black people found ways of fighting back. At times they did so as individuals; in other instances, their struggle broke out into collective forms of challenge to planter dominance. Black people, as they had since slavery and emancipation, employed multiple strategies to survive the plantation system and to secure justice and safety within it. And they created a world separate from the planters that drew from their own political and cultural traditions rooted in slavery and emancipation, in their families, communities, churches, and lodges. Freedom fighters in the post–World War II civil rights movement, like Mrs. Carrie Dilworth and Mrs. Fannie Lou Hamer, were born into a generation of early twentieth-century black communities one generation removed from slavery, and were raised in an egalitarian tradition that stressed the importance of community and an expansive notion of family, of a "profoundly democratic tradition holding that every man and woman, merely by virtue of being that, is entitled to some regard."[10]

The black families who moved into the new lands of the Arkansas and Mississippi Delta at the turn of the century were the immediate descendants of slaves, if not ex-slaves themselves, and thus carried with them remembrances of not only the battles fought during slavery, but also the hopes and disappointments of emancipation and the years that followed the end of Reconstruction. They struggled in the post–Civil War years to retain their hard-won rights of citizenship rooted in the Thirteenth, Fourteenth, and Fifteenth Amendments. Linked to the political rights entailed in citizenship was the economic right to the fruits of one's own labor. Free labor for African Americans, as it emerged after Reconstruction, was free in the classical liberal sense of being able to work for wages, even to own property. Yet in practice, it was more coercive than free. Divorced from the political rights and power embedded in citizenship, free labor was empty of meaning.[11] Indeed, during the 1890s and the early twentieth century legal measures were introduced to divorce voting from citizenship.

The freedom struggle during the period prior to 1945 was shaped by black peoples' lack of full citizenship. At times they fought for issues more directly related to their daily lives; at other times, given the right circumstances, their daily confrontations broke out into broader demands that specifically addressed citizenship in both its political and economic forms. But it is hard to imagine that even in their efforts to achieve justice on the plantation, black people did not also see their actions as part of a more expansive struggle for the citizenship denied them in the late nineteenth and twentieth centuries. Their struggles at times broke out into armed and organized rebellion in the form of labor unions, but most of the time their battles were launched on a daily and more personal basis in the form of confrontations with plantation managers, commissary operators, cotton weighers, and local law officers over issues of daily living—such as getting a just return on a cotton crop, having the right to move freely around the community, protecting oneself and family from physical harm and rape, securing the privacy of one's home, ensuring the right to raise and keep livestock, protecting one's property (both land and material possessions) from theft, and securing a decent education for one's children. These challenges to planter authority mirrored those in extractive industries and of rural workers throughout the colonial world at this time.

The freedom struggle in the Delta during the first fifty years of the twentieth century is linked to the vast changes wrought by two world wars and a great depression. Black people, drawing from their daily confrontations over labor conditions and the plantation system, used these national crises to push their demands for justice and citizenship. Their demands were not always overtly shaped in the discourse of citizenship, though their actions indicated they knew that their battle encompassed both the economic and political rights embedded in a democratic conception of citizenship—the rights to receive a just return on one's labor, to live free from terror, to own property, to have equal access to the legal system and a lawyer, to move, and to vote. In this conception, citizenship applied not only to men, but also to women and the family. The wars empowered black men and women, and both fought for their collective rights.[12]

Like their counterparts in other countries, the contest embraced far more than feigning illness, dragging of feet, stealing crops and food, burning down buildings, and singing the blues. Their "transcripts," as one scholar has called such actions, were rarely hidden.[13] Black people knew what their issues were—and what they were up against—and acted accordingly. The number of planters and field riders, commissary managers, and gin weighers (not to mention a few county sheriffs and their deputies) who were killed suggest that black people were engaged in more than "playing possum." As they had since emancipation, both men and women carried guns and practiced armed self-defense. If, following emancipation, freedpeople had won "nothing but freedom," they fought to regain it in the twentieth century.[14]

The post–World War II civil rights movement cannot be understood outside of the context of these earlier battles for freedom. Studies of the movement in the Mississippi Delta have placed its locus in the local communities, where men and women drew from their own institutions and understanding of justice and citizenship to forge a movement that included the Student Non-Violent Coordinating Committee and the Mississippi Freedom Democratic Party. Freedom fighters like Mrs. Fannie Lou Hamer, Mrs. Unita Blackwell, Mrs. Ida Mae Lawrence, and Mrs. Victoria Earle Gray in Mississippi, Mrs. Carrie Dilworth in Arkansas, and many others, mobilized not simply to secure their civil rights, but also to fight the injustices of the plantation world they lived in. In doing so, they drew from a long tradition of rural protest in the Delta.[15] From the perspective of the twenty-first century, we might say that Delta black people have been engaged in a human rights campaign for an entire century, if not longer—a campaign that continues to this day.

While the people themselves did not always describe their conflicts in terms of securing citizenship, there were moments, usually in times of national crises, when the daily confrontations over labor and its surplus shifted to include the broader questions of segregation and the franchise. Black people had learned since the end of Reconstruction that what the federal government gave with one hand, it could take with another. And they knew from those experiences that citizenship entailed a vigilance that translated not simply into efforts to secure the vote and equal accommodations, but also into daily confrontations with the plantation system that defined the contours of their social and economic world.

The story of the rise of the alluvial empire has not been told; neither the extent of physical and political deprivation that black people endured, nor their valiant efforts to combat an oppressive system, have been articulated. African American struggles for justice and freedom in the twentieth-century Delta took place in a century of crisis in which two world wars and a great depression gave birth to or enhanced existing political organizations and labor unions, and raised the issue of citizenship. World War II accelerated the freedom struggle as it unleashed forces at home and abroad that made segregation and disfranchisement unacceptable. The shifting political terrain of the postwar years, combined with technological changes in the plantation South, rendered sharecropping obsolete. Together, these transformations boosted long-standing efforts by Delta black people to secure their freedom. African Americans then joined with the liberation struggles all over the world to secure their rights and justice in American society. Instead of claiming independence, like colonial societies in the declining imperial world, African Americans, as they had since the end of slavery, looked to the federal government as the guarantor of their rights long ago provided in the Constitution. And they knew from past experience that freedom is never a given. Nor is it handed down by politicians from the highest levels of government. Freedom has been wrested from the federal government through the efforts of those who have witnessed, over generations, the nation's refusal to protect basic human rights for all of its people. That struggle is not over.

1 | The Forging of the Alluvial Empire

The industrial revolution came to the Arkansas and Mississippi Delta countryside only in the early twentieth century. As the "Age of Capital," the heavier phase of the economic transformation, neared its late-nineteenth-century end in the core centers of U.S. industrial capitalism, a sector based on extractive industries shifted southward to a region extending from the boot heel of southeastern Missouri to the Gulf of Mexico. Having exhausted the great stands of trees in the Northeast and Midwest, lumbermen headed South to continue reaping the riches of the forests. They brought to the countryside an industrial revolution, for as they followed the newly built railroads, cleared the lands of timber, and drained the vast swamplands, these lumbermen erected large lumber mills and wood products factories, paving the way for the emergence of large-scale capitalist agriculture that in the twentieth-century United States was matched only by California. The Delta became a periphery of Midwestern, Eastern, and foreign capital, with Memphis as the regional core linked to the metropolitan centers of New York, Chicago, and London. First Mississippi, and then Arkansas, were overrun by hardwood lumbermen who also went into Missouri, western Tennessee, and Louisiana. By the early twentieth century, Memphis had become the center of the world's hardwood production, with Arkansas as its largest producer. The Delta thus mirrored the expansion of western capital into the colonial world at this time, as the imperial powers launched the wealth gained from the industrial revolution into their colonies in Africa, Asia, and Latin America, creating export economies based on extractive industries and agricultural products—and employing various forms of coerced labor to produce the crops and to work in the mines and mills.[1]

Invoking the metaphor of the imperial age in which they lived, entrepreneurs idealized the region as a self-described alluvial empire—a frontier of opportunity but hardly a backward area. It contrasted with the old, flagging cotton economy of the southeastern seaboard with its sharecropping, racism, and resulting overproduction, low cotton prices, and extreme poverty. The alluvial empire, in the entrepreneurs' view, was inhabited by progressive farmers who practiced diversified crop and livestock

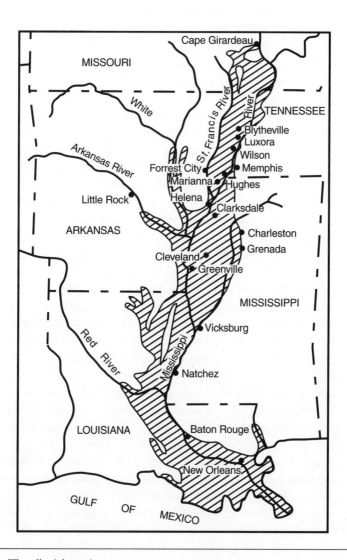

Fig. 1. The alluvial empire

production, employing only the finest varieties of seed and breeds of hogs and cattle. They also claimed that the region contained the latest of modern conveniences: up-to-date homes with electricity and running water; fine schools for the education of children; paved roads on which to drive their new automobiles; and opera houses that provided them with cultural opportunities no different from the rest of the country. This was yet another New South, one advancing beyond the patterns of the Birmingham coal fields and the textile towns of the Carolina Piedmont.[2]

The forging of this "Cotton Kingdom of the New South" occurred along the banks of the Mississippi River and its tributaries as they flowed from southeastern Missouri through Memphis, Tennessee, and down to Vicksburg, Mississippi, and Chicot County, Arkansas. The rich alluvial lands then extended inland for around one hundred miles.[3] Development of the region began first in the Yazoo-Mississippi River Basin following the Civil War. With more than 4 million acres of undeveloped land, the Yazoo Basin offered a major attraction for Gilded Age capital. During the 1880s the federal government worked to establish flood control of the Mississippi River, and an east-west railroad linking the Delta to the eastern seaboard was completed. More importantly, the Illinois Central Railroad purchased the Louisville, New Orleans, and Texas railroad that linked the region with Chicago and New Orleans. Lumbermen came to the Arkansas Delta in the early twentieth century after a massive drainage project—another major technological feat—had begun in the St. Francis River Valley. The growing number of levees and drainage projects allowed for a rapid development of the Delta in the first decades of the twentieth century as lumber companies cleared the land and plantation farming expanded.[4]

The men who carved out an empire from the swamplands rarely claimed an Old South lineage. According to the *Southern Lumberman,* a major trade journal for the Delta timber industry, most of the owners of the lumber mills in Memphis, Arkansas, and Mississippi came from the Midwest, with Indiana supplying the most, followed by Michigan, Ohio, Wisconsin, and Illinois. Rhode Island and Massachusetts also sent many people. Only three of the companies in Memphis were owned by native Tennesseans. Hardwood investors like J. F. McIntyre purchased lands in Mississippi and then established mills in Arkansas. In 1895 McIntyre came from Troy, Indiana, where he had been a lumberman since 1884, to Bigbee, Mississippi, to build a sawmill for a northern company. By 1905, he owned the Memphis Veneer and Lumber Company and in 1910, he opened operations in Pine Bluff, Arkansas, as well. He co-owned another mill and fifteen thousand acres of land in five other counties with an investor from Missouri and Kentucky.[5]

Southern lumbermen and landowners mixed with outside businessmen to form a large and powerful planter class. Some Delta natives who started their own companies to harvest the timber later became large plantation owners. William Alexander Percy, for instance, formed a lumber company with several other partners in Washington County, while J. F. and S. L. Dodd had sawmills in Drew, Doddsville, and Ruleville, all in Mississippi.[6] Few matched the success of Robert E. Lee Wilson in Mississippi County, Arkansas. Born in 1865, Wilson was orphaned as a child. In 1880 he had acquired only two or three years of education and worked as a field hand near Bassett while farming the small homestead his father had left him. He purchased a sawmill and began cutting timber and acquiring land, forming the Lee Wilson Company in 1886.[7]

Wilson's experiences in the early years of clearing the forests attest to the difficulties of the tasks and to how these early loggers had to create additional business and technology to complete them. The logging business led him to build railroads in order to haul the logs out of the woods, placing the tracks on logs that he cut as he cleared the forests and allowing the tracks to float in the water. Teams of mules dragged logs to the train, where a steam loader placed the logs up on the car. As the train moved along out of the forests, the tracks sank beneath the water, prohibiting the engineer from seeing the tracks for at least two hundred feet ahead. The logs were taken to the company's main headquarters at Wilson, where they were cut into timber. Since the town of Wilson was close to the Mississippi River, Wilson built a railroad straight to the banks and shipped his timber by steamboat.[8]

Swamplands posed additional obstacles to overcome. Levees in Mississippi County were not as extensive in the late nineteenth century; most of them were only twelve feet high. Fighting the overflows challenged many an aspiring entrepreneur. As Wilson's son recalled, "Every time the levee would break, it would break him. The river would come up and break the levee. There were bad breaks in 1912 and 1913 on the same day, April the tenth or eleventh . . . It scattered his lumber all over Mississippi County. By the time he got that all picked up and gathered together, he just started all over again." Wilson soon built an empire of 65,000 acres. Unlike owners of the larger lumber companies, he realized the value of the rich land that lay beneath the woods. Most people did not know the value of their lands, and when selling the timber rights to Wilson, simply deeded their land over as well. By the 1920s, Wilson had developed one of the largest plantations in the Delta—indeed, the world.[9]

Few attained the wealth and power of Wilson, yet the Delta hardwoods offered hope to people from all walks of life. Dillie Flagg Veach's grandfather had fought in the Civil War with Union troops that went into Arkansas. Her grandfather liked the people and the rich soil, and when he returned to Ohio, he told his son of the opportunities existing in the postwar South. Veach recalled leaving Cincinnati with her father and family and coming to Memphis on a steamboat. Her family made its way through the thick forests of Mississippi County to a place called Lost Cane where they bought land for twenty-five dollars an acre and hired sharecroppers to clear it.[10]

Some men, like M. C. Pearson's uncle, made their living by contracting to clear timber on other people's land. "We had axes, sludges, wedges, saws and Keiser blades. The man maybe have five acres . . . to clean up. He would pay a dollar or maybe 75 cents an acre." Pearson and his men cut the undergrowth first, then the trees. "We'd trim these trees up, cut about so long, and then we had sticks—just an ordinary stick. We'd roll this log upon these two sticks and take four men, one on each side and tote that log to a pile. We started to pile the logs up in piles. Then we put brushes on top of the pile" and burn them. "Then whenever you get it all cleared up then we have something like what you call a new ground plow. We had a wheel back here behind this here. Whenever the colter get there if the root wasn't too big it'd cut that root, that plow go right on through the root." Others, like Lee Wilson, had so many stumps in their fields that they simply planted around them each time.[11]

The expanding lumber industry in the Arkansas and Mississippi Delta offered possibilities for black farmers as well. The life of Scott Bond in Madison, Arkansas, illustrated the possibilities that many black people found in the Delta following the Civil War. Bond, born a slave, rented the 2,200-acre plantation of a relative of his former master who lived in Tennessee. The owner furnished credit for Bond to buy mules, corn, and tools for the St. Francis County farm. According to Bond, "There were all sorts of people living on the Allen farm. Some half-breed Indians, some few white families and some low, degraded colored people. The whites were no better than the others." He made a profit of $2,500 in his first year. Living in the "big house," forty-two miles from the Mississippi River and with no levees, Bond faced constant overflows that required his moving the workers and livestock to higher ground on Crowley's Ridge. He had rented the farm for eleven years, paying a rent of $16,000, when he decided to buy his own farm. He purchased 320 acres, located in Madison on the St. Francis River, for two dollars an acre. When the Allen family failed to find a manager as good as Bond, they offered to sell him their farm in partnership with a white man. Bond accepted and supervised the place for four years, then sold his interests to the partner. With that money he purchased seven other farms.

Bond became a prosperous planter and merchant with his own gins, merchandise stores that catered to black and white customers, brick kilns, brick homes for his sharecroppers, 445 head of cattle, a concrete plant with its own cable to load the railroad cars, and eight hundred people who lived and worked on his farm. During the late nineteenth century when cotton brought only five cents a pound, he grew ten thousand bushels of potatoes that he sold in Pittsburgh and Chicago for $1.25 each. When cotton prices rose again prior to World War I, Bond shifted back to cotton. In 1914, cotton prices fell again and he diversified his crops and planted wheat, rye, alfalfa, oats, and began to accumulate hogs and cattle. During the years before World War I, Bond sent all of his seven children to college and bought another farm each year.[12]

Like other Delta planters, Bond was engaged in the lumber business. He started with nine dugout canoes and nine men whom he paid $2.50 a day. One man, "Sambo," was paid $3.50 to lead the others because of his knowledge in felling trees. Sambo ordered all of the men to cut ten of the largest trees and then to saw them off at sixty to seventy feet. Each man worked one hundred yards apart to prevent accidents. As they finished sawing the logs, water rushed into the brake and allowed them to float the timber. Men spliced and cribbed the logs and toggled them together. At night, the men slept on a raft, awakening the following morning to water that had risen five feet, covering the stumps and allowing them to float the logs. Each man mounted a log and used his body to steer it into the stream. Bond and his men cut 248,000 feet in eleven days, until the water rose too high for them to work any longer. Over the years, Bond continued cutting his own timber in the swamps, building his own sawmill and selling the lumber directly to buyers, bypassing the middlemen.[13]

Portraying the Delta as a frontier of economic opportunity for all, pioneer tales like those of Veach, Wilson, and Bond tell only part of the story. As recent scholars writing on the lumber industry in East Texas and on the Yazoo Delta in the post–Civil War years have shown, woodsmen, homesteaders, lumber workers, large planters, lumber companies, and agents of the various states and the federal government all initially battled with each other over legal rights to the land. In the end, however, the large companies and plantations drove out the smaller woodsmen and farmers.[14]

Struggles over land ownership and titles existed in Arkansas as well. For example, in Drew, Bradley, and Union counties, farmers combined lumbering with their agricultural work, but lacked capital to develop the timber industry themselves. Eventually, outside companies came in and depleted the lumber. Local farmers did not necessarily welcome the Yankee intruders, as illustrated in 1902, when a Connecticut-owned lumber company sued squatters for cutting timber on their holdings in these counties, suggesting that corporate holdings undercut the opportunities of the smaller woodsmen and farmers. In nearby Poinsett County, a black squatter was arrested for establishing a homestead farm on the properties of the giant Chicago Mill and Lumber Company. In Mississippi, the State Land Commission prosecuted several lumbermen in Issaquena County for cutting timber off of state lands and selling it to lumber companies.[15]

One of the most contested regions centered in northeastern Arkansas, where large landowners like Lee Wilson prevailed in a struggle with the St. Francis Levee Drainage District over titles to the "sunken lands" created by the New Madrid earthquake in 1811–1812. In 1893, the State of Arkansas ceded all of the lands granted by the federal government in the St. Francis River Valley to the St. Francis Levee Board, which sold much of it to large timber companies for a low price, securing money to then drain and ditch the region for plantation farming. In the early twentieth century, ownership of the sunken lands was contested by the federal government, the State of Arkansas, planters, lumber companies, and homesteaders. In 1908, the Department of the Interior opened the lands to homesteaders, unleashing a scramble for land by black and white small farmers hoping to find a new start. Still, the contest over the lands raged, until a series of court decisions and intervention by politicians on the local and national levels privileged the large landowners over the homesteaders. The small farmers fought back, forming an all-white homesteaders' union in 1915 in Poinsett County to represent the interests and claims of the small farmers. Many white farmers blamed black people for getting much of the land, thus explaining why the union excluded black members. Statistics did not support the racist claims regarding land ownership, however. Landless white men, known as whitecappers, also blamed black people for stealing the land, and violently drove many black producers out of the region. Nevertheless, a combination of drainage taxes, planter controlled drainage boards, and favorable legislation secured the land for plantation farming. By the 1920s, homesteads had given way to large-scale production.[16]

The Arkansas and Mississippi Delta saw the emergence, sometimes overnight, of large lumber companies that built towns and recruited workers to live and work in them. Some towns were temporary, as companies cut the timber and moved on, while others became permanent over time. In Leflore County, Mississippi, W. J. Cude purchased seven thousand acres and built a mill where workers flocked in so swiftly that they lived in tents. Not only did companies harvest the timber, but they also manufactured wood products, building mills and plants to manufacture staves and shingles. For example, businessmen from Fort Worth and Memphis organized the Choctaw and Shingle Company in 1907 and set up operations across the river from Memphis in Hubert, Arkansas, where the company built a mill that cost $100,000 and produced 300,000 cypress shingles daily. (Red Cypress, the most precious of hardwoods, was used in making wine presses, tables, and musical instruments.) Logging equipment consisted of twenty-four Davenport locomotives, with Russell logging cars and a Russell skidder, the steam-operated machine used to pull the trees from the woods to the railroad spurs. The company bragged that its town had emerged within one year and had a hotel, commissary, and dwellings for the one hundred male workers and their families. Although the brochure did not specify whether the workers were African American, white, or both, the photographs included in the promotion showed mostly black workers.[17]

Mill towns in Arkansas and Mississippi attracted a work force of both black and white workers, mostly single, some married, but always segregated. Segregation of accommodations flowed naturally from a work force divided along racial lines. Steven Reich, in the only significant study to date on southern lumber workers, described the job segregation in the industry, with black workers employed in the lower-paying unskilled jobs, and skilled positions reserved for white workers.[18] Some mills, like the Ayer-Lord Tie Company creosoting plant in Argenta, Arkansas, built a town with a hotel, homes, and a boarding house, supplying all with electricity. They principally used single black men for this task, but a description that black workers lived "separately in well built frame houses" suggests that married black men also worked there. (Single men lived in boarding houses run by widows or the wives of lumber or railroad workers, while families lived in company houses.)[19] The frontier quality of the industry and its boom towns may have created more opportunity than usual for workers, but it did not mean less rigid segregation than in the rest of the South.

Nor did the frontier smooth over all differences between the laborers. In some instances, white workers violently opposed the hiring of black people. In Anderson Spur—near Jonesboro in northeastern Arkansas—white workers demanded in 1913 that the Hinds Lumber Company fire all black laborers. The mill at first had hired only white workers, but when they proved unsatisfactory had turned to African Americans. According to the mill's manager, the white workers had been "trifling" in their work. The *Southern Lumberman* observed that the white people in Anderson Spur had always opposed black people, making it one of the few Arkansas mill towns where they were not welcome as laborers.[20]

Economic benefits were mixed for workers in the first two decades of the twentieth century, when the timber industry and the emerging plantation economy coexisted. On the one hand, both industries competed for the same labor supply, which led to higher wages, especially when cotton brought a good price. On the other hand, the nature of the industries often proved detrimental for workers. Timber and cotton were subject to a cyclical economy: overproduction and low wages were followed by underproduction and high wages, which created a boom-and-bust situation for workers that could lead to seasonal unemployment. In down times, workers relied even more on the company town and store. In 1907 lumber mills in Arkansas, Missouri, and Louisiana shut down for lack of labor, cash, and railroad cars as well as because of competition from a good cotton crop that year. Mill owners allowed workers to remain in their houses while the railroad car shortage and financial depression prevailed, allocating them food and clothing from the commissary in return for their labor. The problem for laborers came when wages were lower than their living costs. The company benefited from gaining work without paying cash wages, but the workers fell further into debt to the company store.[21]

By 1905 Memphis claimed to be the largest hardwood producing center in the world, with five hundred mills operating within a radius of 150 miles, and one thousand within a 200-mile radius. The city received an estimated 75 million feet by river and 50 million feet by rail each year, selling for $8 million. Nearly 45,000 cars of logs passed through the city annually. In Arkansas, more than half of the state's capital was invested in the lumber industry, employing 36,662 people in 1909—more employees than any other industry. The total number of woodworking establishments in Arkansas—including the cooperage, furniture, turning, and carving industries—was 1,750. By 1919, Arkansas was employing 20,000 people in lumber, which remained the leading industry in the state.[22]

The rapid growth of the lumber industry in the Delta spawned prosperous towns that matched those in other parts of the nation. In Mississippi County, Arkansas, the county seat, Osceola, grew from a small village founded in 1840 to a town of more than 2,500 people in 1902. It boasted one of the most modern opera houses in the South; electric lights; a water works; cotton seed oil, planing, and shingle mills; two ice plants and a bottle works; a wagon and buggy manufacturer; a cotton compress; two banks; machine shops; cotton gins; and an agricultural implement factory. At least fifty houses had been erected in the past twelve months, mostly made of brick. Osceola, located on both the Mississippi River and on the St. Louis and San Francisco Railroad, was only two hours by rail from Memphis, eight from St. Louis, and fifteen from Chicago, linking the rising Delta bourgeoisie to their friends and kin in more cosmopolitan places.[23]

By World War I, the lumber companies had cleared a significant portion of the Delta hardwoods, leaving behind devastation that recalled Sherman's March to the Sea. Smoking stumps and flooded swamps dotted the Delta landscape. Lumber companies pursued a slash and burn policy as they cut the timber and then moved on to newer lands southward, making their way to the Gulf Coast.

Because the lumber companies owned much of these lands, they faced the problem of dispensing with them profitably. In 1916, Delta lumbermen formed the Southern Alluvial Land Association in Memphis to promote the selling and developing of the cut-over lands along the Mississippi River from Cape Girardeau to the end of the hardwood belt in Mississippi and Louisiana. John W. McClure, a lumberman from Memphis, and A. C. Lange, the director of the lands belonging to the giant Chicago Mill and Lumber Company in Blytheville, Arkansas, served as the first president and vice president. McClure aimed to advertise the Delta to respectable farmers capable of turning the land into fine plantations. Many northern banks and corporations, he argued, had entered the region to compete with local farm banks in offering low-interest loans. Above all, McClure saw the association as countering the misinformation about the Delta as an unhealthy place to live because of the heat and bad water, a lack of roads and schools, and the supposed backward people who inhabited the area.[24]

McClure insisted that the founders of the organization "had a broader vision than their own individual needs," aiming to build a new leadership in the alluvial region, that would unite all of the forces within the Delta into "one great co-operative effort for the growth and development of this new empire." Within a year, the association's membership read like a who's who of Delta landowners, bankers, merchants, railroads, and local civic organizations. McClure's efforts received a boost from World War I and the increasing demand for food production.[25]

The selling of the area during the war years differed dramatically from the earlier attempts of the railroads to promote Delta lands. In 1910 the Illinois Central Railroad marketed the Yazoo Delta as a "reincarnation" of the antebellum South. "Nowhere in Mississippi," boasted the brochure, "have antebellum conditions of landholding been so nearly preserved as in the Delta," with its vast plantations where the "Negro is naturally gregarious in instinct, and is never so happy as when massed together in large numbers, as on the Delta plantation."[26] McClure's association, however, presented a different Delta, one composed of progressive farmers who used scientific methods of farming and who welcomed outsiders. *The Call of the Alluvial Empire,* a brochure the land association published in 1919, proclaimed the existence of "twenty million acres of super soil" that made up "the last richest great area of America's undeveloped corn land available for agriculture. It stretches across the Mississippi Valley from the river to the gently rolling hills of Arkansas, Tennessee, Mississippi and Louisiana, a broad expanse of Delta land more fertile than Egypt's far-famed Nile." The Delta represented "a New Eden in the heart of America," where thousands of men of "small means" from the North, East, and West heeded the clarion call of the alluvial empire, paying for farms in short periods of two to five years.[27]

Attempting to overcome the stereotype of the South as a region of disease, ignorance, and poverty, the Southern Alluvial Land Association trumpeted the "chain of titanic levees that have conquered the Mississippi River," the productive farms that had sprung up within a decade on cut-over lands, the "modern towns with comfortable homes, prosperous stores, churches and schools" that had "risen in an erstwhile deserted cross-trails"; and drainage programs that "robbed the mosquito of its lair and is driving malaria from the land." The people of these "thriving towns" were "progressive," as "indicated by their paved streets, modern sewer systems, electric lights and pure water systems." Mud roads were giving way to paved highways. In the Yazoo Delta alone, one county spent $2.5 million during World War I to build roads. The region also boasted an excellent school system with consolidated schools and forty-eight agricultural high schools.

The brochure promoted diversified agriculture, rather than the cotton plantation worked by black sharecroppers, as a way of appealing to grain and livestock farmers of the Midwest. Not only did Delta soil yield a bale of cotton per acre; it also produced thirty bushels of wheat, fifty bushels of oats, and seventy-five bushels of corn per acre. Alfalfa "grows luxuriantly, and yields four to seven cuttings per season." Livestock seemed to grow as large as the high Delta cotton—as illustrated in the brochure's featured pictures of gigantic hogs and cows, which recalled the eight-foot jack rabbits of which Texans often boasted.[28]

The alluvial empire promised quick profits to investors. A director of a large Memphis bank who invested in 1918 in cut-over lands in eastern Arkansas hired a gang of men to cut and burn the brush and stumps. In the fall he sold the cotton and seed for about $200 per acre. While cotton varieties in other parts of the South brought 30 cents, the alluvial cotton commanded 40 to 70 cents per pound. The rice districts also yielded great profits.[29]

A major component of the selling of the alluvial empire centered on dispelling the bad side of the southern stereotype while retaining the finer attributes of white southern people: their culture, manners, and ways of living. Countering the stereotype involved allaying northern fears that southerners resented them, stressing the common characteristics inherent in all Americans. The editor of the *Memphis Commercial Appeal*, C. P. J. Mooney, seeking to calm concerns over anti-Yankee sentiment, insisted that "Southern people are the same as other people." The "southern colonel," he insisted, "with a drooping mustache, long tail coat and string tie is seen only in picture shows, patent medicine shows and occasionally in congress." While he claimed that southerners were not "sui generis," he did think that their good and bad qualities were more accentuated than in the North. "Our people are just a little more emotional because they escape the gloom of long winters and enjoy a plentitude of sunshine. The burden of life is easy in the South . . . the rewards for labor are large."[30] Mooney countered the image of southerners as suspicious of outsiders, observing that the "Southern people are not clannish; neither are they provincial." Nor did the South have a caste system, he continued, for today "a man is measured for what he is. If he is the grandson of a president and is no account he cannot trade upon his lineage." Mooney described a southern social life rich in culture where "good breeding" was a necessary ingredient, yet without any vulgar "snobbishness."[31]

Invoking the history of the region, Mooney said that the southern people had suffered the effects of the Civil War for more than a generation.

"The scars of battle were on the face of the earth, as well as upon men and women. Fortunes were wrecked, families were destroyed and property was wasted. In the nature of things there was bitter resentment." The region had adopted the one crop system by default, but Mooney insisted that farmers now understood the necessity of diversity and applied scientific methods of agriculture. "Loyal to the best traditions of the South, the Southern man today is not sorrowing because of failure in great causes in the past, but seeks to make the South a place wherein there will be opportunity for education, for honest work and for high endeavor." A characteristic trait of southerners was their "application of commonsense to every problem he runs into," though they are "tenacious" of the right to hold and express an opinion. In spite of the lynchings that had swept the South and reports of peonage and convict labor, southerners realized, Mooney insisted, "that the progress of human society depends upon the recognition of supremacy of the laws." Nor did southerners question the supremacy of the nation. "Although his ancestors bore a mighty hand in attempting to dissolve the Union," wrote Mooney, "his dominant trait today is vigorous and earnest Americanism. The Southerner has the ample faith that the American flag stands for all that is best in government and in civilization."[32]

Anyone reading the publications of the Southern Alluvial Land Association imagined a region where people were friendly and welcoming, civilized and progressive, and completely white. Little was mentioned of the labor situation or of racial relations in the Delta, except to note briefly that such matters were not a concern. Yet in most of the photographs included in the brochures of the farming operations, black people were picking the cotton, feeding the hogs, and driving the wagons of cotton to the gins. Henry Grady, the Atlanta newspaper editor who had promoted the first New South campaign in the 1880s, probably smiled from his grave as he watched yet another attempt to sell the "New South" region to northern investors.

The Southern Alluvial Land Association's campaign to sell the South was but another leg of the region's postbellum journey toward a fuller integration into the national economy. The New South of the early twentieth century exhibited many features of the 1880s campaign, reflecting what C. Vann Woodward called the colonial nature of the southern economy. Delta leaders sold alluvial lands to outside capital, much as their forebears had sold the coal mines and steel mills of Alabama and Tennessee. Though many of the new investors came from regions outside of the

South, they soon followed the traditions of the native southerners who had long engaged in the business of extractive industries, operating as "junior partners" to the northeastern bourgeoisie.[33] They adopted forms of coerced labor—peonage and convict labor—and they cheated their labor force with as much acumen as any southern colonel. The Delta planters of the "New Plantation South" did reflect the progressive era of the early twentieth century in one way, however. They employed the methods of scientific management to produce a larger and more efficient cotton crop and, in the process, achieved a control over their labor force that would have been the envy of any planter twenty years earlier. Their "progressivism" merely strengthened an authority that drew not only from a southern tradition of racial and class rule, but also from a national government that condoned disfranchisement and segregation—and it was buttressed by an "enlightened" western colonial ideology that held people of color to be morally and racially inferior. Delta black people were in for some hard times.

The shift in the Yazoo Delta from an undeveloped timber region to a plantation economy in the early twentieth century closed the frontier of opportunity that many black woodsmen and aspiring landowners had achieved by the late nineteenth century, mirroring the experience of their counterparts in other parts of the colonial world. Following emancipation, many freedpeople purchased land in the Delta backcountry. In the 1870s and 1880s, they were joined by hundreds of African Americans who had migrated from the flagging cotton economy of the southeastern states to the labor hungry Yazoo Delta in search of better opportunity. Landowners, eager to find labor to clear the outlying acreage on their plantations and to increase their cotton production, rented land to black farmers for cash rents. Some renters turned the contracts to their further advantage by agreeing to make improvements on the land, or clear additional acreage, reducing the amount they paid for rent. Wealthier landlords paid additional cash for the cutting of cordwood and for building fences and making other repairs. Some renters even secured three year's free use of the land in return for clearing the acreage. Many renters, black and white, became part-time backwoodsmen, selling the trees they felled to lumber mills in Delta towns. Others used the income derived from their part-time lumbering operations to become full-time woodsmen, purchasing portable steam-driven sawmills and moving from plantation to plantation clearing land for cash.[34]

Still others, with the money earned from clearing land, lumber sales, and good cotton crops, became landowners. Indeed, by 1900 more than three-fourths had done so. According to one study, African Americans were from 55 to 80 percent of landowners in seven of the nine Delta counties. Overall, black farmers made up 66 percent of all Delta farm owners at the turn of the century.[35]

During the 1890s, black peoples' economic opportunity and political power declined. Cotton prices collapsed in the depression of the late 1880s, and merchants tightened credit and raised prices for all landowners, forcing many into debt or foreclosure. Black farmers responded by forming the Tchula Cooperative Store in Holmes County. Drawing from the cooperative vision of the Farmers' and Colored Farmers' Alliance movement, black farm owners in the early 1890s bought supplies, purchased loans, and marketed their crops through the Tchula Store. Unlike other creditors, the cooperative did not charge interest on debts or cash advances.[36]

The cooperative movement challenged planter and merchant authority and profits, resulting in a violent massacre in nearby Leflore County. In August of 1889, Oliver Cromwell appeared in Leflore County, urging black farmers and sharecroppers to join the Colored Farmers' Alliance and to participate in cooperative purchasing from an agricultural cooperative that Cromwell represented. Rumors soon spread throughout the Delta of an armed uprising of thousands of Alliance men. White vigilantes from surrounding counties, fearing an uprising, rode into Greenwood. Meanwhile, armed black men gathered in Minter City, twenty-five miles northwest of Greenwood. The county sheriff requested that the governor send in the National Guard, who killed from thirty to one hundred black people, with no reported white deaths. Planters then met and banned the distribution of the Alliance newspaper, the *Vaiden Advocate,* and warned that any future attempts to organize Delta farmers and sharecroppers would encounter massive armed resistance. According to one account, the fear of armed rebellion in the black majority Delta backcountry drove planters to seek the disfranchisement of African Americans in 1890.[37]

Disfranchisement and the dramatic rise in lynchings of Delta black people laid the foundation for twentieth-century white supremacy in the Delta. After 1900, white supremacy was accompanied by the rise of the corporate plantations. As cotton prices rose in 1900, planters looked to expand their land holdings and to secure a cheap labor force. As increasingly more black farmers lost their land, they found themselves working as sharecroppers on newly developed plantations. Disfranchisement deprived black people of political power, and sharecropping enforced their economic dependency. The rapid expansion of large-scale plantation farming and the planters' easier access to credit sealed the fate of black landowners.[38]

During the first two decades of the twentieth century, the Yazoo Delta was defined by large-scale "business plantations." These plantations were known for their use of scientific management, in which a black labor force of sharecroppers and day laborers was closely supervised and its tasks routinized. A 1913 Bureau of Agricultural Economics study described the Yazoo region of "extensive plantations," with the majority holdings running from 360 to several thousand acres, some containing as many as five to ten thousand acres.[39]

The Mississippi Delta Planting Company, later named the Delta and Pine Land Company, was the most celebrated of the business plantations and illustrated the application of scientific management techniques. In 1917, the corporation owned 45,000 acres of cotton land in Bolivar County. The history of the operation illustrated how the region was promoted to outside investors who then hired local managers to run their investments. L. K. Saulsbury, seeing the collapse of land prices after the boll weevil invasion of 1908–1910, went to the Fine Cotton Spinners and Doublers Association in England in 1911 to persuade textile manufacturers to invest in cotton production in the Delta. Saulsbury insisted that cheap land and labor promised a lucrative investment. Four years later, the Mississippi Delta Planting Company, with Saulsbury as its president and general manager, boasted a stock capitalized at $7,400,000, and produced $1 million worth of cotton.[40]

The company was organized along a corporate model, consisting of several plantations: the Mississippi Delta Planting Company at Scott, with 32,600 acres; the Delta Farms Company at Deeson, which had 8,800 acres; and the Empire Plantation at Estill, with 5,000 acres. The Scott plantation consisted of fifteen plantations that were supervised by overseers and handled as separate units of 1,000 to 5,000 acres. Of these, 20,000 acres were under cultivation in cotton and feed crops. Scott had 8,000 acres of timberland, and brought into cultivation each year 600 acres, with the goal of planting crops on all of its timber land in ten years. The company milled and marketed its own timber, using the profits to pay for land reclamation. Twenty-five miles of this "alluvial domain" spanned along the banks of the Mississippi River, where drainage projects were an ongoing enterprise. In 1917, the company worked 1,000 tenant families, with a population of 4,000, and owned 800 mules and 250 mule colts.[41]

Like the steel mills of Andrew Carnegie, the company grew, harvested, ginned, and preserved every last byproduct on the plantation, billing the compressed cotton directly to the plantation's owners in Manchester. Scott had two central gins with compress machinery, one at Scott and one at Lamont—another central depot of the plantation, which in 1917 had ginned 7,500 bales of cotton. An oil mill crushed the lower-grade seed into cottonseed meal and cake. The company also had a sales and purchasing organization and "probably the most elaborate accounting department ever undertaken in any single adventure in agriculture." As one visitor to the plantation noted, "Virtually the company is both producer and consumer, for it sells its cotton to itself and spins the cotton fabric in its mills."[42] As with other corporate plantations, every aspect of the plantation's operations made money. For example, on Oscar Bledsoe's plantation in Shellmound, Mississippi, the mule account in 1913 was treated as its own business that bought and sold mules to the plantation. The hog enterprise sold pork to the commissary and the feed business sold cornmeal to the store.[43]

The company, like other plantations in the region, employed managers and agricultural scientists with degrees in various aspects of agricultural science and engineering. For example, J. W. Fox, the general manager of the company's plantations, had previously been on the faculty of the Mississippi Agricultural College at Starkville, and he made a salary of $7,000 a year. The company also employed a full-time agricultural scientist to develop new and finer cotton seed breeds, especially one resistant to the boll weevil. He used sixty acres just for his seed experiments, worked "in close touch with the Government experiment station near by," and traveled "almost constantly through the Cotton Belt scouting for new varieties and getting data on new results."[44]

The managers met each month and reported on the operations of their plantation units. Each plantation had a separate commissary with its own account, and each week the store manager sent every tenant's current charges to headquarters in Memphis, enabling the accountants to balance the weekly accounts. At the monthly meetings, the managers and the accountants discussed the accounts, general matters of policy, labor problems, stock and feed issues, and the sanitary and health reports of two resident physicians. According to Fox, "During cotton picking time it is necessary to have these meetings each week. We must know just how much cotton is picked on each plantation during the week so as to provide against labor shortages. If there is not enough labor available on the plantations for the picking we must send for it. Ours is a big machine that must be kept under steady headway; we cannot allow any part of the machinery to slow down."[45]

Unlike most other Delta plantations, the Mississippi Delta Planting Company provided written contracts and in 1913 employed three kinds of African American labor. First of these were the renters, who fell into two categories: one paid money for renting both corn and cotton land, and the other paid rent in the form of one-quarter of the cotton crop (in both lint and seed) and seven dollars an acre for corn land. Both classes of renters furnished the stock, implements, seed, feed, and labor, with the landlord providing only the land, improvements, and the necessary cash advancements to produce the crop. Under this arrangement, the tenant retained greater control over the crop and the production process. They also usually lived on the far ends of the plantation, escaping the closer supervision given to sharecroppers and day laborers.[46]

Sharecropping was the second form of labor whereby the company furnished everything but the labor, with the tenant and landlord sharing "equally" in the crop. Sharecroppers were basically wage workers whose wages were paid in the form of the crop, usually one-half, and who brought only their labor to the agreement. The landowner furnished everything—the tools for production, feed, seed, fertilizer, food, housing, and clothing. Each of these was charged against the sharecropper's account, ensuring that few made a profit at the end of the year; in fact, most usually went deeper into debt. Unlike a factory worker who may have lived in a company town but did not pay for using the factory's machinery, sharecroppers had to pay not only for their subsistence, but also for the tools of production. Planters thus rarely had to pay actual cash to their workers since the croppers lived off the commissary at a subsistence level. Landowners got a labor force for the price of subsistence, and a bare one at that. The third system was day labor, whereby the company worked four thousand acres of cotton, cowpeas, corn, and alfalfa with workers who received a daily wage of fifty cents plus lodging.[47]

The company preferred wage labor to any other arrangement because it allowed the closest supervision. Wage laborers, however, were usually single men who floated from one plantation to another in search of better wages. Thus, in an effort to secure a stable working force, the company employed mostly sharecroppers, allotting them more acreage than on other plantations to allow families to raise their own crop and to earn wage labor. In 1913, sharecroppers worked 10,500 of the 14,000 acres planted in cotton, in contrast to the one thousand acres of cotton grown with cash renters and 3,800 of cotton produced with the one-fourth renters. Each plantation employed only fifteen wage workers, who either lived in bunkhouses or boarded with sharecropping families.[48]

Fox had each plantation manager organize the croppers into plow squads as soon as the cotton was harvested, "because we cannot rely upon our tenants to do this." The plow squads, composed of day laborers and tenants, plowed the croppers' land for so much an acre, with the cost then charged against the cropper family's account. Tenants who owned their own teams and plowed in the squads earned enough money to pay for the plowing of their fields. While the use of squads aided the company in getting its crops in early and reflected the corporate drive for efficiency and maximum profit, it also seemed to woo croppers who, having harvested their crops, were not ready to work again without wages. Each plantation manager recruited and managed the squads that were also used in crop rotation, drainage, and clearing.[49]

According to Fox, the company had enough work to employ day laborers for the next twenty-five years just from drainage and clearing projects. Both men and women sharecroppers worked on these projects, with the men earning one dollar a day and the women fifty cents. Sharecroppers also hired out in squads for boll weevil pest control, picking the weevils by hand from the infected bolls. Other wage labor came at picking time, when managers hired outside workers to harvest the cotton that cropper families could not. Managers also hired croppers after they had picked their own cotton.[50]

After picking the cotton, the cropper brought his or her bales to the gin, and received a paper with a cotton sample on it. The cropper then took the sample to a man on the Scott plantation who graded the sample and determined the price of the bale, which he then credited to the cropper's account. Settlement days were posted on each plantation and the croppers were allowed to take their cotton for settlement only on those days. They presented the slip for each bale to the main office, obtained credit toward their debts, and then received cash for each bale beyond this amount. As with the majority of Delta plantations, croppers could not sell their cotton through anyone else, enforcing the notion that the crop belonged absolutely to the company or planter.[51]

Food and clothing further tightened the control of the Mississippi Delta

Planting Company over its workers. Sharecroppers received their food and clothing from the commissaries. Managers provided each family with a monthly advance of seventy cents per acre in cotton that also covered feed, and croppers were expected to perform day labor to pay for clothing. Each plantation was assigned a time to go to the store every other Saturday, and croppers were not allowed to leave work to shop at any other time. The advances began on February 1, when the families received coupon books of two and five dollars, and continued until the account had been paid off. The store did not advance any more credit until the cash received at settlement time or from day labor had run out.[52]

Two commissaries served all of the company's fourteen plantations. One store operated on a cash basis and employed three clerks, who sold the latest consumer items to the families of the overseers and other white workers. Croppers and day laborers, however, were bound to the other store, known as the "time" or credit store. This store did not carry consumer items; it had only large piles of salt pork, sugar, beans, flour, and shoes. All other clothing was sold at the cash store, where croppers brought their wage slips and cash to pay for them. Such a system allowed the company both to provide the subsistence provisions for credit, thereby ensuring they received payment at the end of the year, and to guarantee the absorption of any cash croppers may have earned, for they shopped at the company "cash" store rather than in town. Indeed, at Runnymede Plantation, in Leflore County, tenants had to sign an agreement to trade only at the commissary.[53]

The unit managers were key to the success of the corporate plantations. They had the most direct contact with the labor force, supervised the daily work, and authorized croppers' requests to purchase clothing at the commissary. As G. W. Hardin, manager of the Mississippi Delta Planting Company, observed in 1913, the solution to the labor problem rested "entirely with the super and managers; it is beyond the power of this office to aid in its solution. Some of the plantations have plenty of labor on them, while others are very short. The securing of more labor on the latter depends largely on the personality of the managers."[54]

Securing and retaining enough labor remained a problem for planters. Some managers encouraged tenants to convince their relatives to move onto the plantation, hoping the proximity of family members would create a more stable tenantry. In other cases, when croppers could not secure enough outside labor to help pick their crops, the manager advanced money for them to return to their former homes and recruit labor, often in the northeastern hill region of the state. The cost of securing and hiring these outside pickers, however, was charged against the croppers' accounts. The hiring of outside labor remained a contested issue for sharecroppers, who resented this extra cost and who knew the planter simply wanted to harvest the first and most valuable part of the crop as soon as possible, regardless of the costs to the cropper family. On some plantations, sharecroppers contracted for more acres than they could harvest, then subrented to other sharecroppers, often family members, thus creating a tier system even within sharecropping.[55]

A final aspect of the corporate farms' strategy to maintain close supervision of their labor entailed the centralization of tools and livestock. For example, the Runnymede Plantation rented over a hundred mules to the tenants for a cost of twenty-five to fifty dollars a year. The renter cared for the mule, furnishing the feed. If a tenant lost the use of his mule for any reason, he or she had to hire another one; if an animal needed rest, the tenant had to replace him with a fresh one. If a tenant abused the mule and rendered it unworkable, he or she faced legal charges. Mule rentals amounted to about $4,000 in annual income for the plantation, allowing the operation to make a profit off the tools of production as well as the labor. Single plowing was also prohibited, forcing the tenant with only one mule to borrow another, adding even more to his or her expense. Centralized control of the mules also served to restrict cropper mobility, preventing them from riding the creatures to visit other plantations or nearby towns. Planters sought to control their workers' leisure time as fully as possible.[56]

The corporate plantations also centralized the tools and machinery used to plant and harvest the cotton. For example, in 1916 Runnymede Plantation charged its tenants five dollars a year for the use of special machinery such as the double section spike tooth harrows, stalk cutters, all of the cotton planters, and the guano distributors. While this allowed for a more efficient use of the tools of production, the system added to the debts of the croppers and prompted closer supervision of the workforce by the overseer. For example, a plow boy followed the croppers with plow points for immediate replacement of a broken point, to prevent the cropper from ever leaving the field.[57]

The corporate plantations, as they emerged in the early twentieth-century Mississippi Delta, sought to tightly circumscribe the life and work of their black laborers. Nevertheless, black workers, while having few options under the corporate system other than leaving for such work on another farm, pressed the system where they could. While most preferred to work as renters free from any supervision, planters insisted on a system of labor that rode the workers as hard and closely as possible. Few black people secured a renter's status, though where severe labor shortages existed, some families managed to insist on and receive a share renter's contract.

Despite the inequities of the system, cropper families shaped sharecropping. For example, they refused to work the grain crops as part of their sharecropping arrangement, insisting on wages. As a Bureau of Agriculture investigator found in 1916, on plantations where the cropper system predominated, planters found it necessary to raise a part of the feed for the mules with wage labor, for as one owner put it, "It would take a world of land to raise the corn for the croppers' mules if the croppers were to raise it. The negro tenant is a very poor corn producer and although since the coming of the boll weevil more emphasis than formerly is placed on the corn crop, the tenant seldom raises enough even to feed his own mule." Knowing that the real profits came from cotton production, croppers simply did not work the feed and seed crops except for wages. Even though croppers resisted growing corn, some planters, like Alfred H. Stone of Dunleith Plantation in Washington County, required the workers in 1916 to rent land for ten dollars an acre to grow the grains, whether they actually produced a crop or not. Thus croppers paid for corn production, one way or another.[58]

While planters often preferred working their crops with wage hands—which offered the closest supervision—women especially insisted on having a sharecropping contract because the arrangement insured subsistence for the family. This strategy thus allowed women and children to work the family's crops while allowing the men to engage in as much wage labor as possible. And when the crops had been laid by, women also hired out for wages. They knew that wages gave them some latitude in securing the needed items for their families' existence that went beyond the bare subsistence provided for them at the commissary. From experience, croppers knew that planters made double profits off the commissary by selling them goods at high prices and then charging them exorbitant interest rates, as high as 25 percent on food and 35 percent on clothing, creating a system designed to keep them in debt. But wage labor bought them some space, however small it may have been.

The Yazoo-Mississippi Delta, then, as it emerged in the first two decades of the twentieth century, became a center for large-scale plantation agriculture, worked largely by black sharecroppers who formed a majority of the population. In 1910 the black population in these counties was 94.2 percent in Issaquena, 90.7 percent in Tunica, 89 percent in Sharkey, 88.8 percent in Coahoma, 87.4 percent in Bolivar, 85 percent in Washington, 84.4 percent in Leflore, 80.9 percent in Sunflower, and 76.5 percent in Quitman.[59] A 1913 study of 878 plantations in the region found that 92 percent of the plantations were operated with tenants, and 95.4 percent of them were African American. Further, 86.3 percent of the sharecroppers made an annual income that ranged from $100 to $399, with the average being $333.[60] The contours of the Yazoo side of the alluvial empire were thus set for most of the twentieth century, for it remained a region defined by a majority of black poor people who lived in the midst of large plantations ruled by wealthy planters—a scene that could be found in most of the colonial world.

The Yazoo-Mississippi Delta was well on its way to becoming a center for large-scale corporate plantations. Meanwhile, across the river in Arkansas, the clearing of the forests had only begun. In comparison with its neighbor, the Arkansas Delta retained a frontier quality well into World War I.[61] By the end of the war, however, the Arkansas Delta would mirror the corporate plantations in the Yazoo region with its large-scale holdings owned often by outside capital and worked by a predominantly black labor force. Still, there were key differences. For example, sections of the Arkansas region had larger percentages of white sharecroppers and tenants than did those on the Mississippi side.

The Arkansas Delta in some ways reflected the national divisions between North and South. A land tenure study conducted by E. G. Nourse during World War I noted that the northeastern counties of Clay, Craighead, Greene, and, to a lesser extent, Poinsett and Mississippi, had attracted large numbers of white settlers from Missouri, Illinois, Indiana, and Tennessee who began as sharecroppers and share renters and worked their way into landownership. Consequently, this area was "free from the trammels of financial Bourbonism and economic caste lines," possessing an economic life that "bespeaks an intention to 'live and let live.'" Tenancy and cotton production prevailed in this area, noted the investigator, but it was not "ignorant sharecropping," for black people were absent from most of the counties and living in only limited sections of others. Some counties like Craighead and Poinsett had upland sections inhabited by white people and bottom lands where black tenancy prevailed.[62] Large timber companies like the Chicago Mill and Lumber Company and the Tri

States Lumber Company had created settlement programs to divide and sell their cut-over lands to white tenants at low prices. Consequently, entire sections of Cross, Poinsett, and Mississippi counties were developed for whites only in the years prior to and during World War I, as indicated in the census returns. In 1910, the following percentages were listed for the black population in the counties of northeast Arkansas: Craighead, 4.8 percent; Poinsett, 16.6 percent; Cross, 43.6 percent; and Mississippi, 4.2 percent. These percentages changed slightly in 1920.[63]

The southeastern section of the Arkansas Delta, the largest sector of the plantation economy, had a very different look with a black majority of sharecroppers and tenant farmers, as well as significant numbers of black landowners. This began with the southern section of Mississippi County and extended down to Desha County and the Louisiana state line. The black population contrasted with those of the northern counties. In 1910, the African American population in Chicot was 80.4 percent; in Crittenden, 84.6 percent; in Desha, 79.4 percent; in Lee, 78.4 percent; in Phillips, 78.6 percent; and in St. Francis, 68.8 percent.[64]

The investigator was struck to find so many landowners of both races in the plantation regions, noting, "Such small holders are likely to find their lot relatively hard in the older plantation sections and to meet many handicaps in the securing of supplies or credit upon favorable terms or in disposing of their crop." Such farmers were "cotton farmers like their neighbors and find it difficult to raise their standard of living much above the level of tenants in the same neighborhood." Even when they made their houses "a little more habitable or attractive," the roads, schools, and public improvements remained the same for all. He contrasted small black and white landowners in the southeastern district with the more prosperous ones in the northeastern counties, and especially in the rice growing districts.[65]

The region also had some common characteristics throughout. Nourse noted that in most of the plantation counties, the upland sections had passed into the hands of white landowners who practiced diversified farming and livestock production because high cotton prices had pushed larger numbers into ownership of tracts of 80 to 160 acres. Simultaneously, factors (marketing agents), merchants, bankers, and businessmen of the larger towns had purchased great tracts of land, operating them with managers on a "strictly commercial basis"—for example, Little Rock businessmen had purchased in 1918 a 25,000-acre plantation in Chicot County that included five smaller plantations, two towns, and seven gins, all to be operated under a "highly industrialized" form of management.[66] Also, the economic trend in the Arkansas and Mississippi Delta favored corporate plantations. Nourse found that the average size of a plantation was around 1,000 acres, with 5,000 acres not infrequent and others much larger. The largest consisted of 100,000 acres. Obviously, the very large land holdings were cut-over lands in the process of developing into actual cotton production.[67]

Thus, it appeared that the plantation economy on the Arkansas side of the Mississippi River differed from that of the Yazoo Basin only in terms of degree and stage of development, having a twenty-year lag in terms of the actual clearing and developing of the land. In 1915 Barton W. Currie, on behalf of the *Country Gentleman* magazine, visited plantations in both Pine Bluff and Mississippi counties and then traveled across to the Yazoo Delta. He compared the great strides he saw in Mississippi over the past few decades to those he found in Arkansas, observing that "it struck me that the over-the-river valleys had made scarcely more than a beginning." He insisted that much more drainage work had to be done in the St. Francis Valley, requiring a comprehensive scheme. A "more intelligent, scientific Government aid is required in levee construction," he wrote, "and less of the pork-barrel method of obtaining funds." Currie also saw the different migration patterns that had shaped the region, noting that the settlers from Tennessee, Kentucky, and Illinois had brought with them the traditions of farming and a preference for using white labor, compared to the southeastern district that employed black labor. Like Nourse, he saw the plantation region beginning in southern Mississippi County, noting that in the Osceola district there "is more of the Old South, though it is a New South at that."[68]

The securing of a large pool of unskilled labor, available when needed and for cheap wages, drove the planter class in the first half of the twentieth century. Like the producers in export economies in the colonial world, the planters' capital was fixed—invested in land and geographically confined. Labor, however, was mobile, and unlike capital, consisted of human beings who had a will of their own. Hence, landowners never had enough labor willing to work on their terms of cheap wages in an exploitative sharecropping system. Delta planters wooed laborers through promises of high wages and decent conditions. But black people, once they had arrived and worked on the plantations, saw the illusiveness of their opportunities and left in search of better options, either on neighboring plantations or in the lumber industry.

Delta planters in the years prior to World War I pursued a number of strategies to secure a stable labor force. Some followed the path of their counterparts in the colonial world and recruited immigrant workers, as did Alfred Holt Stone, who secured Italian families for his Dunleith plantation in the Yazoo Delta. The Italians quickly learned, however, as had the black sharecroppers, the impossibility of making a decent return on their labor. Eventually, the Italians became landowners in the Arkansas Delta and in other parts of the state.[69]

In its efforts to solve the labor problem—the refusal of black workers to remain on plantations they deemed unfair—planters turned to harsher forms of labor control. Despite the boosterism of the "New Plantation" cotton kingdom, convict labor and peonage underwrote much of the Delta expansion. Prior to 1900 in Mississippi, a tenant who failed to pay his debts had to work them off or be sold to another planter. Planters did this to prevent sharecroppers from leaving before the harvest without settling their accounts. Many sharecroppers realized, after planting the crop, that they would not break even at the end of the year. Thus they often moved off the plantation, sometimes sneaking away at night, in hopes of finding a fairer landlord. Often a planter assumed the debt of a sharecropper he hired, adding further to the workers' debt.

In 1905 the federal courts outlawed holding people for debt and levied heavy fines for guilty landlords. After this decision, landlords faced a labor force that now left in the middle of the crop, usually moving to another plantation in search of a new contract. Unable to arrest them for debt, planters had tenants jailed for other offenses, such as bigamy or bootlegging, and especially vagrancy. While Arkansas outlawed convict labor in 1893, planters still found ways of employing this form of labor, as did Austin Corbin, a New York banker who owned the Sunnyside Plantation in Chicot County. Corbin made a "sharecropping" contract with the state in 1894 for 251 convicts who worked for one-half of the crop, paid directly to the government.[70]

The search for a cheap source of labor drove Delta planters, who believed they never had enough workers and were willing to coerce, beat, cheat, and steal to find and retain them. The web of debt, peonage, and convict labor ensnared all sorts of people. Unsuspecting people often found themselves arrested for loitering or vagrancy and ended up on a plantation working out their sentences. A. C. Hervey wrote that a Mr. Frank owned two rice and cotton plantations in Hickory Ridge, Arkansas, where he leased convicts from the county. Frank worked with local justices of the peace and sheriffs who, in one case, arrested a one-legged man who had been sitting on a truck for drinking. The man served a twenty-six-day sentence on Frank's plantation. J. C. Harris of Illinois was also arrested in Wynne for obtaining a delivery rig under false pretenses. According to Hervey, both black and white people were held "in slavery."[71]

Others were lured by agents promising high wages, as were the thirty-six black families living in 1912 on the Poinsett County plantation of Orley R. Lilly, Daniel H. Robertson, and Robert E. Bailey. Once lured, men, women, and children worked on an island under overseers with guns and pistols, in all kinds of weather—rain, snow, and sleet. The families worked on Sundays, never received any money, and never were given a settlement. As in slavery days, some men ran away and later sent for their families. Guards threatened to kill anyone who tried to leave or who came to take the people away. Although Lilly, Robertson, and Bailey were arrested and tried for peonage, a Jonesboro jury acquitted them after one hour of deliberation. The U.S. attorney for eastern Arkansas said that an impartial jury would have convicted them, but the atmosphere was "unfriendly, not to say hostile, with sympathy clearly resting with the planters." There was a "feeling that if they were convicted in this case, it would demoralize the negro help." Revealing the frontier atmosphere of the region, the attorney noted that this was the first federal court ever held in the town, thus a "laxity" in the administration of the law prevailed. In the lawyer's view, the people were uneducated in the ways of the court.[72]

Similar cases existed all over the Delta. A lawyer in St. Louis represented twelve black people who had signed a contract in Memphis to work on a plantation in Arkansas. Once on the plantation, they were held in peonage from January until they fled in May 1912, walking thirty miles through the swamps. Levina Shaw and her husband escaped from a farm in the "swamp district" of eastern Arkansas and reported their case to the U.S. attorney, while another report came from Luxora, in Mississippi County, regarding peonage across the river.[73] Planters never hesitated to cross state lines to track down a worker, as did Lige Alexander of Aberdeen, Mississippi, who went to Oklahoma and forced James Warren back to his plantation. Warren, a sharecropper, had raised a crop, and after realizing that Alexander would seize his cotton, left the state.[74]

While black people were the most likely victims of convict labor, planters and local sheriffs took any stranger whose misfortune it was to be in the Delta. A German citizen, George Scharmer, was arrested for trespassing when he jumped a train in Malvern, Arkansas, ending up on Frank Tillar's farm in Drew County where prisoners worked for seventy-five cents a day.

In addition, he had to work out a fine of twenty dollars combined with court and arrest fees of one hundred dollars. His sentence required him to work from December 20, 1908, until April 20, 1909, but he was still on the farm in October 1909.[75]

The case of a Russian Jew, Joseph Callas, drew national attention. Callas was making his way from Colorado by train. While standing in the railway station in Little Rock, a man approached him, placed a gun to his head, and asked where he was from, if he had a job, and if he had any money. Callas replied he had ten cents. Arrested for vagrancy and locked in a barn with other vagrants, he was shipped to southeastern Arkansas and charged a ten dollar fine, plus the costs of the food he ate in transit, the guards who brought him, and the railroad fare, with a total debt of ninety dollars. When he and the others arrived, six black men surrounded the prisoners and placed them in a wagon followed by the superintendent and the whipping boss who worked eighty-five white and black men. Black guards with guns marched them to the fields with cotton sacks tied on their backs, followed by an overseer with a three-foot-long whip and a black man with a pack of bloodhounds. According to Callas, black people knew how to pick the cotton, but the white men did not, as in the case of one German, Schmidt, who received a whipping because he did not move fast enough. Another man sought to escape and was shot while another was whipped to death. "We were put to different works. We gathered cotton, we dug ditches, tilled the ground, built fences around the fields . . . There was not one day in which someone would not be flogged. Two or three were flogged each day, and sometimes this number rose to ten," while a super often beat people more and harder when under the influence of alcohol.[76] Callas, unlike most of the convicts, managed to escape from the harsh labor camp. He wrote numerous letters to the U.S. State Department, which eventually sent an official to bring him home. Callas then told his story to *Colliers* magazine.

Lumber companies often used convict labor or engaged in peonage. The Bryant Lumber Company in Fourche, Arkansas, recruited twelve unsuspecting Hungarian immigrants from New York City who spoke no English. The company paid the transportation costs and $1.50 in wages. When the immigrants arrived, the company seized their luggage and all of their clothes and forced them to live in a guarded boarding house run by an outside party. When people tried to run away, they were arrested.[77]

The Arkansas Delta became known as a place where people disappeared. When several families in Mt. Carmel, Illinois, had relatives who had left the town and had not been heard from, they requested that the Justice Department investigate and find out if they had become convicts in Arkansas. Apparently, several had been recruited to work in Arkansas, but when they arrived had been arrested for vagrancy and sent to work in the lumber camps.[78]

Some of the most well-known incidents of peonage occurred in the Mississippi Delta, where federal investigations revealed the widespread existence of coerced labor. Perhaps the most celebrated case involved the Sunnyside Plantation owned by O. B. Crittenden and the prestigious planter and politician LeRoy Percy. In their mission to secure labor, Crittenden and Percy had contracted several northern Italian families to work on their plantation. These Italians came to America to improve their status, however, and thus refused to work under the exploitative conditions associated with black labor. Sunnyside became the object of a Justice Department peonage investigation conducted by Mary Grace Quackenbos, a northern reformer.

Despite Percy's efforts to initially charm and then intimidate the Yankee reformer, Quackenbos found evidence of peonage. While Percy fancied himself a civilized man, he undoubtedly engaged in the practices of his fellow planters. As the leading scholar of peonage noted, Percy "charged the immigrants for transportation, sold them mules at inflated prices, used the payoff system, marketed their cotton at some forty percent per pound less than they would have received in Greenville, kept their seed money, forced them to trade at his commissary (at ten percent flat interest), screened their mail, prevented them from leaving until they paid their debts, and when they did try to leave, had them arrested and returned." Revealing the national power that some Delta planters wielded, Percy called on his friend President Theodore Roosevelt to reign in Quackenbos. But Percy did not limit his campaign against federal investigators with a visit to the president. He intimidated an immigration agent and ruined his investigation in the region, prompting the Mississippi congressional delegation to attack Quackenbos as similarly biased. By the time the Immigration Commission Report appeared in 1911, Percy had taken a U.S. Senate seat, personally signing the report. Out of the forty-two volumes, only seven pages dealt with peonage.[79] LeRoy Percy's confrontation with Quackenbos and his ability to use the instruments of the federal government, indeed of the presidency itself, revealed the power that Delta planters exercised on a national level. They controlled not only the local officials, but those at the state and federal levels as well.

As the alluvial empire materialized on the eve of World War I, its contours were not much different from those of other western empires: a wealthy and powerful few lived off the sweat of a predominantly "coloured" labor force. The accumulation of capital in the Delta had led, as it had in other regions of the world, to oppressive labor conditions that drew on peonage, convict labor, and eventually murder and torture. As in other colonies, workers were stripped of any access to citizenship. They had no legal rights, and not only did they lose the fruits of the their own labor, but they also lacked the basic protection of civil rights. People worked without pay, people disappeared, and no one was held accountable. The enlightened face of progressivism and science that characterized the early-twentieth-century culture of the region masked an oppressive racism.

2 | Tensions of Empire

World War I changed the map of the world, collapsing some empires while adding to others. Above all, the global conflict unleashed the anticolonial struggles that would shape the rest of the century. President Woodrow Wilson, by calling in 1917 for an end to empires and the formation of nations along the principles of self-determination, buttressed colonial demands for independence. The western imperial powers thereafter lived on borrowed time, until another world war destroyed their empires forever.

The United States, while emerging as the leading power of the world, did not escape the social upheaval that the war produced. In the alluvial empire, the war ushered in changes that lasted for several decades. The central tension that pulled at the core of the empire's political economy was the changed position of Delta black people. The war opened up new opportunities for them in northern factories, in the military, in Delta towns, and on plantations. Moreover, black people had new sources of political information and support from outside the region, especially in the campaigns of the National Association for the Advancement of Colored People (NAACP), the major civil rights organization in the country. Delta black people formed local chapters of the NAACP and, through this and other venues like the *Chicago Defender,* they were linked to the vast changes sweeping not only the United States, but the world. Emboldened by President Woodrow Wilson's claims for a war "to make the world safe for democracy," African Americans who had remained behind to work in the fields, lumber mills, and local industries joined with returning veterans to demand more democracy at home. The much feared defiant and militant "New Negro" of the North had a counterpart in the South.

Wilson's lofty rhetoric placed the issue of citizenship and democracy on the table, and black people seized their war-induced leverage to press their own claims. Thus daily confrontations with planters over labor issues now had larger implications. The requirements of fighting a global war entailed the rise of a liberal national state whose goals were to coordinate productive resources, both human and natural. This centralized state required the service of black people, thousands of whom left the cotton fields for northern factories, with many men joining the military. While they had a stronger position from which to press for better wages and conditions, they aimed much higher. Their participation in fighting the war for democracy was predicated on claims to citizenship that included not only their economic rights, but their political rights as well. Through their affiliation with the NAACP and through their fraternal orders that taught self-worth, improvement, and political equality, Delta black people had new weapons with which to fight planters and their Jim Crow empire.

Within the context of the collapsing imperial world of the postwar years, planters of the Delta were uncertain which fate would be theirs. For the first time since the Civil War they faced competition from a force far greater than their own, as the federal government demanded patriotism before economic gain. These demands came from a growing liberal state whose interventionist policies touched southern life in ways not experienced since Reconstruction, raising the old specter of federal challenges to their cherished way of life, which was rooted in white supremacy. Planters now struggled to control not only their labor, but also the federal policies that they believed threatened their authority over their black subjects. Their fears were justified, and not simply as they related to a growing national power. For one legacy of the war was an internationalism that manifested itself in many ways, especially in the creation of an international body, the League of Nations, where colonial peoples hoped they might have a voice. And while colonial claims for independence were not realized as quickly as many had hoped, new international channels emerged that enhanced their struggles for nationhood and for an end to the exploitative labor conditions they endured. Through the Pan-African Movement, people of African descent the world over had a voice on the international stage. And in the 1920s, the League of Nations asked the International Labor Organization to investigate forced and compulsory labor in the colonies. While the League did not consider the Mississippi and Arkansas Delta as part of the colonial world, the question of coerced labor remained an international issue, signaling to the imperial powers the limited future of such practices.[1]

Delta planters may not have imagined the war's final outcome, but they realized enough to rethink their labor strategy. Some continued with their rule of terror, but others followed their counterparts in industry by introducing welfare capitalism to the plantation world. And the more prescient, realizing that the liberal state would not recede after the war's end, found ways to shape federal policies as they related to the plantation economy. The world of the alluvial empire would not be the same after the war's end. The "New Negro" would not go away with the signing of the Versailles Peace Treaty.

The Great Migration of southern black people formed one of the major historical developments in twentieth-century U.S. history. While the country did not enter the war until 1917, signs of economic mobilization appeared in 1914, after the war began in Europe. For the first time since emancipation, southern black workers had major options beyond the plantation and white supremacist South. In 1917, the *Literary Digest* reported that Arkansas had lost in the summer 23,628 African Americans, while Mississippi and Tennessee had had 35,291 and 22,632 go elsewhere.[2] Over 400,000 black southerners went north during the war years, with Mississippi losing 100,000 of its black people from 1915 to 1920.[3] They went in search of economic improvement, better education, housing, and a chance to exercise their civil rights. Above all, they sought to escape the terror, poverty, and oppression of the plantation South.[4]

This movement of laborers could not have come at a worse time for planters in the Delta. With the U.S. entry into the war, demands for food and cotton led to the rapid development of thousands of acres of new land, especially in the St. Francis River Valley. The Southern Alluvial Land Association stepped up its activities to sell and develop the cut-over lands in response to demands for cotton and foodstuffs. Wartime necessities led to further expansion and reclamation of lands, causing timber companies and plantations to need labor more than ever just when workers were leaving the region. Simple mobility in a wartime economy provided workers with a weapon that threatened the downfall of an empire. Consequently, many Delta planters continued to mistreat their workers, making few concessions. In 1917 in Leflore County, Mississippi croppers complained that landowners denied them space to raise their own gardens and livestock, forcing them instead to buy all of their necessities at the commissary. Since the plantation store also served as the post office, planters withheld the mail until the crops were gathered to ensure that workers remained on the land, while a Greenwood landowner retained his laborers' pay until both the crop was gathered and the next one had been started. One tenant protested that he had made eighteen bales and received no money. He assumed that his employer aimed to hold on to it until he was drafted, then steal the money from his wife.[5]

Despite the abolition of peonage in the early twentieth century, Delta workers still confronted an oppressive web of debt, coercion, and violence when trying to earn a living on the plantation. As five laborers discovered in 1917 in Coahoma County, it was the "law" on all plantations that croppers could not question the price they received for their cotton. According to state laws governing the sharecropping system, the landlord owned the crop and thus had full responsibility for marketing the cotton. Thus, croppers were required to sell their cotton to the landlord.[6] When the five croppers questioned the low price that their cotton received at the end of the year, the landlord answered the complaints with a severe beating. When yet another cropper sought to sell his cotton independently, the employer shot and killed him without fear of punishment.[7] Still, some croppers, undaunted by fears of planter retaliation, simply stole cotton from various plantations and sold it independently on the market. Few, however, escaped arrest for the offense.[8]

To escape these oppressive conditions on the plantations and to take advantage of rising wages, many laborers moved from the countryside into Delta towns and cities, but these locations had their own forms of equally severe oppression. When a group of preachers traveled in the Mississippi Delta in 1917, they reported to the NAACP that the "whipping of Negroes has gotten to be a mere pastime." Traveling from Leland to Cleveland, Mississippi, they arrived around 2:00 A.M. and had to wait until 4:30 for another train. While waiting for the train, "two white men came in posing as officers, flashing revolvers and kicking our grips [baggage] over and over, using all kinds of oaths and making threats. Finally, a grip was found with some liquor in it (No one in our party owned it) they carried it outside the depot, drank the liquor and threw the suitcase and its contents on the ground. They came back and cursed the whole crowd out." The minister also observed that a white man at Shelby had sent a colored man to Vicksburg for two quarts of whiskey and when he got off the train, a few men ordered him to stop. When the man refused, they shot him to death. And in Hollywood, a white doctor killed a "leading colored man" for merely disputing a small account. The physician shot the man three times in the back, then battered his head with an axe handle. The murder occurred at noon right in front of a large store owned by the Tunica County sheriff.[9]

Police harassment wore many down, often creating conditions reminiscent of peonage. City officials paid justices of the peace and constables by the number of arrests they made, thus encouraging officers to arrest men under false pretenses for petty offenses. In Vicksburg, Mississippi, for example, a young boy received a fifty-dollar fine and was sent to the chain gang for stealing one dollar, while another received a five-year sentence for stealing a bicycle. City police in the state capitol of Jackson hired stool pigeons to entice black people into playing craps. They then raided the games and arrested the players, sending them to the county farm. As many as thirty men were arrested on Friday evenings, sending boys as young as thirteen years old to the chain gang.[10]

African Americans in Greenville, a major commercial center on the Mississippi River, complained about the treatment they received at the hands of the city's "red neck" mayor. City officials were reportedly fined for dragging and beating people as they boarded the northern bound trains, though the police chief had claimed that every "nigger" could leave before he would stoop to beg him to stay. White migrants fleeing the depressed hill sections worsened tensions by engaging in whitecapping—driving black landowners off their property—and other forms of racial intimidation. Such were the abuses that sent more than one thousand of the city's people northward in 1916. For many, migrating meant the possibility of never returning, at least not safely. Those who left feared that they may never see their extended families again, knowing if they returned for a visit, their northern-inspired independent ways would only threaten local white people. As a prominent physician observed, "These things have got us sore. It is not so much the older generation that it chafes. We are inured to it."[11]

Despite these conditions, many black people remained in the Delta, for the increased need for foodstuffs and cotton created new opportunities and promised higher wages and prices for cotton crops. The migration northward increased the economic leverage for those left behind. Many moved within the region, from the countryside into towns or cities like Memphis, or back and forth across the Mississippi River, in search of higher wages and fairer prices for their cotton. Wartime demands for cotton led to cotton prices that climbed from eleven cents per hundred pounds in 1915 to twenty cents in 1916. By 1917, cotton had climbed to twenty-eight cents, peaking in June 1919 at forty-three cents per hundred pounds.[12] Sharecroppers benefited from this, even when their landlords paid them far less than the market price. Half of twenty-eight cents was far better than a portion of the eleven cents that cotton had brought prior to the war. Faced with new job options outside of the plantation, too, laborers who remained on the land bargained for better cotton picking wages, driving them in 1917 from a prewar sixty cents to two dollars per hundred pounds picked. Daily earnings in the companion industries of cotton oil, compress, and lumber shot up from $1.25 to $2.00.[13] By 1918, daily wages earned by picking cotton or working in the related industries had climbed on both sides of the river to $4.50.[14]

The increased competition for labor allowed workers to test planters' authority over them. Sharecroppers in Arkansas refused to accept the traditional arrangement that paid croppers once a year at the end of the harvest. As planters complained in 1917, "Negro farm hands" had been "demanding and receiving weekly settlements, and upon being paid quitting work until their money was spent."[15] In Desha County, landlords blamed high wages for "irregular" work habits. "Negroes," they mewled, who "used to gladly work six days in the week now work three or four and idle about the rest of the time, or work a few days at one place and quit and go to another."[16] Weekly cash payments gave sharecroppers and cotton pickers a newfound independence, allowing them to work on their own terms and spend their money when and wherever they wished.

The newly acquired economic leverage that rural laborers achieved during the war had ramifications beyond the issues of wages and hours. As sharecroppers gained greater economic independence brought by higher wartime cotton prices, they made broad demands that challenged planters' control over their lives. For example, employers spent as much time complaining about their workers' purchasing new cars as they did about paying high wages. A Coahoma County, Mississippi, planter whined in 1917 that sharecroppers had received generous cash settlements from the year's twenty-eight-cent cotton crop and had squandered them on expensive automobiles. One worker, he said, had "bought a machine costing twelve hundred dollars, ran it to a wreck inside a few months, burning the roads up and sold it finally for forty dollars." Even worse in his eyes, the cropper still had enough money to stay home from work.[17] In Greenwood, a planter ordered twenty-eight Fords for his sharecroppers, hoping both to retain their cash wages and to absorb any surplus income that might be used to leave. Local car dealerships, seeing a market that might not come again, pitched hard to sharecroppers eager to purchase mobility. Car ownership thus became another source of tension between planters and croppers. In the case of accidents, black drivers were expected to pay all or most of the damages. And cars became yet another possession that creditors could seize, or in some cases, steal outright.[18]

Most troubling from the planters' view, car ownership gave African Americans the mobility to drive wherever they pleased, back and forth across the Mississippi River, in search of higher-paying jobs. More than one Mississippi planter blamed the automobile for his tenants' migration to Arkansas. Cars also allowed workers to participate in leisure activities in towns, such as playing in pool halls or attending minstrel shows and circuses. Or workers could simply hang out in public places as a provocative reminder of their refusal to bend to planter demands for cheap labor. They also exercised their consumptive power by shopping outside the plantation commissary, a particular concern for landowners who drew great profits from their stores. In Leland, Mississippi, planters asked the sheriff to arrest Greek and Italian growers who drove to black churches and sold their produce—landowners had needed to open their stores on Sunday to compete.[19]

Arkansas planters faced similar problems. In 1917 a reporter for the *St. Louis (Missouri) Star* described the prosperous times that black sharecroppers enjoyed in Jefferson County, especially the areas surrounding the town of Pine Bluff. No longer in debt to their landlords, wartime wages allowed many a sharecropper to wake up overnight "almost to discover he is 'flush'"—a realization that would lead him to "splurge in reckless and sensational extravagance." He was amazed that "never before in the commercial history of Jefferson County have the negroes aspired to be owners of automobiles until now." Nor had they ever bought until now "pianos, organs, talking machines, buggies, saddles, guns and other luxuries of life so profusely." All sorts of patent medicine vendors and "hordes of carnivals and negro minstrels" fleeced the croppers on the streets of Pine Bluff. In the view of the reporter, however, it was the "city merchant, the supply house and the automobile man" who skimmed the "cream of the surplus coin."

The reporter found extraordinary the success story of Files Sanders of Ladds who owned forty acres and rented a few others. After paying off his debts in 1917, Sanders had $1,500 "he doesn't know what to do with" until "a few days ago, when the idea occurred to him to buy a second hand automobile. So anxious was he to be an autoist that he paid the owner just what the machine cost when new and then gave his order to the local agent for a next year's model." In that same year, Drew Sims, a tenant on a plantation at Tucker, bought for cash a seven-passenger car "after seriously considering the car for a period of five minutes." S. B. Adams, a black-smith, came to Pine Bluff "flashing a roll of $20 bills as large as the ankle of a fat girl in a sideshow," and left driving a $1,250 car. Down the street, a local hardware firm's salesman was shocked when a black farmer bought a wagon for eighty dollars, asking if the "cap'n" could cash a check for a thousand dollars. Another tenant posted four hundred dollars with his planter's commissary for a new car. When the car did not arrive in two weeks, he, "itching for an auto bought the bookkeeper's car for this amount and would have paid $100 in addition to have obtained it, but for the white man's fair-mindedness." The reporter presented these stories as revealing examples of "what a substantial percentage of the negro farmers in the cotton belt are doing with their extra money."

Furniture houses, dry goods stores, and standard business concerns had also made more money, like the two dry goods stores on Main Street that reported receipts totaling from four to six thousand dollars at the end of many business days. "A host of smaller clothing stores are reaping com-mensurate profits from the negro's lavishness. Music houses have had a steady upward climb in receipts for the past month and will be in Novem-ber and December. The natural love of the black man for music manifests itself in his desire for a piano or talking machine. Gladly he will kick in $200 or $250 for a standard piano. Organs are his second choice and pho-nographs third." Among the rural white residents, observed the reporter, "organs are the main desideratum, but the darkey remains unswervingly devoted to the piano."

Wartime cotton prices allowed for these "acts of extravagant buying and folly that characterizes the negro at this season of the year." Receipts to date, according to the reporter, revealed the extent of the increase in wartime cotton production. Within a year, production had increased by roughly 25,000 bales, with each bale bringing $115 to $125. As usual, planters expressed the paternalistic concern that "the extravagance of this autumn may be a lesson for the black man in succeeding years and should prosperity visit the cotton belt next year, he trusts that the negro farmer will learn the golden lesson of thrift," the "only policy for him to adopt would he earn the economic freedom to which he is justly entitled."[20]

The reporter reflected all of the stereotypes of African Americans as spendthrifts, childlike, indulgent, and naive when it came to business mat-ters. He also expressed, if only indirectly, the landowner's fears of increas-ing worker independence: their mobility, ownership of automobiles, and freedom to shop, buy, and consume when and where they wanted and in whatever quantities they desired. Planters no longer controlled as fully the food that workers ate, the clothes they wore, the furniture they owned, or the music they played and listened to. Workers no longer had to wait for the commissary days on every other Saturday to buy their goods. They now had cash that was good at any store in the nearby towns, where they could shop on any day they chose. In short, landowners were losing control over the consumptive power of their workers and the profits that followed. If wartime wages continued after the conflict ended, the planters stood to see an important part of their authority eroded, something they might never be able to recapture.

Rural laborers' refusal to work on planter-defined terms, and their determination to claim their family and leisure time as their own, concerned not only employers, but also the federal government. Through a draft and various boards to control the economy and loyalty of citizens, national wartime mobilization spawned a liberal state apparatus that touched southern life in ways not experienced since the Civil War.[21] But although national officials established policy and even directed the economy, they still allowed local agencies to handle the implementation and administration of programs. In the South, this meant that the planter class and their minions—comprised of landowners, businessmen, bankers, and agricultural extension workers—made vital decisions through the state and local councils of defense, branches of the National Council of Defense. These local councils mobilized labor, aided local draft boards in securing inductees, conducted Liberty Bond drives and food conservation campaigns, instilled loyalty, and monitored communities and plantations for subversion.[22]

Such an all-encompassing mission allowed planters and local officials to extend further their power into plantation community life. Concerns centering on labor control underwrote all other aspects of the mobilization effort. People accused of sedition were often labor organizers or agents, while many draft dodgers were croppers who refused to work for low wages. County agricultural agents formed most of the Mississippi local councils because they had clerical help and travel expense accounts.[23] Indeed, the U.S. Department of Agriculture required its county agents to report to the War Department on the morale of their subjects as well as their attitude toward the military and the draft, making agricultural agents spies, if only in an informal sense.[24] Federal wartime agencies, then—like the Committee for Public Information, the secretary of war's Military Intelligence Division, and Herbert Hoover's Food Administration Conservation Campaigns—by operating through a decentralized structure of local committees, handed enormous power to a regional elite that hardly needed empowering.

One of the major duties of the local citizens centered on drafting their men, ensuring they answered Uncle Sam's call. While black people voluntarily went North to work in the factories, it is not clear that they voluntarily went into the military. Federal and Delta civic leaders worried that African Americans would not support the war, especially when 66 percent of those drafted in Arkansas did not answer the call.[25] Arkansas governor Charles H. Brough argued that the failure of black men to enlist resulted not from disloyalty but from ignorance, illiteracy, and their "moving disposition."[26] A local postmaster may have been closer to the truth when he observed that many men had simply left their notices in their mailboxes, hoping that "through ignorance they believed they will not be drafted."[27] Few efforts to resist the draft matched the scale of defiance across the river. When police in Memphis rounded up "recruits" at a 1917 registration day, more than three thousand African Americans tried to flee across the Mississippi River to Arkansas. U.S. marshals came and dragged them off the boats. According to one editorialist, someone was "working up" the black people, implying that outside agitators had encouraged them not to support the war.[28]

The "slacker" problem persisted in the Arkansas Delta for the war's duration. In the summer of 1918, Phillips County draft officials blamed their low recruitment numbers on the labor agents who had recruited "hundreds upon hundreds of Negroes" to places all over the country. Thus, many "slackers" may actually have been employed outside the region, though none had left forwarding addresses.[29] A national draft inspector found that the Arkansas Selective Service had a "higher degree of activity . . . in regard to deserters than has yet come under his observation." Perhaps this diligence prompted the major newspaper in Phillips County to observe that black men, many of whom could not read the posters or letters they received, had become easy prey for bounty hunters who had received fifty dollars for apprehending each slacker.[30]

Arkansas's "slacker problem" represented the overall resistance that characterized black and white southerners' response to the war and the draft. Southern resistance to the war revealed not simply the racial, but also the class divisions within society. President Woodrow Wilson had promised farmers deferments to match those in industry, and he had expressed the hope that only single men would be called. The Selective Draft

Act of 1917, however, yielded different results. Provost Marshall General Enoch Crowder administered the draft. He created four categories of eligibility for men twenty-one to thirty years of age, with single men following into the first, and all others into the remaining categories. He appointed local draft deferment boards to determine which men should receive deferments. Crowder argued that deferments should be based on dependency rather than marriage. No man should be exempt if his relatives could provide for his family in his absence or if his wife could rent land for income. In addition, no deferment was awarded to a husband whose military pay of thirty dollars per month could support his family. In other words, for rural laborers and sharecroppers who rarely made any money, a monthly pay of thirty dollars represented an improvement in their living condition. This ruling ensured that poorer men would fight the war. Further, Crowder tied agricultural deferments to production. A farmer had to produce beyond the subsistence level in order to receive a deferment, a ruling that favored wealthier farmers. The draft law as administered by Crowder thus pitted poor southerners of both races against the wealthy. It also exacerbated regional divisions within states, for most farmers in the mountain and hill sections of the South were white families who produced closer to a subsistence level. They thus competed with the predominantly black sharecroppers in the Delta whose powerful landlords saw that their workers did not join the military.[31]

The federal government's system of allocating draft quotas added further tensions, and combined with southern white peoples' racial prejudices worsened the effect of conscription upon the region. As one scholar has shown, the federal government "set quotas based on a state's population of draft-age men and on the number of volunteers a state had already sent to service. States with many men already in the National Guard and the regular services received low quotas." While southern white men had not "rushed to volunteer," southern black men had not been allowed to. "Most southern states had no black National Guard units, and the federal government stopped accepting recruits to the black regiments in the regular army in the spring of 1917. Therefore state draft quotas were higher in proportion to population in the South than in other parts of the nation."[32]

The consequences of this policy meant that African American men were drafted in disproportionate numbers, with one-third of black registrants conscripted, as compared to one-quarter of the whites. In five southern states, including Mississippi, more black men were drafted than white men. But "even a color-blind draft board would have drafted more black men because they were disproportionately the poorest." Few black men had any choice in the matter, for in the plantation regions, landlords made sure that their workers received deferments and remained on the farm. Thus most black men received their deferments based not on dependency, but through the intervention of their employers. A Little Rock attorney complained, "The injustice is all the more flagrant because if the Negro is a tenant or works for some influential white man, 'he can't get by the board' as they put it. The Negro who is somewhat independent, has his own farm or business, is the one who is hard hit."[33]

The nation's demand for conscripts, then, raised sensitive questions about the racial composition of those drafted.[34] And while the planter class influenced the draft boards, the federal demand for soldiers trumped the landowner's need for cheap labor. Planters intended to do whatever they could to keep their workers on the land. Mississippi planter and politician LeRoy Percy predicted early in the war that a draft requiring each state to send two out of every five men would result in Mississippi sending all of its white males. In the Delta counties, the black majorities of men would receive agricultural deferments, and given the rate that black people were migrating, "there will be no town darkies much left."[35] Statistics bore out Percy's concerns. Arkansas in 1917 had to send 40 percent of its white population in order to meet its draft quota. Delta counties did not have enough white men to send, meaning that other portions of the state had to contribute much more than 40 percent to achieve the overall goal.[36] Predictably, the effort fell short and Arkansas failed to send the required number of white draftees.[37] Delta draft boards, always worried about a labor supply, saw it differently, insisting that black workers with families as large as six children had been drafted when, because of ignorance, they failed to claim legitimate deferments. Consequently, the majority of men certified were black inductees.[38]

Delta planters became embroiled in conflict with local and state draft officials over exemptions for both their labor and for family members who ran commissaries or managed plantations. In Mississippi, planters bribed state officials to defer men over the objections of the local draft board. Others bargained with boards for their laborers' exemptions. The owner of an oil mill in Leland, Mississippi, confronted with the loss of six workers, promised that "if the board would give them four of the darkies, . . . the mill would give the board two." With no apparent consultation with the workers, the board accepted the deal.[39] Still other planters lobbied with politicians to secure deferments for their relatives who worked as managers or accountants on family-owned plantations. Nor were draft boards devoid of politics. A member of the Mississippi County, Arkansas, board accused the sheriff of drafting his enemies and deferring his friends in preparation for a future election.[40] Local Delta draft boards often competed with each other over labor requirements and exemptions. According to the board in Bolivar County, Mississippi, surrounding counties had deferred all married men, prompting planters to feel "very much put out by the fact that their neighbor's tenants, living just across the line are marrying, and securing deferred classification while their tenants are being put into Class I by us."[41]

Planters often invoked paternalistic concerns when attempting to shelter their labor from military conscription. Mississippi U.S. senator John Sharp Williams wrote to President Woodrow Wilson on behalf of E. D. Cavett, "an old confederate soldier who belonged to a family of men who were good masters when slaveholding was in fashion." One of Cavett's "darkies," Walter Graham, had failed to register for the draft and had served part of a sixty-day sentence when he was sent back to his local draft board, which then granted Cavett's request for the deferment. Graham still received a draft notice, however. Graham, claimed Cavett, was a "good negro," a "splendid hand and good farmer," but was not worth the fifty-dollar allotment the military paid to his family each month. Senator Williams told President Wilson that the "darkey" had not intended to break the law. "I am surprised that more of these poor negro creatures out of ignorance do not do what he did, or fail what he failed to do." He pleaded with the president to send Graham back to the plantation.[42]

Not all Delta draft officials were as paternalistic in justifying deferments. In Craighead County, Arkansas, the draft board protested against drafting black men at all. The "negro soldier," it insisted, "is a danger to any community; the officers seem unable to control them, and their natural brutality asserts itself when in pack and with arms." Black men "are quite necessary as laborers, and should stay home and work. Military training of the negro will certainly intensify the race problem in the south. The South will do the negro's fighting, if he is left in the fields."[43]

The struggle over the draft and agricultural deferments illustrated one way that planters sought to retain control over their labor force in the face of growing wartime options for black people. They watched with alarm as wives, sisters, parents, and grandparents received the thirty-dollar monthly allotments paid to black soldiers. Women especially gained economic latitude, allowing them to exercise their rights as free workers during the war by responding to market conditions for their labor. According to one observer in Desha County, Arkansas, "the worst feature of the labor question is the domestic, or Negro women labor," who had practically quit work due to the increasing earnings of menfolk or because of allotments from relatives in the military. This travesty, he continued, had undermined the war efforts of women who had worked for the Red Cross, Liberty Loan drives, and other wartime organizations. "It looks hard that the white women who are striving so hard to assist in the war should sacrifice so much and undergo so many hardships and the Negro women live in ease and idleness." Moreover, black women refused to work in other jobs they considered demeaning. For the first time, small businesses like steam laundries employed white women. To the consternation of employers, they could not compel black women to work; their independent income sheltered them from vagrancy laws.[44]

For white women, the world had turned upside down, for the coercion of black women to work as domestics or in the lowest of unskilled jobs had allowed both men and women to have jobs that paid more, and to have clean homes and cooked meals when they returned from work. But black women's refusal to work for low wages had serious implications on the plantations as well. Planters had always relied on family labor to harvest their crops. Without the mothers and wives, there were no children to chop and pick the cotton. Thus the military allotments, perhaps more than anything else, levied a serious blow to planter efforts to control their cheap labor force.

Confronted with the challenges created by the draft and other economic opportunities, planters turned to the local councils of defense for help in securing and retaining a labor force. The councils sent prominent black leaders into plantation communities to instill loyalty to the war, raise funds for Liberty Bonds, and encourage croppers to remain on the land rather than to head North. Many of these leaders, who were members of the black middle class, followed the accommodation and self-help philosophy of Booker T. Washington and viewed the black working class with paternalistic concern and as subjects for bourgeois uplift. During the war, most of the black bourgeoisie in both the North and the South followed W. E. B. Du Bois's plea for African Americans to "close ranks" and support the war. Like the middle classes in other colonies, they may have hoped that by sending their "natives" to fight in the war, the home governments might privilege them with citizenship. In any case, their cooperation with the planters clashed with workers' efforts to improve their condition.[45]

Superintendent of black schools P. L. Dorman, on behalf of the Arkansas State Council, used black community institutions like the churches and schools to create support for the war. He wrote to black ministers, requesting that they preach "patriotism and loyalty to your country, both in your sermons and in your private conversations." A "man's loyalty," Dorman cautioned, "is sometimes questioned from his silence." He urged the ministers to teach their flocks to sing "America" at least once a month in services.[46] Appealing to black people posed potential dangers for some, however. Some white council members feared that "it was dangerous to organize the negroes too thoroughly."[47]

In Mississippi, planters invited similarly prominent black leaders to speak to their croppers in an effort to raise money for wartime causes and to encourage them to remain on the land. A favorite speaker in both Arkansas and Mississippi was W. E. Mollison, a lawyer and orator who had served as chancery clerk in Issaquena County for twenty years. Mollison spent his own money and time urging black people to remain in the South, though he had moved to Chicago to practice law.[48]

In Moorehead, black workers gathered in the Mount Arratt Baptist church to hear a local judge praise their contributions to Delta life. The "negro could always be depended upon to do his duty," said the judge. "He took care of the masters in slavery, not that he wanted to be kept a slave, but he could not afford to betray a trust." The Reverend E. Z. McGee followed by reassuring white people: "It is our war, we are with you," said he, "we did not come to this country; we were brought here, and we are not going away, whatever is against you is against me." Each of the nineteen men and women attending gave one dollar to the Red Cross.[49] Leland residents met in their schoolhouse to hear local senator and planter J. L. Hebron promise that officials would "show no mercy upon those who would not do their best to uphold our Government." N. S. Taylor, a black lawyer, asked his people to back up their "white friends" in whatever they were asked to do. He then collected forty-five dollars from the attendees.[50]

Local newspapers ran stories extolling black people's devotion to their white patrons. For example, Annie Hinds, who had worked twenty-one years as a cook on O. J. Hersh's plantation, gave her life savings of $1,000 to buy Liberty Bonds.[51] When McGee, Dean, and Company settled with their tenants, the workers then "cheerfully" gave $570 dollars to the YMCA fund drive, while on a neighboring Arcola plantation, forty-three families donated $430 dollars, and sixty-three families on another contributed $680 dollars. Each of the donors saw their names printed in the local paper.[52] Black employees of a local lumber mill raised $3,500 of their company's $5,000-dollar contribution for Liberty Bonds.[53] Black farmers were urged to use their bales of cotton to buy bonds: "Every Liberty Bond is an insurance policy on freedom for the United States," waxed a Sunflower, Mississippi, editor, "and at the same time is a splendid investment and an opportunity for many farmers to become self- sustaining and independent." The war "presents more than one opportunity for the men in the United States of America to become absolutely free. Do you want to be your own man and do business like the best businessmen in America?"[54]

While black civic organizations endorsed the war, some often did so with qualification. In Phillips County, Arkansas, the National Negro Business League, which included members of fraternal lodges, formed "war clubs" to mobilize support for the war.[55] When one of the strongest organizations, the Woodmen of the Union, held its convention in Helena with fellows from both Arkansas and Mississippi attending, it proclaimed loyalty to the flag, yet insisted that "lynch law does violence to organized society, civilization, and Christianity."[56] In Doddsville, E. C. Morris of Helena, Arkansas, president of the National Baptist Convention of America and known as the "Black Moses of the Baptist Church," spoke to more than 2,500 people from all over the Mississippi Delta for a schoolhouse dedication. He implored the Sunflower County officials to provide funds for black education, noting that inadequate education "for the Southern negro has made it hard for him in this war," forcing him into the trenches "while the Northern negro holds most of the non-commissioned officers and clerical positions."[57] Similarly, Joseph A. Booker, a prominent lawyer and an official of the National Negro Baptist Convention who lived in Little Rock, spoke to the association's local meeting in the Arkansas Delta counties and noted that the war allowed black people to show their usefulness and loyalty. Although he pleaded with people to remain on the land, he also insisted that white leaders provide better schools, teachers, "protection of life and property, and better pay for honest service rendered."[58]

One could only wonder how black people received these appeals from various leaders to support the war, especially since efforts to sell Liberty Bonds to workers probably bordered on coercion for many. But black people had their own minds about the war as indicated in the migration statistics, the refusal to work for low wages, and the high rates of those who refused the draft. Even some of the leaders had qualified their support for the war by calling for better education and the end to the violence and terror under which black people lived.

To retain their labor force, planters not only used black spokesmen and appeals to paternalistic loyalty, but also sought internal changes on the plantation. World War I accelerated welfare capitalism in industries throughout the United States. Planters pursued a strategy of improving living and working conditions in the interests of achieving tighter scientific management and labor efficiency. They also sought to win over a labor force eager for better working conditions. Landowners used the newspapers to publicize and advocate for improved social and economic conditions for black people. Articles described "model" plantation owners who treated labor fairly, built decent houses, and provided better education. And planters bragged about their financial support of schools and churches, paying ministers to help retain their workers.

A reporter for the *Country Gentleman,* John Roland, interviewed fifteen Mississippi Delta planters and managers in 1917 to discover their methods for retaining labor. His report revealed the attitudes of some of the more "progressive" planters toward their workers. He found that Dr. T. J. Atterbury, for example, had successfully applied his labor policy for forty years in Washington County. Out of twelve cash tenants, only one had been working for less than ten years, some had been there as long as twenty-five years, and one, age thirty-eight, had been born on the place. The twelve tenants had twenty-four share hands of their own, and lost only one-sixth of them during the year. In addition, Atterbury had twenty of his own share hands. Atterbury led the reporter around to visit with some of his tenants, such as John, who had two acres of alfalfa pasture, three fat mules, a grade jersey cow and heifer, a two-story barn that also housed a stalk cutter for sugar cane, and a two-row cultivator plow. He lived in "a well built house surrounded by a lush vegetable garden." Since he and his wife had no children, they hired hoe hands and pickers, though they also had a share tenant.

Atterbury attributed his success in "holding labor" on his fifteen acres to the following: "every renter and share hand has a comfortable house with a garden, a sweet potato patch, and a small pasture. Then I encourage them to own hogs, chickens, and cows. In short, I urge them to make practically all of their living on the place." Atterbury informed each tenant that he "is not content with them making money just for me, but that I want him to clear money for himself also. In case the man is a poor farmer, I do my best to help him learn to be a good one. If after a fair trial he fails to learn, I make him leave, explaining that a tenant who doesn't make money for himself isn't a good advertisement for the plantation and for my treatment of him."

Atterbury farmed the land nearest his home on shares. The renters lived in a community of their own and paid ten dollars an acre rent. High cotton and corn prices had led him to shift his share tenants over to renting on one-fourths, allowing the tenants to reap the benefits of the higher prices by paying only one-fourth of the crop as rent. He paid wage hands one dollar a day, provided a house and a garden, and allotted wives five or six acres for their own sharecrop as a means for keeping labor the year round. He also allowed the men to work off the plantation during slack periods. Atterbury insisted that he aimed to make money as a planter, not a merchant, and thus his commissary supplied tenants on credit for what he seemed to have thought was a fair rate of 20 percent interest. For years he provided each tenant with a copy of their commissary accounts, but had recently stopped since everyone agreed that his mathematics were accurate.

When they passed the plantation church, Atterbury explained that when the church had burned down and the insurance had not covered fully the rebuilding costs, he had loaned them money on condition that they use an architect and the finest supplies for an attractive building. He bragged how they had almost repaid him. The church owned three acres and a burial ground of its own that had never been part of the plantation. A believer in education, Atterbury had also built a "fine school house" for "his negroes."

In Roland's view, Atterbury proved that "labor management in the Delta has the double object of keeping the laborer hopeful and of winning his confidence and goodwill." He retained his labor by "seeking the welfare of his tenants, by encouraging their development as farmers and as human beings, and by using sane and efficient methods in the management of both the store and the plantation . . . Instead of exploiting the land and defrauding the laborer of a chance to live, Doctor Atterbury has increased the fertility of his plantation and taught his laborers that the calling of the human being is growth."[59]

Sheriff L. D. Dean of Bolivar County represented another management style. He advised Roland: "We must never forget that the negro is a child and that he should be treated as a child." A number of planters had mentioned Dean as one of the finest managers in the Delta, and he had credited this statement as the key to his success. Roland contrasted Dean's philosophy with Atterbury's. Both agreed that the Negro must be treated as a child, noted Roland, "but their ideas as to proper treatment of the child differ." The sheriff did not allow his laborers to have cars: "It ruins them—takes them out of the crop when they are needed there. Besides, the ma-

chines are too expensive and use up money needed for their homes."
Atterbury, on the other hand, "rejoices" that four out of every five of his
tenants had cars. "The Dean method certainly protects the laborer against
himself; but the Atterbury way promotes the development of a person
who can protect himself against his own whims. At the outset the tenant on the Dean place will have more cash, but the tenant on the Atterbury plantation will grow more quickly into a self-directing and intelligent man." Roland concluded, "It is the difference between infancy and
youth."

Like other planters, Dean required his tenants to market their crops
through him. "Parts of my profits come from buying the tenants' shares of
the cotton and selling it again," he said, "I make a profit of one to two
cents a pound in this way. This is only enough to furnish a reasonable return for the service of marketing. And it is understood when the tenant
comes to me that I am to have the privilege of purchasing his cotton." All
of his tenants had paid their debts over the past five years and had money
in the bank.

An important feature of Dean's management centered on his "regard
for the comfort and health of my negroes. The provision of first-class
housing is hindered somewhat, however, by the constant expansion of my
plantation. But as rapidly as possible, I bring the houses on my newly acquired plantations up to my standard." He wanted his "tenants to feel that
they have a real home: I furnish them materials for making permanent improvements and allow no other kind to be made." Each tenant must keep
his house and yard in good condition, and each was required to plant fruit
trees. "I recognize the community interest of the negroes by building for
them good churches and schoolhouses. And I make it a point to help them
choose preachers who will stress good behavior and contentment," teaching tenants that they must obey the laws of the state. Dean also insisted
that all couples living together must be married, and he forbade whiskey,
stealing, and "disturbances." The Bolivar County agent summed up the
significance of Dean's management: "Negroes on that plantation know
that they have a home for a lifetime."

Oscar Bledsoe, owner of the 3,600-acre Shellmound plantation, had a
management style supposedly marked by his "humourous friendliness and
his keen enjoyment of negro character." Bledsoe "paid attention to developing a cordial relationship between managers and tenants." As proof of
the trust that Bledsoe had developed among his workers, Roland noted
how, as leader of the Liberty Bond drive in his district, Bledsoe had agreed

to underwrite $15,000 of the bonds. He then called all of his workers together at their church, telling them how important it was to purchase the bonds, hoping to sell them around $5,000 worth. More than one hundred of his tenants opted for the bonds, far exceeding Bledsoe's expectations.

From his visit to the Delta, Roland concluded that "the problem of labor management on Mississippi plantations is at bottom a problem of human nature. In the solution personality is of equal value with method." Different though these men were, they had certain things in common: "They are good farmers so that the tenants who work under their supervision have plenty to eat and clear money when the crop is sold. They are firm, just men, who take a friendly interest in the personal welfare of the negroes. But those are most readily successful who add to the essential qualities of justice, humanity and efficiency, [and] a humorous delight in the whimsies of negro character."[60]

Anyone reading these articles might wonder why black people were leaving the Delta so rapidly. In the face of African American demands for decent wages, better living conditions, decent education, and an end to lynching and other forms of violence, planters insisted that such conditions already existed on the plantations. Indeed, none of these articles dared mention peonage, lynching, or planter theft of croppers' cotton and property. Either the planters engaged in self-deception or they simply lied—as in the case of Atterbury, who thought that charging his tenants 20 percent interest at the commissary was a good deal, or Dean, who hired preachers to discipline his labor force for him, shrouding it in the rhetoric of benevolence. Planters spoke of their workers as if the laborers had no minds or wills of their own.

The improvement of living conditions had started before the war as part of the expansion of the business plantations. Once the war had started and labor had begun to leave, however, planters stepped up some of their efforts to screen houses, provide cleaner water, and lower commissary prices, especially since more croppers had money to spend in town stores. Yet all of these "improvements" still fell under the rubric of greater supervision. As the general manager of the famous Delta Planting Company told Roland: "By doing this [providing teams of mules, seed, implements, better housing, screened windows] we can keep the labor of the tenant and its results under closer supervision. We are trying so far as possible to extend this supervision to living conditions, to provide better sanitation and to keep down the spread of disease. We want to have all our cabins screened and to keep them screened. We cannot force cleanliness in the cabins, but we can encourage it."[61]

Planters and their managers never conceded that black people hated the close supervision. Plantation improvements operated always under the assumption that management would determine the nature and extent of the changes without consulting their workers. The portrayal of workers as children needing direction always guided planter actions, and planters presented changes on the plantations as gifts to the workers. Yet Atterbury, for one, clearly made concessions to worker demands by shifting to a one-fourth rental system with his share tenants that allowed them to take a much greater share of the crop, and by providing the wives of wage workers with their own sharecropping acreage to retain them on the land.

Finally, the reporters who traveled in the Delta never consulted the tenants except in the presence of management, and even then, reported the conversations in their white versions of black dialect without ever quoting the planters in their southern accents, which often differed little from those of their laborers. In the end, migration statistics belied their claims of good working conditions and friendly relations. Black people, as these figures revealed, had their own say about the conditions on the plantations and management's use of "psychology" to keep them on cheap terms.

The Mississippi Council of Defense also sought to persuade black people of employers' good intentions by issuing a resolution in August of 1917, on the eve of the cotton harvest, calling upon the white people of the state "to express positively, the general, though semi-dormant feeling, that the liberty and property rights of the negroes should be scrupulously regarded by all our people." Only "contented and intelligent labor will make for prosperity, while discontent and ignorance carry with them ultimate economic disaster." The council "strongly" urged the state legislature to "amend its laws pertaining to the administration of justice in the minor courts as to remedy the evil existing in them," and it recommended the employment of county agricultural agents whose sole duty was to teach black workers the principles of agricultural and home economics. Speaking for the council, Frank H. Andrews of Vicksburg said that black people should "be paid for their services liberally, promptly, and regularly, and not be subjected to the piratical and blood-sucking propensities of those who profit most by their little peccadillos—the professional, fee-grabbing constables attached to justice of the peace courts. As long as the fee system for compensation of constables remains as it is," continued Andrews, "just so long will the district or beat justice courts remain as they are, courts of injustice and persecution for the personal aggrandizement of these leeches who live and thrive on costs and so forth which are extracted from the negroes."[62]

As a symbol of progress in "race relations," in the summer of 1917 planters formed the Bolivar County Community Congress to promote the economic and social development of the Delta. The association appointed twelve white and five black people to study working and living conditions on local plantations, resulting in a contribution of $25,000 to build an agricultural high school.[63] Other planters in Sunflower County funded W. F. Reden's Delta Industrial Institute as proof that "the Southern white man is the negroes' best friend." The institute educated black people in Washington's Tuskegee tradition of "moral, religious, industrial, and literary uplift." Reden, in a contradictory view that apparently escaped him, stressed the importance of maintaining schools and churches, for they have always "nurtured" the ideals of American "human rights and liberty."[64]

The most extensive organization formed to combat the black migration was the Mississippi Welfare League, whose membership spanned planters and businessmen in Arkansas, Louisiana, and Memphis. It aimed to halt the flight of labor by encouraging planters to pay decent wages, improve living conditions and schools, and oppose lynching and other forms of violence directed against black people.[65]

Some African Americans saw white people as their protectors and friends, but most tenants surely thought otherwise, hence the Great Migration. A joke published in the *Pittsburgh Courier* may more accurately have revealed their views. A Mississippi planter asked one of his tenants why he wanted to go North. "Don't you know that the Southern White Man is the Negro's best friend?" The tenant replied: "Yes, Boss, Ah' reckon you am right, but when a Southern Nigger can't agree with his best friends he don't quarrel with dem—he just naturally pick up an' leave dem."[66]

Planters did not stop at persuasion and paternalistic charity in retaining a workforce. As wages continued to rise and men and women laborers, emboldened by appeals to support a war for democracy, demonstrated increasingly more independence, landowners looked to the federal government for assistance in securing workers. In the summer of 1918, Provost Marshal Crowder issued a "Work or Fight" order to all local exemption boards, allowing them to draft men who were not engaged in employment essential to the war. Local councils of defense helped identify "loafers" and turned them into the local exemption board. In a sense, Crowder's order federalized local vagrancy laws that had empowered constables, justices of the peace, mayors, and sheriffs to arrest whomever they deemed a vagrant. In Arkansas, justices of the peace and constables were "deriving great profit from the Work or Fight Order" by "arresting negroes and ignorant whites" and virtually "placing part of our citizens in a terrorized state of mind, because they have no understanding of the distinction between State and Federal jurisdiction and they naturally believe that a Constable or a Justice of the Peace is the embodiment of power, both State and Federal."[67] Reports from other communities found planters and businessmen applying the work or fight order to women, even though they did not fall under the jurisdiction of the draft boards.[68] One deputy sheriff arrested thirteen women, listing them as prostitutes for refusing to work, implying, one might suppose, that a black woman who was not in some white woman's home could only be a prostitute. It was entirely possible that these women had an independent income.[69]

Mississippi County, Arkansas, had an especially active labor program, its chairman of the defense council reported: "We are getting the labor situation well in hand, have had public demonstrations with a parade of business men thro [sic] various of the rendezvous of the idlers and speaking by prominent and influential citizens and have given the vagrancy Statutes publicity." Although farmers paid two dollars a day and board and sawmills paid $1.75 a day, plus a 10 percent bonus for working six days a week, government works had taken "many by their fabulous offers." And in Desha County, the local chairman reported that "people in this county are anxious to start something to force labor to work."[70]

In Mississippi, local councils of defense requested from the national branch the authority to "tell our negro labor to stay on the job six days in the week or they will be inducted into service, or if ineligible for military service, they will be properly punished." The council believed that sufficient labor existed in the Delta, but that "many of the negroes are idle from two to four days out of every week." A national council official maintained that Crowder's work or fight order provided the means to "use pressure upon the negroes to remain diligently at work," and urged local councils to leave "no effort unexpended which may keep the negro population at work." Regretting that the national council had no authority to force men to work, he encouraged the state council to invoke vagrancy laws.[71]

With the encouragement of the National Council of Defense, Delta councils on both sides of the river adopted a card system that required all men and women to carry a document listing their place of employment. As a federal Labor Department official discovered, however, the card system operated only against black wage workers. If the U.S. Department of Labor accepted this, he reported, it "would be promoting labor conscription for private profit." Many planters may have shared the views of a Sunflower County editor who suggested inviting the Ku Klux Klan in to compel idlers to work.[72] Instead, Sunflower County planters formed the Self-Preservation Loyalty League to enroll workers of every kind, serving as a labor bureau to "compel idlers and vagrants to do their part in the war."[73]

The work or fight order proved to be the turning point in the labor problems of lumber companies in Phillips County, Arkansas. "It has been felt all along that, notwithstanding the inroads made upon local industries by the operation of the Selective Service, there were still enough laborers in the immediate vicinity to supply the needs of local manufacturers, the chief difficulty being the method to be pursued to get these men to work." The lumbermen "elaborated and perfected" the local council of defense order to "suit the needs of this particular section." Their guidelines aimed to "register all male labor, both white and black, and at the same time issue to the men so registered a card, showing such registered man's name and place of occupation. Space is provided on each ticket for each day of the month and all foremen or others directly in charge of labor will be expected to punch the day of the month out of each employee's ticket when he reports for duty." The local defense council kept the cards in its office to show the exact hours of each worker, allowing the monitoring of loafers and idlers. The foremen, as soon as they determined their labor needs each day, called the central office, which then sent specially deputized men to find out why a person was not at work. If a deputy discovered a worker "laying off," then he arrested him for vagrancy. If he claimed illness, the worker had to prove without a doubt his sickness. All deputies were empowered to "accost all men between the ages of 16 and 55 and request them to show their registration cards." Ten days after the system had started, local mills reportedly had to turn away ten to twenty-five workers each day. Larger mills reported that they started their operations on Saturday with the same crews they had from the previous Monday, indicating that common as well as skilled labor were working at least six days a week.[74]

Officials also restricted the leisure time of black workers. In Marked

Tree, Arkansas, the defense council requested help in closing two pool rooms and several soft drink stands, hoping to then force the owners to work in the fields.[75] The Arkansas State Council recommended that local officials refuse to grant any new licenses for pool halls and to persuade those current owners to change their line of business.[76] Planters were especially concerned about the traveling circuses and Negro minstrel shows, which had drained workers of their money. In 1917, Arkansas had seventy circuses visit the state, prompting Governor Brough to ask the state council to discuss ways of restricting these activities.[77]

Planters also sought to prevent labor organizers from adding to their woes over an adequate labor supply. No sooner had the war started than Arkansas councils found evidence of organizers working among plantation workers. In Latour, Phillips County, two men received a five-hundred-dollar fine for supposedly threatening seventeen black workers if they did not walk off their jobs. Since the men failed to appear for work the next day, officials assumed they had been chased away.[78] The Industrial Workers of the World (IWW) struck the greatest fear in planters' hearts. The Arkansas State Council of Defense addressed an entire memorandum to the activities of the union in the state, instructing local councils to utilize the military intelligence committees to monitor the radical movement. According to council member C. T. Carpenter in Poinsett County, the IWW was quite active, "using a good deal of seditious language."[79] The extent of the IWW's involvement in the Delta could only be measured in the expressed fears of employers, however, since few traces remain of their activity among workers.

Equally vexing to employers were labor recruiters for wartime industries. In Arcola, Mississippi, planters tarred and feathered a man who had circulated fliers promising higher wages. The labor agent was then arrested and interviewed by federal authorities for making seditious statements.[80] In another county, two labor recruiters were arrested for carrying "several carloads of negroes to work" on Arkansas plantations.[81] Local anti-enticement laws favored planters in their efforts to prevent workers from reaping the benefits of wartime employment.

To some planters' relief, the federal government intervened to prevent industries from poaching rural workers, by organizing the U.S. Employment Service to coordinate the movement and distribution of labor throughout the country. Each county provided a quota of unskilled labor for war industries, thus preventing the development of an unfair shortage in the countryside.[82] The employment service had representatives in each

Delta region to coordinate labor quotas. But many planters saw government agents as no different than private ones, and refused to allow any workers to leave. According to one official, unless the government agents could operate "unmolested," recruiting efforts in the South would have to stop.[83] The agency further outraged planters by using rural mail carriers to distribute applications for jobs, making the mail carriers, in the landowner's view, farm labor agents.[84]

Faced with rising cotton picking wages in the fall of 1918, planters in Mississippi County, Arkansas, took matters into their own hands when they met and established a wage ceiling of $1.50 per hundred pounds and a five-and-a-half-day work week. They urged surrounding counties to do the same. Gins refused to accept offenders' cotton and local officials arrested violators. The Mississippi County Council of Defense enforced the plan as a means to control the smaller farmers and sharecroppers, who paid high wages to harvest their small crops early. By November, wages had risen in some nearby areas to four dollars per hundred, and some planters were complaining that workers refused to work for less. But the local council held firm, claiming that the larger planters reaped great profits as a result of the ceiling.[85]

The massive efforts of local defense councils to control both the labor and the personal and cultural realms of their workers' lives implied that rural peoples contested not only the war but also the power relations governing them at home. A government that simultaneously called on people to participate in patriotic ceremonies and purchase war bonds, while requiring field laborers to work six days a week for low wages, or that invoked "work or fight" laws, surely led African Americans to question whether the war would make the Delta safe for democracy. Appeals for Delta black people to remain in the South with their white friends held no more sway than did the scare tactics of local newspapers and planter organizations regarding the racist conditions that migrants confronted up North. One can only wonder what went through the minds of Phillips County black people when the local newspaper printed the song "Dixie" next to the "Star Spangled Banner" on its front page on the day of a draft call.[86]

Delta families also knew of the treatment their men received in the military, either through letters from their loved ones or by reading newspaper articles that described the condition and treatment of black troops. For example, an article in the *Helena (Arkansas) World* described how white officers treated local recruits who had arrived in Camp Pike, outside of Little Rock. "Come on lets go see the niggers drill," yelled a white soldier. The

Helena World seemed certain in 1917 that "war, or the prospect of war and the many hours a day of drill has no effect on the negro, so long as he has an audience." According to the *World,* "The white boys have been raised with the negro. They know him, appreciate, and if the truth be told, absolutely love him. This affection is mutual, though not displaced in terms of endearment, nor by outward sign, but you cannot keep a southern boy away from the negro nor the negro away from the white boy. The negro knows his place," the writer insisted, "and the white boy of the South knows how to keep him in it. That is why Southern training camps are ideal for the task of transforming a good field hand into a strutting bit of ebony in a uniform." Immediately after registration, the black soldiers received their "first shower and free application of soap that is warranted 99%." Unlike white recruits, black soldiers were uniformed without delay, while the white men went through a ten-day quarantine without a uniform. Anyone familiar with the "psychology of the negro enough [knows] that the best way to put a negro through his paces is to dress him up . . . like a Thanksgiving Turkey." Without any apparent irony, the *World* insisted that the white officers had "shown a disposition to grant the negro the right of being a soldier, and the privilege of taking part in the world's war for Democracy."[87]

A 1918 investigation into the war conditions at Camp Pike revealed the self-serving dishonesty of the newspaper's report, if not the delusional views of the planter class. While the investigator found that black soldiers generally got along with their officers, at least a thousand men were held in a stockade, quarantined for venereal disease. Although rules for quarantine were the same regardless of race, black soldiers received different treatment. The men did not receive adequate medical care for their illnesses, and white officers beat defiant soldiers, referring to them as "you niggers." The investigator recommended that the secretary of war issue an order requiring officers to refer to black soldiers as "you men" as a means of lifting the morale of black troops.[88]

One African American soldier from the 409th Reserve Labor Battalion described the conditions in Camp Pike as his unit experienced them after the war had ended. After working in the Camp for eight months, he wrote that he and his comrades "wants to go home to our families and start life anew. We are in this organization taking all kinds of abuse. Poor food. Hard work. Such as ditching and cutting down trees. Hauling stumps and all sorts of hard chores and many of us is without proper bed clothes and rude treatments. Not one to console us whatever and further more we feel that it is our time to go home as the other boys have done. We are just the same as prisoners. Nows we are denied passes to town to visit our wives." He said that the white officers had been discharged, but their commanding officer had told them that "you niggers" have to stay and work. Of the men in his unit, 80 percent were illiterate and all were from Arkansas. His own wife in Little Rock was ill and needed him; she had little food or fuel and no one to care for her. "We don't believe that the Secretary of War or the Adjutant General knows that we are being treated so."[89]

Delta black people did not sit quietly in the face of the affronts accorded their soldiers, nor did they ignore the possibilities that World War I created for their struggle for equality and citizenship. One of the signs of black people's increasing determination to secure their citizenship rights was the organization in the Delta of NAACP chapters. In Mississippi the first chapter was organized in Vicksburg in 1918 and in the following year, another was formed in the African American community of Mound Bayou.[90] The Arkansas branches embraced both towns and plantation communities. By 1918 important chapters coalesced in Little Rock, where the supreme commander of Woodmen of America had visited, urging people to join, and in Pine Bluff, a Delta commercial center; one year later, ninety-nine farmers belonged to the chapter in the all-black community of Edmundson where a member of the Memphis chapter had helped them to organize. Affiliates emerged in Grand Lake with eighty-five members, and in Jonesboro with fifty. Significantly, those who joined in the Delta towns or villages were not middle-class professionals as in cities like Memphis or Little Rock, but were porters, laborers, domestics, and other members of the working class. Efforts to organize, whether successful or not, indicated that poor people knew of outside agencies that existed to secure their rights.[91]

Even though most chapter offices were located in towns or cities, rural workers still had access to the NAACP's activities. The seasonal nature of plantation work required men and women to seek employment in nearby towns for part of the year. Fraternal orders, churches, and kin networks also yoked the countryside to the towns. Even if rural people did not join the NAACP, they learned of the organization and its strategies to fight Jim Crow through literature circulated among their various networks. It would be logical to assume that branches organized in Arkansas Delta commercial centers—like Pine Bluff and Jonesboro, or the Yazoo Delta town of Vicksburg—had links to plantation communities.

Through their reading of the *Chicago Defender,* the *St. Louis Argus,* and the *Crisis* (the official organ of the NAACP), as well as their local newspapers, and through letters from kin and friends up North, many Delta black people on even the remotest plantations knew of political struggles occurring outside of the South. Whether they read these publications, or heard about them through their ministers, fraternal orders, or relatives who had gone North, many knew that W. E. B. Du Bois, editor of the *Crisis,* had urged his readers to support Woodrow Wilson's war to make the world safe for democracy. In return, Du Bois hoped that the president would reward African Americans' participation and loyalty by supporting their struggle at home to achieve full citizenship—an end to segregation, disfranchisement, and the violence and terror under which they lived.[92] But many may also have read Du Bois's articles, such as the earlier cited "We Should Worry," which warned white southerners that the war would change the position of African Americans, both politically and economically. And others read or heard about his investigation of black troops overseas, which detailed both the discrimination they faced and the valor they displayed. Du Bois described the respect that African American troops had won from the French army, and how they had fought side by side with Senegalese, Congolese, and West Indian troops, comrades in arms who also hoped that their service in the war would bring freedom.[93]

The politically awakened and assertive "New Negro" of the urban North, then, rose up among black men and women in the plantation South. Delta leaders anxiously observed this increasingly defiant attitude among their workers. According to a member of the Arkansas State Council of Defense, "We have noticed for some time a very perceptible difference in the hitherto respectful demeanor of the colored people of this locality." While arguing that German propaganda was partly responsible for "upsetting the racial situation," the member was sure that the widespread circulation of the *Chicago Defender* was a major cause of unrest.[94]

African American servicemen provided further tension, especially when they arrived home. Having offered their lives in service to the nation, the soldiers expected their full citizenship rights—that they would have equal access to public accommodations and the vote. Delta leaders suspected as much and saw in these uniformed men the erosion of the status quo. Consequently, P. L. Dorman carefully instructed community leaders to "tak[e] all precautions to see that our soldiers be rightly informed and encouraged to maintain at all times the correct deportment and attitude that should be theirs, to carefully avoid doing anything that might bring reproach upon them or the community in which they are." He noted that numerous incidents had been avoided because of "prompt and conservative action on the part of some of us." Ministers had been instructed to see that at all times the "proper kind of speakers appear before their people, who will give sober and wholesome advice, rather than the radical agitator."[95] Reverend J. P. Holmes in Leland, Mississippi, "pleaded with his race to be discreet in their conduct and to give no comfort to the lawless elements of the race."[96]

Fears about the frame of mind of returning veterans arose well beyond the Delta. In other southern states, civic leaders argued that African American veterans should not receive a homecoming, but should return individually, so as not to call attention to themselves as a group. They also sought to prevent discharged black men from exercising the right to wear uniforms for three months. Fred Sullens, a Mississippian and a captain in the Military Intelligence Division of the Department of War in Washington during the war, described the problems of mobilization from the white southern perspective. When a number of southerners visited his office, Sullens found that they "do not believe that negro troops should be brought into the South as such; that their homecoming should be as individuals, and not in uniform, if this can possibly be avoided." Sullens acknowledged that this was an "extreme view" and "at the same time a denial of the right accorded by the War Department to discharge soldiers' wearing of the uniform for a period of three months after discharge." While the problem reverted to the states "after the negro soldiers leave the service," there "is a growing belief in the South that the Federal government should not leave it wholly to the states; that plans should be formed now whereby this prospective trouble will be reduced to a minimum, and it can only be accomplished through close cooperation and thorough understanding between Federal and state authorities before the negroes return."

Sullens continued, "It is needless to point out that the negro soldier returning from France will not be the same sort of negro he was before donning the uniform. The Military Intelligence Division is well acquainted with the new ideas and social aspirations our negro troops have gathered in France, and particularly from his associations with the French demi monde. Obviously, if he attempts to carry those ideas back into the South —and some of them unquestionably will—an era of bloodshed will follow as compared with which the history of reconstruction will be mild reading, indeed." The governor of Alabama had already called a "secret conference of citizens" to discuss the issue, and the American Protective League "is to take an active part in the program being formed." Sullens was certain that any "person familiar with the South, and its ever-present race problem need not be reminded that the negro soldier strutting about in uniform three months after his discharge will always be a potential danger, especially if he happens to be of the type inclined to impudence or arrogance. It is needless to discuss the 'rightness or wrongness' of the Southern white man's attitude toward this type of black. That is an established condition, and cannot be dealt with as a theory." Sullens proposed that officers "thoroughly conversant with the South, and particularly the negro problem," be sent to visit governors of southern states to ascertain plans for demobilization. The governors and federal government must adopt a policy "of tolerance and conservatism toward the returning negro soldiers" and a "system of propaganda planned that will instill into the minds of whites and blacks alike a proper attitude on the subject." Sullens urged the enlistment of the black clergy in the work, for the "negro has no political leaders. His preacher is always his surest and safest guide."

Sullens cautioned that "if those in authority wait until the negro troops have been actually returned and demobilized, it will then be everlastingly too late. Speaking now as a citizen who knows the negro and the troubles that have beset his pathway in the upward climb from slavery, I feel that it would be a gross injustice to the race to turn the negro soldiers loose without some precautions being taken, both for their restraint and their protection. They went into the army willingly, and have served faithfully," he continued. "If many of them have had false ideas instilled into their minds during the period of service it is more a misfortune than their fault. Also, it should be borne in mind that thousands of these negroes who return home will not be trouble-makers, yet they are likely to become the innocent sufferers for the ignorance, arrogance and wrong aspirations of others. They were ready and willing to sacrifice their lives in time of war. Certainly, they should be protected in time of peace."[97]

As the Military Intelligence report revealed, a profound fear existed among white southerners that returning black soldiers would spread the social aspirations and political ideas they had acquired in their service abroad. Yet Sullens also reflected the contradictions of southern white thought regarding black servicemen. Having supported the use of black troops to fight the war for democracy, white people now feared the consequences. They knew from the Spanish-American War in the late 1890s that returning veterans provoked white repression, and some even recalled that during the Civil War black soldiers who fought to save the Union had demanded their freedom. Even more, the soldiers' experience with other ways of living and thinking about race threatened social mores, and therefore, power relations in the South. Mississippi governor Theodore Bilbo spoke for most southern leaders when he warned that those servicemen who had been "contaminated with Northern social and political dreams of equality" need not return: "We have all the room in the world for what we know as N-i-g-g-e-r-s, but none whatsoever for 'colored ladies and gentlemen.'"[98]

Bilbo's approach, while shared by many, added to planter labor woes as the country demobilized in 1918 and 1919. Hoping to retain their wartime profits from high cotton prices, Delta planters searched for ways to lure workers back to the cotton fields. The Mississippi Welfare League stepped up its activities in the spring of 1919 by calling together leading businessmen and planters for a meeting and by raising $100,000 for the organization. One businessman noted that the labor problem had become grave and required the devotion of the "best thought." Isaiah Montgomery, who came from the historic black town of Mound Bayou and who had supported the 1890 Constitution that disfranchised black people, hastened to assure the gathering that social equality was not included in the program.

The members of the Welfare League discussed the vast problems they saw confronting their region. All agreed that venereal disease had become so widespread among "negroes in Mississippi" that "unless the white man came to the black man's rescue in a hundred years the negro will be no more as a race . . . Poison blood is developing rapidly into tuberculosis and the negro is dying three times faster than the white man." Dr. M. T. Auerly of the State Board of Health pleaded for more funds to counter venereal disease. Another businessman noted that venereal disease had reduced the efficiency of the laborers by one-third. He then told of a planter who had 90 percent of "his negroes" afflicted with the disease, allowing very few births. Dr. Auerly noted that "to society at large, the most fatal diseases are not the most costly," but those that prevented a man or woman from working. These proved the most costly "both to the individual and to society in general."

Charles Banks, a black banker of Mound Bayou, turned to the issue of lynching and reminded white southerners that the "debasing acts of lynching mobs are dealt with too leniently and indifferently . . . Whatever may be the provisions of the statute, be it state or federal, I am of the opinion that healthy public sentiment must be built up for the maintenance of law and order, and it is largely upon such men as you, the leaders of the white race in this section, the makers and executors of the law, as well as the makers and developers of public sentiment and opinion, that the burden rests." Executive Secretary Jack Wilson agreed, noting that recently white people had stood by while four innocent men were lynched. "Will you as a Mississippian or as an American stand for this?" he queried.[99]

The Welfare League found support in Memphis, where the Chamber of Commerce urged all employers of "negro" labor to pay a two dollar tax, matched by each worker to form a fund to improve conditions of black workers in Memphis. The city's branch of the Welfare League claimed that in the past, Delta black people had migrated to Memphis in search of work, but during the war they kept heading North. Memphis had a new automobile body plant and a number of other industries that required common labor. The powerful Lumberman's Club, representing all of the major lumber mills in the Delta, strongly endorsed the campaign.[100]

In conjunction with the Southern Alluvial Land Association, the league devised a program to bring workers home before cold weather began. The plan aimed to establish offices in Chicago and St. Louis to recruit those black workers who wanted to come back. They organized a "publicity campaign to offset the evil and unfounded propaganda issued by big industry and political forces that are the real agencies in alluring and holding southern negroes in the North."

Jack Wilson spent ten days in Chicago, meeting with Mayor "Big Bill" Thompson, police heads, leaders in the Chamber of Commerce, organized labor leaders, and federal employment agency heads. He found that men in city politics worked hard to hinder the return of black voters to the South. Wilson decided after the trip to recruit a committee of white and black people to visit the Delta and to determine conditions for themselves.[101] The committee, consisting of members of the Chamber of Commerce and the Federation of Labor, reported having found "exceptional happiness, contentment and prosperity among the Negroes of Mississippi." Churches, schools, housing, and race relations in general appeared good. Indeed, they found that the "industrious Negro is afforded excellent opportunities to become a landowner. No police oppression, imposition or lawlessness was found." Delta Negroes carried committee members around in their own automobiles to see conditions for themselves.[102] The committee also reported that "railroad accommodations for Negroes were adequate and uniform, irrespective of locality"; that "treatment ac-

corded Negro passengers by railroad officials was courteous throughout";
that Negroes had free use of the sidewalks; that they were prosperous,
some owning as much as $175,000 worth of property and averaging
$1,500 a year in crops; that public school terms were nine months in the
city and eight months in the country for white and colored alike; that
many modern homes were being built for black people, and that the
strongest possible human ties between planter and worker existed. The
visitors found no trace of racial friction, especially compared to conditions
in Chicago where 17,000 black people stood in breadlines in one day
alone.[103]

The Chicago Urban League investigated the truth behind the report,
and the author of its findings decided that the committee of "alleged Negro leaders from Chicago was so very nauseating to us that I regret to refer
to it. These fellows, whoever they were, were guarded by those who had
charge of them as if they had been convicts. They were not even allowed
to have the privilege of purchasing their own tickets." The league's investigator concluded that the "major thing they found was that blacks walked
on sidewalks. Let me assure you once and for all that racial conditions are
worse in the South today than they have been in all the years of my life, all
of which have been spent there, and anyone who reports to the contrary is
false and a traitor to the cause of humanity." His "advice to any Race man
who can make bread across the line is that he remain there and it would be
an outrage for the people to be deceived and brought back here." The
Chicago Defender also insisted that all of the black people who had spoken
to the visitors from the city had been forced to promise beforehand that
they would not mention a desire to secure the vote.[104]

Planters, however, did not want just any "negroes" from the North. As
the vice president of the Chicago Mill and Lumber Company made clear:
"We would not hesitate to pay the expenses of a hundred or more Negroes
from Chicago and other northern cities to our place if we can get southern
Negroes, particularly Negroes who have gone from Mississippi, Arkansas,
and Tennessee." A. C. Lange continued: "I think it is safe to say that every
southern Negro in the North would be brought back without expense to
him if southern farmers and plantation owners knew where and how to get
in touch with the Southern born. We don't want and will have no northern Negroes."[105]

The war revealed the contradictory nature of social relations in the
Delta and the ideology to which they gave birth. A writer for the African
American newspaper *New York Age* acknowledged that many "of the con-

tradictory positions taken by the white South on the race question would be very puzzling to any one not familiar with the fact that whatever position the white South may take on the race question, its eyes are fixed upon just one point." The white South "lays down the declaration that the negro is incapable of rising, then it adopts every possible precaution to keep him from rising. It would seem needless to take precautions to keep down a people incapable of rising." White southerners constantly complained that black peoples' inefficiency and ignorance held the region back economically, yet the region fought fiercely to keep them from leaving. "Of course," he continued, "anyone who knows anything at all about the South knows that it does not want to get rid of the Negro; it wants to keep him, but it wants to keep him on its own terms."

The author concluded by noting an article in the *Memphis Commercial Appeal* describing the reasons that black people left—education, housing, segregation, disfranchisement, and poverty. The Memphis writer, however, rather than conceding these as legitimate issues for migration, blamed the North for stealing black labor. "It is not to the credit of northern manufacturers and employers of labor to record that they sought to exploit for their own selfish advantage whatever of discontent there was among southern Negroes." As the *New York Age* reporter noted, "Can you beat it? It was wrong for the northern manufacturers to offer inducements of good wages and a place to work where he would have equal schools and would not be subjected to lynching." Yet the southern writer had "no doubt that the Negro would prefer to remain in the South" because of the warm climate and to be near the southern white man, "his best friend."[106]

Plantation reforms and espousals of white affection to the contrary, events in 1919 showed that brutality, violence, and oppression continued in the alluvial empire. One southerner wrote to the *Crisis* in 1919, saying that even as a "white son of Miss., when it comes to the place that negra's are to be treated as they are here, I feel that I should speak out, negra's are being whipped here, as they were in the days of slavery, and these poor defenseless beings cannot speak out."[107]

Returning black veterans confronted southern white people who saw their military service in Europe as a threat to the southern way of life. Thus, when Flinton Briggs returned to his home in Star City, a town just outside Pine Bluff, white people immediately sought to impress on him the importance of returning to his subordinate position in local society. While walking down a sidewalk in early September 1919, Briggs stepped aside to allow a white couple to pass. Apparently, the white woman brushed into Briggs, scolding him that "Niggers get off the sidewalk down here." When Briggs replied "This is a free man's country," the woman's escort seized him until others came with an automobile that carried Briggs outside of town. Unable to find a rope to hang him with, the mob took the automobile chains, tied Briggs to a tree, and riddled his body with bullets. Briggs's murder was the fifth lynching that had occurred in Arkansas in 1919.[108]

Numerous other lynchings followed the war as well. Beginning in January 1919, with the murder of an African American soldier in Memphis, people were tortured and burned all over the Delta. At least eighteen lynchings of men and women in Arkansas and Mississippi were reported to the NAACP in 1919, some involving the murder of more than one person. While some of the men were killed for alleged violations of white women's honor, many instances centered on the actions of returning veterans.[109]

African Americans were not silent or passive observers. Having rendered their lives in service to the nation, whether as soldiers abroad or as workers at home, black men and women knew that their efforts to fight a war for democracy implied citizenship. In countless ways, they expressed this recognition of their rights, whether by joining the military or by withholding their labor at home for decent wages and working conditions. And they were mindful of their political rights, as revealed in their forming of NAACP chapters, whose purpose was to secure citizenship for black people. As Flinton Briggs said, "This is a free man's country."

African Americans' understanding of their rights of citizenship clashed inevitably with those of southern whites. As Alfred Holt Stone told his fellow members of the Welfare League in 1919, "We have proclaimed from the very beginning that the Southerner was the best friend that the negro ever had." Giving him a "square deal does not mean giving him the ballot . . . The white man is in power."[110] But the question of black citizenship did not rest entirely in the hands of planters like Stone. African Americans had their own views about the issue that had been enhanced during the war by the expansion of the NAACP, and after the war, by the rise of the Pan-African Movement that sought to unite all peoples of African descent and to forge a war for liberation. African American soldiers had fought along the side of other "coloured" soldiers, and like them, returned to fight a war for freedom at home. The struggle for justice and equality did not recede, in the face of either increased terror or benign attempts at reform, as planters had hoped. The New Negroes—men and women—had returned "fighting."

3 | The Killing Fields

Social upheaval followed in the wake of World War I in 1918 and 1919. Many who endured combat witnessed the unnecessary slaughter of their comrades and despaired of the possibilities for peace. Inspired by the Russian Revolution of 1917, some war-weary workers and soldiers organized strikes in 1918 and 1919 that challenged the monarchies and democracies alike. England and France experienced anticolonial uprisings. And while Europe did not follow the Russian revolutionary path in these immediate postwar years, the emerging anticolonial struggles the war had unleashed brought issues of racism, exploitation, and oppression to the fore.[1]

The United States did not escape the upheaval the war had wrought. In 1919, violence and terror erupted across the nation as the federal government moved to destroy the momentum of labor. Corporate heads and their government partners crushed workers in the massive steel strike that swept the country in 1919, labeling the 250,000 workers as Russian-inspired communists intent on overthrowing American capitalism and democracy. The first Red Scare accompanied this attack on labor, as Attorney General A. Mitchell Palmer used federal power to deport radical labor leaders and imprison others. The federal government and employers also sought to force African Americans back into their prewar subordinate position, whether in the job-segregated North or in the white-supremacist South. Racial confrontations swept the country in what was known as the Red Summer of 1919, and not only in the urban centers of Washington and Chicago, but also in the hinterlands of Omaha, Longview, Charleston, and the plantation region of the Arkansas Delta. Emboldened by a war that intended to make the world safe for democracy, African Americans returned to Delta towns and villages to demand with their families citizenship and justice. In Phillips County, Arkansas, this struggle directly challenged planter dominance, triggering a massacre in October 1919 of hundreds of African American men, women, and children.[2]

African American struggles for citizenship in Phillips County were inter-twined with the countryside's rapidly developing cotton and timber indus-trial economy. An estimated one thousand African American men from Phillips County had served in the military.[3] Soldiers returning to the town of Elaine and the surrounding region found friends and family who had reaped the benefits of wartime wages in the lumber industry, and share-croppers and tenants who had welcomed higher cotton prices. Black veter-ans brought back to their plantations a determination that life could and would be different. The experience and political will of black veterans, combined with the wartime aspirations of their family and friends who had remained behind, forged a collective will to secure a more just life in the alluvial empire.

With men returning from war and others coming home from their war-time jobs, landowners braced themselves for a more assertive working class. Many sharecroppers and tenants, while never making a just return on their crops, had made some money during the war by receiving their per-centage of rising cotton prices. Compared to the seven cents per hundred pounds that farmers had received in 1914, cotton prices had climbed to forty-three cents per pound by the summer of 1919. Families used their newly acquired income to accumulate property, including livestock, furni-ture, pianos, and automobiles. Some had purchased Liberty Bonds, while others had acquired land.

Planters aimed to retract the wartime gains of their workers. But share-croppers and tenants, determined to hold on to their wartime gains and to secure their fair share of production, challenged the planters' right to mar-ket their crops. Tired of landowners who took their cotton and paid them a lower price than the market value, Delta workers demanded that they be allowed to sell their own crops directly on the market. With this in mind, several men and women in the region surrounding Elaine, Arkan-sas, joined the Progressive Farmers and Household Union of America. The ensuing clash between planters' efforts to control labor and profits and workers' attempts to secure their just reward led to a horrific confron-tation. Black men, women, and children engaged in a determined strug-gle, and many died for it.

The conflict in southern Phillips County mirrored that of any industrial setting where labor squared off against capital over wages and surplus, ex-cept that the planters' response was distinctly southern. What made this region of southeastern Arkansas different from northern areas was an ap-proach to race and labor relations rooted in slavery and its aftermath. Although the industrial class of southern Phillips County came largely from regions outside the South, and seemingly held no claim to the southern legacy of paternalism, they had no trouble adopting the attitudes or the harsh methods applied to black labor. Like the northern planters who invaded southern plantations during the Civil War and Reconstruction, these Yankees willingly adopted the southern stereotype of black Delta workers.[4] More significant than the regional roots of the owners was that these men used southern-born managers who were experienced in "handling negroes" in the most direct and coercive fashion and who could thereby reinforce the southern "way of life," rooted in segregation, disfranchisement, and sharecropping. For all of its newness and industrial innovation, much of the region's contours were still drawn by southern history.

Southern Phillips County represented a microcosm of the changes that had taken place in the area during the first two decades of the twentieth century. At the turn of the century, it was an undeveloped swampland and forest. With some of the most fertile soil in the world, this region was nestled between the White and Mississippi Rivers, whose overflow continually layered the earth with more sediment. While slave owners had managed to farm sections of the county along the Mississippi River, the overflow of the rivers prevented any extensive settlement. Bounded on the north by Helena and on the south by the village of Snow Lake and the Laconia Circle Levee in Desha County, the area was about fifty miles by twenty miles. The Helena Businessmen's League boasted in 1913 that their city was surrounded by 30,000 square miles of unharvested lumber.[5] By the end of World War I, the expansion of railroads, levees, and drainage projects had made this region the second largest hardwood center in America.

The region's development brought together elements that were to feed tensions and raise the stakes of power to a dangerous level. Southeastern Arkansas was taking off economically during the war. Planters wanted to drive labor hard to make as much money as they could, but labor in the region had changed with the new aspirations and standards of living that the war had allowed. "Ours was a primitive and pioneer country," observed Gerard B. Lambert, a prominent landowner in the region, "where racial hatred was close to the surface. Here we had a tinderbox to be set off by the slightest spark," in part because of the numerical imbalance where black workers outnumbered the white people at least ten to one. "White men," he continued, "with their families on their minds, were constantly alert for the first signs of what they considered danger to their women and

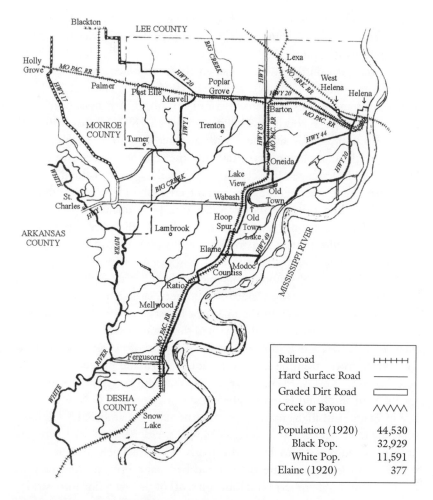

Fig. 2. Phillips County, 1919. Prepared by Butler Center for Arkansas Studies, Central Arkansas Library System, using the Midwest Map Company Arkansas Highway Map (1920), Blaisdell's Map of Arkansas (1919), and Ohman's Standard New Map of Arkansas (1930).

children. And the Negroes knew this. If they got out of line, they realized that there would be no compromise with sudden death. It was the old law of self-preservation at work."[6]

The area surrounding Elaine opened to development when the Missouri Pacific Railroad built an extension in 1903–1907. Harry E. Kelly, an industrialist and real estate banker from Fort Smith, Arkansas, purchased extensive acreage in southern Phillips County in 1892, and by 1901, he owned 16,000 acres individually, with another 19,000 in joint partnership. After the completion of the railroad, the state legislature created the Yellow Banks Drainage District, appointing Kelly as one of the directors. The expansion of the railroad line, and the creation of levees and drainage ditches, launched a timber and cotton boom. Kelly formed a partnership with E. M. Allen from Fort Smith to develop 4,000 acres surrounding Elaine, to cut the timber and to begin cultivation of cotton. Together, they laid out the town of Elaine in 1911 and began selling lots.[7]

Other planters and timber companies soon followed Kelly and Allen, the most prominent being Gerard B. Lambert, owner of Lambert Pharmaceuticals in St. Louis and the maker of Listerine. With the encouragement of his father-in-law, Lambert visited the region while a law student at New York University. Enthralled by the prospect of developing the land for cotton production, he left law school in 1913 and purchased 21,000 acres six miles west of Elaine, next to the White River. He paid $500,000 for the land and hired Harry Holbrook, a carriage maker in New York, to live in Elaine and manage the plantation he named Lambrook.[8] Lambert built his own railroad to his property, hiring independent Irish workers known as "humpers" to build the roads. The Irishmen lived in tents, worked on their own laying the railroad beds, and proved "unwilling to tolerate a boss."[9] Lambert built four spurs off of the main line into various sections of land that allowed him to send four flat cars into the woods. Mules hauled a gigantic "skidder" that pulled the logs to a steel crane which then loaded the logs onto a flat car. As many as thirty carloads of wood traveled daily by train to the Chicago Mill and Lumber Company in Helena.

Within eight months, Lambert had cleared 1,200 acres of land; built houses, a company store, a blacksmith shop, and a gin; and started planting and raising cotton. Like other planters in this region, he turned to black sharecroppers for his labor source, hiring black families and allotting them from twenty to forty acres of land with a new house. Lambert soon had four thousand acres under cultivation employing six hundred black and fifty white workers with a semiweekly payroll of five thousand dollars. Like most of the large landowners in the area, he had his main office in Elaine, where he also stayed whenever he was in Arkansas.[10]

Unlike other developers, Lambert had come from Virginia fully equipped with the racial views of his upbringing. Prejudice and paternalism were important parts of his character. In his early youth, Lambert recalled, he had lived "surrounded by Negroes . . . where they were nearer to us than members of our family. We trusted them and loved them. When they were ill we attended them personally." Drawing a distinction between the Old South of the eastern seaboard and the New South of the alluvial empire, he found that at Lambrook the men "employed for manual labor held no such position in our affections."[11] Paternalism would have no place in the large-scale plantations of the rapidly developing southern Phillips County economy.

By the outbreak of World War I, numerous newly developed plantations had engulfed the town of Elaine, along with a timber industry that provided wage labor for male sharecroppers who sought work during the less labor intensive or "lay-by" seasons of the cotton crop. Elaine represented a bustling New South center, a fine example of the growth and riches pouring out of the area right after World War I. The town had the largest white population in the region, with a population in 1920 of 377 people, including 61 African Americans.[12] Yet the region also had a frontier quality about it, like that of western boom towns with their dirt streets and newly built houses and stores. Paved roads did not come until the early 1920s; the commercial center was yoked to the countryside through a series of mud roads and trails or railroad tracks and spurs.

The war affected the Elaine area as it did other parts of the Delta. Wartime demands led to greater production needs, requiring a full-time labor force. While many workers crossed the river into Mississippi in search of higher wages and fairer landlords, many other black people headed north or to other southern towns and cities, especially Memphis, in search of better paying work. During the war the Helena Businessmen's League protested to the U.S. Department of Labor regarding outside recruiters who came from the Midwest and other places to steal their labor in Phillips County. Labor agents had secured several hundred black people to work in a Little Rock army cantonment where soldiers were temporarily housed. After working in such government jobs, many "negroes" became "dissatisfied." Planters and lumber mills thus experienced a labor scarcity that led them to allow women to work in the lumber mills for the first time. One company complained about the state law that prohibited them from working black women the traditional ten-hour days. Planters and lumber operators also complained that laborers worked irregularly and that women refused to work as domestics in white homes when they could make higher wages picking cotton or working in the lumber mills. To retain a cheap labor force, these employers pursued a very active "work or fight" program.[13]

The government took steps to reassure planters. In 1918 the U.S. commissioner of labor released eight to nine thousand black workers from working on army cantonments, with five hundred returning home to Phillips County. The commissioner also assured the businessmen that the government would not recruit any more black workers from the region. In spite of this order, labor recruiters continued to "steal" black labor—and employers responded accordingly. In 1917, a labor agent recruited 117 black people to a government plant in Nashville, Tennessee. When he returned, the Helena police ran him out of town, and then passed an ordinance requiring all federal agents to pay a five-hundred-dollar fee for the privilege of recruiting workers in the city.[14]

Phillips County employers also feared the intrusion of unions. The *Helena World* filled its front pages with accounts of the activities of the Industrial Workers of the World ("Wobblies") throughout the nation, fanning fears of radical elements at home. Businessmen insisted in 1917 that western laborers recruited to work in building the army cantonment in Little Rock had brought with them the radical ideas of the Wobblies. Apparently, federal intelligence agents had warned officials in Helena to place extra guards around factories, mills, and compresses. The agency had arrested an IWW organizer in Clay County, who supposedly had planned to organize in Phillips County. When a dredge boat blew up in Crittenden County, officials discovered that one of the accused had sent a trunk to Helena with plans to blow up mills in the region. Federal agents then found the trunk full of nitroglycerine. Another mill was also blown up in nearby Cross County. The agents also claimed that the Wobblies had caused telephone trouble in several Arkansas cities. And in Latour, just a few miles outside of Helena, two men had received five-hundred-dollar fines for trying in 1917 to entice eighteen black men to leave their jobs in protest of the low wages they had received.[15]

Underneath the booster mentality of Elaine, then, lay some rather unsettling facts for the planter class. It is not clear whether or not the IWW had influenced black workers in Phillips County. A federal government investigation in 1916 in Arkansas, however, predicted that "as a result both of the evils inherent in the tenant system and of the occasional oppression by landlords, a state of acute unrest is developing among the tenants and there are clear indications of the beginning of organized resistance which may result in civil disturbances of a serious character."[16] Planters were aware of this unrest that had been accelerated by the war, and they feared the influence of outside forces such as labor unions. They braced themselves for a postwar conflict rooted in contests over the surplus that high wartime cotton prices had produced.

Landowners were also concerned over the wartime accumulation of property, which had fostered greater independence for sharecroppers. For example, Ed Ware and his wife cultivated 120 acres of cotton and he owned a Ford car that he drove daily to Helena as a taxi service when his crops were laid by. The Wares owned two mules, one horse, a Jersey cow, a farm wagon, all of their farm tools, a harness, eight hogs, and 135 chickens. Ed Hicks was also doing well. He rented one hundred acres from Stanley and Moore Brothers that he and his brother had farmed in corn and cotton. He and his wife owned four mules, a wagon, and farming tools. Alfred Banks worked thirty-two acres of cotton, eight acres of corn, and one acre of truck crops. Frank Moore, just returned from the war, worked with his wife fourteen acres of cotton and five acres of corn; they also owned $678 worth of household goods. And Ed Coleman, seventy-nine years of age, farmed twelve acres in cotton and six in corn. He had obtained a number of household items and owned fifteen head of hogs.[17] The acquisition of property by so many families threatened planter dominance and especially their control of the wartime surplus. They wanted to keep as much of the wartime high profits as possible. After the war, when men and women returned from the cities and battlefields, planters no longer had to compete for labor with factories or the military, so they returned to their traditional methods of stealing their workers' crops and possessions.

One of the principal ways that planters sought to reassert their power involved a problem that faced sharecroppers from the very beginning— who controlled the crop, especially its marketing. By state law, planters owned the cotton crop and the croppers had to sell their cotton to the landowners. Further, since most contracts were oral rather than written, each party often had a different interpretation of the agreed-on distribution of the crop's profits. Planters may have insisted that the cropper had agreed to receive one-half of the crop, after all debts had been paid to the landlord. Some laborers, however, may have thought that they were working as share tenants who furnished all of the labor, equipment, and seed in return for three-fourths of the crop. Whether workers signed up as a cropper or share tenant, or rented land as a tenant, they were usually treated as sharecroppers, thus blurring the distinctions between the various rental and labor arrangements.[18]

During the war, planters had reaped most of the benefits of high cotton prices, continuing to pay their croppers a relatively low price for their crop. The 1919 cotton harvest proved to be the most lucrative yet, producing the South's first $2 billion dollar crop.[19] Sharecroppers knew this and many did as Ed Ware. On September 26, 1919, Ware's merchants, Jackson and Longnecker, came to buy some cotton he had just ginned and offered him at first twenty-four and then thirty-three cents per pound. Ware refused the price, saying he intended to take his cotton to Helena and sell it himself for the market price. Warned that the merchants planned to "mob" him, Ware refused, when invited, to enter their store. On September 29, Ware went to Helena and hired an attorney, Ulysses S. Bratton, who was known to have represented tenants in their efforts to secure settlements, to represent his interests.[20] Bratton filed suits on Ware's behalf, without any results.[21]

Another time-honored technique for denying workers their due involved planters and landlords using the sweat of their workers to put in a crop and then finding ways, sometimes violently, to drive them off the land without settling for the wages (they would typically hire other workers to help harvest the crop). Owners gained tremendously because they benefited from the high prices of cotton during the war without paying labor. And by law, if a cropper abandoned the crop, he or she lost all claims to its profits. Planters could be ruthless, as in the case of one cropper who refused to be driven from his cotton crop. The landowner retaliated by burning down his house.[22]

Planters' refusal to allow their workers to market their own crops or to pay them a fair price for their cotton, combined with evictions of people and the theft of their crops, led sharecroppers and tenants in the villages surrounding Elaine to join, in the spring of 1919, the Progressive Farmers and Household Union of America (PFHUA). Families from plantations and villages such as Ratio, Hoop Spur, Modoc, Old Town, Mellwood, and Ferguson aimed to secure a fair settlement from their landlords. Tenants knew that cotton was selling for around forty cents and they demanded their share of the profits. The founder of the union, Robert L. Hill, lived in neighboring Drew County. The union, according to Hill, had been organized in 1865 under an act of Congress as the Colored Union Benevolent Association in the District of Columbia. The association's charter had a section providing for the purchase of real estate for the organization.[23] Hill and V. E. Powell, a physician, had incorporated the organization in Winchester in 1918. According to the articles of the constitution, the object of the union "shall be to advance the interests of the Negro, morally and intellectually, and to make him a better citizen and a better farmer."[24] The union's structure resembled fraternal orders like the Masons, having a password, door words, and grips and signs for its members, which changed every three months to ensure the order's secrecy. Each lodge had a door keeper who refused entry to anyone who did not know the password. The union provided for a joint stock company with a capital stock of one thousand dollars. Members bought shares for a dollar each, with the aim of building at least a two-thousand-dollar base to allow the organization to invest in real estate for the order. The order elected a salaried deputy to hold office for six months; duties included organizing clubs in the county.

The "business of this Grand Lodge," read the constitution, "shall be to further advance the cause, uniting the race into a perfect Union in various counties. And to levy special taxes on subordinate Lodges for the purpose of purchasing land." Slogans at the end of the constitution read "WE BATTLE FOR THE RIGHTS OF OUR RACE; IN UNION IS STRENGTH; We Champion the Moral, Material, Political and Intellectual Interest of Our Race." At the top of the constitution, beneath the title of the union, was "The Negro Business League," which may have led prospective members to think that the organization belonged to the National Negro Business League organized earlier in the century by Booker T. Washington.[25] It also had the usual provisions of benevolent associations in that its aim was to purchase real estate, though the goal of these investments was not stated. It is entirely conceivable that Hill and his partners intended to form not a labor union, but a fraternal order that assisted rural people in purchasing land.

The fraternal characteristics of the union were significant on many levels. Sharecroppers and farm owners in the Elaine region belonged to the Masons as well as other lodges such as the Odd Fellows and the Mosaic Templars, headquartered in Little Rock. Traditionally associated with the middle class and with efforts of racial uplift, fraternal lodges reached beyond the confines of bourgeois respectability. These lodges, since emancipation, had served as sources of information that linked sharecroppers to organizations and ideas outside of the region. While most lodges provided burial and other benefits for their members, they also created spheres of civic participation for black men and women, who belonged to auxiliaries where they discussed political issues and the struggle for equality. Share-croppers in such organizations had opportunities to travel to regional and national meetings, held various offices, and even wrote their own calendars to reflect not only national holidays, but also important dates in African American history. The societies also provided business experience and offered credit to those unable to obtain loans from racist banks. Further, they were linked to churches, with ministers often forming the lodges through their congregations and holding the meetings in rural churches. Together, the churches and lodges formed the foundation of black civic and cultural life in the Delta. Finally, during World War I, the lodges had served as venues for black migration, and most of those who formed and belonged to NAACP chapters were also lodge members. Thus, by forming a lodge rather than a labor union, Hill stood to reach more people in the Delta. Many of those who did join came from the fraternal orders.[26]

The organization, then, did not appear to be a labor union at all. Yet to planters, it mattered little whether the organization functioned as a union or as a fraternal society. To them, it had only one purpose—to steal their enormous profits, undercut their authority, and threaten their very lives. When Hill hired a lawyer from Little Rock to represent the claims of the croppers, planters saw not just two men but a collective challenge to planter authority in the Delta. And they lashed back with a fury that surpassed any of the other uprisings of the Red Summer.

Members of the PFHUA decided in the fall of 1919 to sue their landlords for their fair share of the largest cotton crop in southern history. They secured the legal services of Little Rock attorney Ulysses S. Bratton. Of all of the firms for them to contact, that of Bratton represented, from the planters' perspective, the worst one imaginable. Bratton, a Republican, had served as an assistant U.S. attorney during Theodore Roosevelt's administration, and earlier had successfully prosecuted Phillips County planters for peonage. Bratton was also known as a supporter of black people's efforts to secure their rights. In September, a cropper from Ratio approached Bratton to represent sixty-eight PFHUA members who worked on the northern-owned Theodore Fauthauer plantation, where the manager had refused to issue itemized statements of accounts and had sold their cotton without any compensation. The croppers agreed to pay a lawyer's fee and to meet in Ratio on Wednesday, October 1, with Bratton's son, Ocier Bratton, an accountant who had just returned from the war in France.[27]

On September 30, Bratton's son traveled by train to Ratio to meet with Hill and other lodge members regarding their cases. Bratton had begun a journey that would take him down an unexpectedly violent and horrible path. Twenty-five to thirty black men and women met him by the side of the railroad, where Bratton sat and heard them one by one as they told how much cotton they had planted and how much they expected to make. Some men threatened not to bother picking their cotton, but Bratton urged them to harvest it and to keep an account of the weight. He asked each one to sign a contract and to make a down payment for his father's services. Most paid five dollars, though two put down fifty, and another twenty-five dollars.[28]

After he had been there for about forty minutes, six to eight white men with guns rode up on horses. Bratton observed that "the Negroes were surprised at this turn, and some of the women, there being several who had cases like the men, were pitiful in their abject terror; in fact I was talking to one when the men came up and she was crying as she talked to me. These Negroes, I do not believe, knew or contemplated any of the things which were so shortly to follow." The heavily armed men told Bratton the meeting was over and then took him nearby where six cars were parked that were surrounded by about thirty men. They demanded to know why he had met with Mr. Fauthauer's workers without consulting his plantation manager. The men then drove Bratton to Elaine where an angry mob awaited, shouting threats of lynching. His captors ushered him to a brick store, chaining him to two black men from Ratio. The guards searched him and then waved an IWW newspaper and another union newspaper in front of him, screaming, "Isn't he a pretty son-of-a-bitch; he's the ring leader." A deputy sheriff told Bratton not to worry, that he would protect him—and sent him on a train to Helena. At some point, Bratton learned that there had been a shooting at Hoop Spur, about three miles outside of Elaine, between a number of black people and some white men. Once on the train to Helena, Bratton heard the guards tell everyone to put their heads down as they passed Hoop Spur. Bratton remained in the Helena jail for thirty days.[29]

While Bratton was meeting with sharecroppers in Ratio, another group of union members, including men, women, and children, had gathered in the nearby Hoop Spur Church to discuss hiring his father as their representative. Several armed black men stood guard outside the church. During the meeting, shots were fired into the church. The guards returned the fire, killing W. A. Adkins, a white special agent of the Missouri Pacific Railroad. He was accompanied by Deputy Sheriff Charles Pratt and Ed Collins, a black prisoner who was a "trusty" from the Phillips County jail. After the shooting, Collins ran to nearby Wabash to get help. When Phillips County sheriff Frank F. Kitchens received news of the shoot-out, he immediately deputized a posse of three hundred men, organized them into squads under the leadership of World War I veterans fresh from combat, and sent them to Elaine. Meanwhile, planters around Elaine had begun to organize their own posse. Mere hours after Adkins was killed, planters burned down the Hoop Spur Church and headed for the fields in search of the union members.

Elaine planters had immediate reinforcements. By the morning of October 1, from six hundred to one thousand landowners, managers, sheriffs, and veterans from all over the Mississippi and Arkansas Delta, including the Helena American Legion, brought their guns to combat the insurrection. Many men came from nearby Clarendon, Marianna, and Marvell, Arkansas, and joined with those from Lula, Tunica, Friars Point, and Clarksdale from across the river in Mississippi to police Helena's city streets on the evening of October 1.[30]

Terrified of what the local white people called an insurrection, county judge H. D. Moore and the sheriff's office in Helena contacted Governor Charles H. Brough and requested assistance. Brough then received permission from the secretary of the Army to send in federal troops. All telephone lines from Elaine were cut.[31] On the morning of October 2, Governor Brough personally escorted 583 federal troops, including a twelve-gun machine-gun battalion, that had just returned from France. Some members of that battalion had fought in the Second Battle of the Marne and represented what one writer has called "a rolling killing machine." Colonel Isaac C. Jenks, a World War I veteran who had earlier fought against Native Americans in the West, commanded the troops. In an effort to prevent the killing of white people, Jenks, upon arriving in Elaine, immediately ordered the disarming of all black and white people, and sent all of the white women and children by train into Helena. He ordered his troops to shoot on sight those black people who refused to surrender. Jenks and his troops then pursued the black people, covering a two hundred mile radius. On that day, three white men were killed—veterans Clinton Lee and Lewis Tappan, both of the Helena American Legion posse, and Orley L. Lilly, real estate agent and member of Helena city council—along with seven black men, including Dr. D. A. E. Johnston of Helena and his three brothers.[32]

It is doubtful that all of the vigilantes left the region upon Jenks's orders. According to several accounts, acts of barbarism were committed by both the vigilantes and the troops. One witness, a prominent white citizen of Miller County who had taught school in Phillips County, saw "twenty-eight black people killed, their bodies then thrown into a pit and burned." He also witnessed sixteen African Americans hanging from a bridge near Helena. "Not a single one of the victims," according to the teacher, had been associated with the uprising, since they lived miles away from Elaine.[33] A white reporter from Memphis described a similar situation on October 2, after the troops had arrived. When following the posse and troops into the canebrakes in search of "negro desperadoes," he saw dead bodies "lying in the road a few miles outside the city. Enraged citizens fired at the bodies of the dead negroes as they rode out of Helena toward Elaine." He found that when the troops rounded up the people, few of them were armed. The soldiers were certain the insurrectionists had hidden their guns. He also saw troops surround a group of black people, but the officer in charge had not received orders to use the machine guns. While holding the people at gunpoint, he sent word to headquarters for permission to fire. After receiving confirmation of the order, he then fired into the crowd, immediately killing two people and forcing the rest to surrender.[34] Other witnesses described the barbarism of "cutting off the ears or toes of dead negroes for souvenirs and the dragging of their bodies through the streets of Elaine."[35]

A distinguished journalist from the *Arkansas Gazette,* Louis Sharpe Dunaway, later observed that the soldiers had "left a path strewn with orphans and widows and made a mockery of the laws they were sworn to uphold and obey . . . the soldiers marched rough-shod over the vast community inhabited principally by negroes, and shot them down in cold blood without any reason or excuse—thus manifesting a blood thirstiness without any parallel disclosed in the history of civilization." The writer was certain that Governor Brough had not condoned the "death dance," but the "appalling practice of killing innocent Darkies continued until a fair count showed 856 dead negro bodies with a wounded list probably five times greater."[36]

Gerard B. Lambert, perhaps the largest landowner in the region, later recalled how the union members were treated on his Lambrook plantation. Enroute to Lambrook on October 4, he saw that white men had spread throughout the woods, firing at any suspicious person. "A steel gondola car was hauled back and forth on the railroad track, the men inside firing from the shelter of the steel walls of the car. Several Negroes had been picked off in this way. When I arrived," he continued, "the death toll stood at 22 negroes and five white men."[37] Troopers apprehended and brought one of his "extremely insolent" sharecroppers, who was the alleged ringleader of the Lambrook local of the union, to the company store and tied him with a stout cord to one of the wooden columns of the porch. The troopers, enraged by the loss of two of their men in the woods that day, pressed the captive with questions. As the sharecropper continued in his "arrogance," one white man hoped to make him speak up by pouring a can of kerosene over him. As the sharecropper refused to talk, another one tossed a lighted match at him. "The colored man went up like a torch," recalled Lambert, "and in a moment of supreme agony, burst his bounds. Before he could get a few feet he was riddled with bullets."[38] As Lambert's account revealed, both troopers and employees of the plantations engaged in torture and murder.

Over the next several days, hundreds of black men, women, and children were arrested and taken to the Elaine schoolhouse where they were interrogated and tortured by troops, planters, and officials until they were cleared of any wrongdoing. Lambert recalled some of the brutality he witnessed at the newly built two-story schoolhouse. When he arrived he saw two armed troopers guarding the steps of the school. Lambert entered a large room where a number of troopers, an officer, and his own plantation superintendent sat at a pine desk and interrogated the detainees. "One by one colored men were brought from an adjoining room, questioned, and either held or released. It was cotton-picking time, and everyone was anxious to get the men back to work. It would seem that cotton was more important than convictions."[39] Lambert then heard a burst of shots come from the floor below. Everyone ran down the stairs of the schoolhouse. "It was all over when we got there," he recalled. "One of the lower rooms was being used to hold some of the worst offenders. Two armed men were at the door of this room and one in the hall. One particularly bad fellow had been insisting that he was 'going out.' The troopers warned him of what would happen if he tried. But he finally made up his mind. He rushed from the room and tore down the hall. He was soon full of bullets but he kept on going, finally diving off the front porch steps like a deer shot in flight, stone dead." Lambert then saw "a horrible thing happen. Two men calmly picked up the man's body and carried it to a spot beneath the windows of the room where the others were confined." They then dropped the body and "looked up at the staring faces of the negroes in the window and told them this should be a lesson to them." Later, Lambert saw the man's body still lying in the same place.[40]

Eventually, the majority were discharged and given passes to carry with them at all times; freedom, however, was contingent on the authorization of their planters and managers. Not all of those captured even lived in the Elaine area. Many people must have found themselves in a situation like that of Ed Glass, who had caught the train from his home in Snow Lake into Helena to take his daughter to the doctor. As the train passed through Elaine, men pulled him from the car, taking him to the schoolhouse where he was held until his planter arrived to vouch for him. His daughter managed to make her way back home.[41]

The Johnston brothers were not as lucky. When Dr. D. A. E. Johnston, a black dentist from Helena, had gone on a hunting trip with his brothers—L. H. Johnston, a physician visiting from Oklahoma; LeRoy Johnston, who had just returned from France where he had been wounded while serving with the Fifteenth New York Infantry; and a younger brother—they found themselves in a treacherous situation. On October 1, they were driving back from the countryside into Helena when a man told them of a riot in Elaine, suggesting that they leave their car and board a train. When the train passed through Elaine, some white men boarded and took the brothers off, placing them in a car driven by Orley A. Lilly, a Helena real estate dealer and member of the city council. County Treasurer Amos Jarman, Deputy U.S. Marshall W. H. Molitor, and Lilly's chauffeur were also in the car. According to Jarman, "We had no handcuffs so we chained the Johnston brothers' feet and hands together and placed them in the rear seat of Mr. Lilly's automobile."[42]

What followed in the car en route to Helena remains unclear. But the result ended in the deaths of all four Johnston brothers and Lilly. Jarman claimed that one of the brothers had reached over and grabbed Lilly's pistol from its scabbard and emptied it into his body, though it is hard to imagine how this might have happened, given the brothers were chained. In any case, the men dumped the Johnston brothers' bodies on the side of the road where they remained for several days until Dr. Johnston's mother-in-law was allowed to recover them. Officials then broke into Dr. Johnston's office and drugstore in Helena where they supposedly found a large stock of rifles and ammunition—proof, they insisted, that the men had been part of the conspiracy.[43] While the details of the Johnston brothers' murders remain unknown, it is worth noting that Johnston was a prosperous man, known for his outspoken views on black equality, and that he was married to the daughter of Reverend Abraham H. Miller, a prominent black minister who had been elected in 1864 to represent the Helena district in the state legislature. No one was arrested for their murders.[44]

Colonel Jenks's troops brought those men and women who had been deemed "insurrectionists" to the Phillips County Jail in Helena. On October 31, a grand jury indicted 122 black men and women, 73 for murder, and the others for various crimes that included night riding. Ironically, night riding had traditionally consisted of white men driving black people off of the land. The presiding judge, J. M. Jackson, began the trials on November 3, dispensing with them in a matter of days while troops from Camp Pike in Little Rock guarded the courthouse. The jury took eight minutes to return a guilty verdict on Frank Hicks, accused of killing Clinton Lee, even though the *Helena World* had initially reported that both Tappan and Lee had been killed accidentally. Eventually, twelve men received death sentences for the murders of Adkins, Tappan, and Lee, and sixty-seven others got from one to twenty-one years in prison for various offenses related to the "insurrection." The twelve men convicted of murder were Ed Ware, Will Wordlow, Albert Giles, Joe Fox, Alfred Banks, Jr., John Martin, Frank Moore, Frank and Ed Hicks, J. E. Knox, Ed Coleman, and Paul Hall.[45] Nineteen other defendants, all from Lambrook, were tried as a group. According to the officials, these people had gone directly to Frank Moore's house on the day of the insurrection with the goal of murdering a prominent citizen, B. F. Cunningham. The prosecuting attorney had expected the defendants to plead guilty; instead they demanded a trial and were convicted.[46] The demonized Robert Hill escaped to Kansas and successfully defeated planter efforts to extradite him to Arkansas. Ulysses Bratton was convicted of barratry for encouraging unwarranted complaints and lawsuits from the croppers, and had to leave Arkansas for the remainder of his life.

On October 7, Colonel Jenks declared the insurrection over and withdrew his troops. He issued a memorandum "To the Negroes of Phillips County" that order had been restored, that "no innocent negro has been arrested, and those of you who are at home and at work have no occasion to worry." He told black people that all "you have to do is to remain at work just as if nothing had happened." Echoing the planters' view, the colonel said that "Phillips County has always been a peaceful law abiding community, and its normal conditions must be restored right away. STOP TALKING! Stay at home—go to work—don't worry!" One week later the troops returned to Little Rock.[47]

In the report Colonel Jenks filed on his mission to Elaine, he mentioned that only two black people were murdered, while he had lost one corporal, with another soldier wounded. His report was devoid of the actual details of his troops' actions once they had arrived on October 2, nor did he describe how the troops had disarmed the white mobs or the black insurgents. An account in the *Memphis Press* on October 2 suggested that more had happened. "Many negroes are reported killed by the soldiers. Two soldiers are seriously wounded. The negroes are surrounded in the woods near Elaine by nearly 500 soldiers and have refused to surrender. A battle to the finish is expected. The negroes are well drilled and armed. The soldiers have trained machine guns on them. Constant fighting now in progress."[48] Even the *Helena World* reported that while the number of dead had not been ascertained, a member of the posse had said on the evening of October 1 that "there are plenty of them." The newspaper on October 5, however, placed the total number of black people killed at twenty-five.[49] Indeed, final estimates of the number of black people killed have ranged from two hundred to 856. Jenks's failure to report the many deaths of black people has led a lawyer to suggest recently that Jenks and the Army covered up a massacre. "One has to wonder," writes Griff Stockley, "how many blacks were killed on October 2 by the military and why Jenks failed to report that even one shot was fired by his troops. Armed with seven machine guns, the troops had plenty of firepower. One can only surmise that reporting the actual number of blacks killed and wounded would have raised a red flag in light of the Army's casualties." Jenks's report conveyed the planters' insistence that union members had planned to murder twenty-one landowners, and he attached copies of articles from newspapers that praised his troops' behavior.[50] Surely the cutting of the phone lines on October 1 made any accurate reporting of the actions of the vigilantes or the troops almost impossible. While the exact details of Jenks's mission to Elaine will never be known, press reports of the troops' atrocities eventually were supported by outside investigators. Meanwhile, Phillips County planters and businessmen developed their own narrative of events.

Faced with the reality of untold numbers of dead black people, and of emerging accounts of atrocities committed by the white mobs and federal troops, prominent officials and businessmen moved quickly on the evening of October 2 to develop their version of events to present to the press and the public. With Governor Brough's support, they appointed themselves to a Committee of Seven. Its members included Sebastian Straub, acting sheriff of Phillips County; H. D. Moore, county judge; Frank F. Kitchens, sheriff of Phillips County; J. G. Knight, mayor of Helena; and E. C. Hornor and T. W. Keese, prominent Helena planters and businessmen. E. M. Allen, real estate dealer, president of the Helena Businessmen's League, and treasurer of the Gerard B. Lambert Company, served as chairman. By October 6, they had constructed a narrative of events and an explanation of the causes of the "insurrection" that would appear in the nation's white newspapers. Their efforts to prevent the truth of the massacre from becoming public was aided by the self-censorship of Delta newspapers.[51]

The committee insisted that "the present trouble with the negroes in Phillips County is not a race riot. It is a deliberately planned insurrection of the negroes against the whites" directed by a union "established for the purpose of banding negroes together for the killing of white people." In their view, Robert Hill had misled poor, illiterate sharecroppers in order to steal the high profits that workers had made from their wartime crops, especially the money they had invested in Liberty Bonds.[52] Promising them land, the narrative continued, Hill encouraged the sharecroppers to murder their landowners and managers. Couriers called "Paul Reveres" had been selected by union leaders to spread word of the uprising. The committee expressed "amazement at the definiteness with which the coup had been planned and organized with prospective victims' names set down in writing and a certain date selected for the slaughter." It noted that the union's slogan was "We Battle for Our Rights."[53]

According to the committee, Hill had also told the sharecroppers of Secretary of the Interior Franklin Lane's plan to provide homesteads for veterans in cut-over lands, insisting the plan had not been carried out for black as it had for white soldiers. Negro soldiers at Elaine, said the committee, had sold their discharge papers to Hill for fifty to one hundred dollars, believing their service in the military had qualified them for forty acres of government land.[54] The committee expressed shock and dismay at the ingratitude shown by some of their oldest workers: "A remarkable thing about the development is that some of the ringleaders were found to be the oldest and most reliable negroes whom we have known for the past 15 years. He had made them believe that he had been entrusted with a sacred mission which had to be carried out regardless of the consequences."

So far "as the oppression is concerned many of the negroes involved own mules, horses, cattle and automobiles and clear money every year on their crops after expenses are paid." Local leaders also blamed the *Chicago Defender* for encouraging sharecroppers to demand better working conditions and political equality. The Hoop Spur incident, according to the committee, occurred when three men en route to arrest a local bootlegger had stumbled upon the union meeting, prompting the black people to fire on them. The committee stressed the history of good race relations in Phillips County, noting that the county had never had a lynching and praising local white people for their restraint in quelling the insurrection: they had relied on the legal system and federal troops to bring the guilty to justice rather than simply lynching them.[55]

The Committee of Seven's report was published in major newspapers throughout the country as the most accurate account of events. In the words of the *Arkansas Gazette,* the insurrection occurred because of the "cupidity of rascals" who had fleeced ignorant black people. In order to organize the people, Hill had to "inflame them with lies" promising them the property of the planters. The entire problem arose when northerners recruited southern labor with promises of high wages. "The South attempted to stop the exodus by reasoning with the negroes, and made some headway until the manufacturers, or some of them, produced the money to make possible a newspaper edited by Northern negroes and having for its purposes the inflaming of Southern negroes against the whites and against conditions in the South." Referring to the *Chicago Defender,* the writer insisted that the paper "is circulated today throughout the South. Each issue is filled with vicious lies and few negro leaders have taken the trouble to make the investigations that would prove the falsity of the paper's statements and counteract the harm it is doing. After the manufacturers produced money to finance this vicious sheet, certain Northern Republican politicians chipped in aiming to bolster up their political fortunes by controlling a new source of Republican votes." Thinking of the "riots" in other cities like Chicago and Washington, the *Arkansas Gazette* noted: "Each outbreak will mean more decided action against the negroes until finally an outbreak will mean annihilation of the negroes in the infected district. The negroes who are making money out of this newspaper are paving the way for ignorant Southern negroes to go to their graves."[56] What the Committee of Seven's narrative had left out was the longstanding fear of a sharecroppers' revolt. As Harry Anderson, a former resident of Phillips County, explained to Governor Brough on October 7, "Even twenty years ago when I was a rough rider citizen of that county, the very thing that happened was frequently talked of and feared."[57]

Challenges to the planters' version came immediately. Both Walter White of the NAACP and the famous antilynching crusader Ida Wells-Barnett traveled to the region and uncovered a different explanation of the "riot." White went to Phillips County a few days after the massacre, passing for a white reporter from Chicago. He interviewed a number of prominent participants, including Governor Brough and Committee of Seven member E. M. Allen. His findings, published in December 1919 in the *Crisis*, the *Survey*, and the *Nation*, reflected the views of the sharecroppers. White blamed the conflict on the sharecropping system, which had allowed the planters to control the crop and deny the workers a just return on their crops. When in 1919 the croppers exercised their constitutional rights and hired a lawyer, the planters repelled their efforts with the utmost force. White argued that the rise of cotton prices to forty cents had made it more difficult for the planters to keep their croppers in debt. Tenants, aware of higher prices, demanded itemized settlements. Planters, in return, had seized in October of 1918 many tenants' cotton from the previous year and had refused settlements until July 1919. White also argued that another union had sprung up to organize cotton pickers for higher wages. In the saw mills, black men had received higher wages during the war and had refused to allow their women and children to pick cotton, though he failed to note how black women had also made good wages in the mills.

According to White, more than one thousand black people were rounded up from October 1 to October 6 and kept in the "most disgusting, unwholesome, and unsanitary conditions." They were denied attorneys and interrogated by the Committee of Seven and their associates, who released none unless vouched for by a planter or employer. Those independently employed or who owned land remained in custody. Once in the Helena jail, he concluded, the prisoners were tortured and electrocuted to secure their confessions. Another study, by Monroe N. Work of Tuskegee Institute, endorsed White's view of the massacre.[58]

When White's articles appeared, prominent citizens of Helena, such as E. M. Allen, denied that White had been in their region. Since White had passed for a white reporter, neither Allen nor Governor Brough knew they had spoken to him. Allen insisted that White had been spreading lies and in particular, that no electric chair existed to torture the defendants. "Remember," he wrote to a University of Arkansas professor investigating the affair, "most of the negroes were men we had known for several years, and when they finally realized what they had done they were very anxious to clear themselves before the white folks who had been taking care of them for some many years." He insisted that the twelve men condemned to death were "bad eggs," and, if they were set free, "many of the negro families around Elaine would leave immediately, as they have been afraid of these men for years, and the negroes themselves say the country is well rid of them." Allen blamed the northern papers like the *Chicago Defender* and the *Crisis* for providing an opportunity for the "bad negro, the agitator, to stir up hatred and racial feeling, and they should either be suppressed or censored. The I.W.W. has been feeding their sort of stuff to all the negroes of the South for the past year, and a lot of harm has been done. If the professional negro agitators," he continued, "the low grade preachers, the self-appointed trouble makers who address white meetings in the North (men like White, Du Bois, and the like) could be suppressed there would be no trouble here." Allen noted that the sharecroppers at Ratio had sought to secure a settlement on the plantation owned by Theodore Fauthauer of Chicago, "a northern man and a Republican who was simply trying to apply business methods to a Southern farm. He was sincere and honest, but the old Southern methods are much the best." Allen, who was born and raised in Minnesota, insisted that the "southern men can handle the negroes alright and peaceably if let alone." Allen apparently saw differences, as had Lambert, between the old paternalistic, face-to-face management of labor that many imagined had characterized southern labor relations in the past and the managerial approaches used in the New South plantations.[59]

The most extensive account from the perspective of the sharecroppers came from Ida Wells-Barnett, who published her findings in 1920 in a pamphlet. Wells had been driven several years earlier from Memphis because of her efforts to fight mob justice. Returning clandestinely to the Delta, she interviewed the wives of the imprisoned, as well as the men and women prisoners themselves. She found that croppers had joined the PFHUA to hire a lawyer, to create a treasury to buy a tract of land for themselves, and to get croppers to hold their cotton for a higher price. The union had distributed information regarding the pending American Cotton Association's meeting in New Orleans, where five hundred cotton growers from ten states met to discuss ways of controlling cotton production to maintain high prices. One of these methods, which union members sought to employ, entailed withholding cotton from the market to drive up prices. Wells-Barnett saw the union's actions as a "Declaration of Economic Independence, and the first united blow for economic liberty struck by the Negroes of the South. That was their crime and it had to be avenged!"[60]

According to Wells-Barnett's calculation, if cotton had sold for forty-five to fifty cents a pound, a five-hundred-pound bale of cotton would have brought $250, and five bales, $1,250. "No padding of accounts nor inflation of prices could use all that money for supplies and leave the Negro in debt and subjection. Another way must be found to do this, and keep the Negro's wealth from him." She found that landlords had driven their tenants from the land once the cotton had been laid by. But some had picked their cotton by October 1, and had ginned and stood ready to market it. The planters, however, wanted their surplus: "What they could not do lawfully they did unlawfully with the aid of public sentiment and the mob. They are now enjoying the result of these Negroes' labor, while the Negroes are condemned to die or stay in prison twenty-one years."[61]

Wells-Barnett conveyed the testimonies of the men and women in jail, which provided a vastly different picture of the violence than did the accounts of planters. According to Ed Ware, when the union held its meeting at the Hoop Spur Church, men fired into the church and killed several people, burning it down the next day with the bodies inside. After Ware had returned to his home, 150 armed men came and stormed his house, breaking open trunks and drawers and taking all of his secretary minutes for the union and his Masonic lodge books. As they surrounded his house, Ware, Isaac Bird, and Charley Robinson began to run away. They shot Robinson, who was too old and crippled to run fast. The white men carried Robinson to Mrs. Ware's bed, where they left him to die, and took all of Ware's livestock and household goods.[62]

When Joe Fox and Albert Giles also saw 150 men coming toward their homes on October 1, they took their sisters and ran into the woods for safety. The men ran them down, shot at the women, killed three other men, and wounded Fox, Giles, and Alfred Banks. "They were so thick around us," recalled Fox and Giles, "that we heard them say, 'We are killing our own men.'" The posse took all of their household goods and livestock. John Martin hid in the woods for two days until the soldiers found him. They locked him in the Elaine schoolhouse for eight days before carrying him to the Helena jail. "It was not the union that brought this trouble; it was our crops. They took everything I had," he said. "Twenty-two acres of cotton, three acres of corn. All that was taken from me and my people. Also my household goods. Clothes and all. All my hogs, chickens and everything my people had. I was whipped twice in jail. These white people know that they started this trouble. This union was only for a blind. We were threatened before this union was there to make us leave our crops."[63]

William Wardlow hid eight women and children with him until the soldiers arrived, and then he carried them to the troops, hoping to prevent them from being harmed. He said that "just as fast as the Negroes lay their crops by they are driven from their homes and farms. When we were under arrest, the white people went and burned the church down to keep from showing up what they had done. We was not taught to kill no one," he said, but they had joined the union to "farm and to buy government land." He claimed that over eighty men, women, and children were "burned up by fire."[64]

Veteran Frank Moore supported the view that the massacre began over economic concerns and that white people instigated the violence as a means to tighten control over the region. Moore ran home after the Hoop Spur shooting and awoke the next morning to hear that white people "were coming down there and 'kill every nigger they found.'" Three to four hundred armed white men had arrived by noon, some walking and others driving in cars. According to Moore, "When we saw them shooting and burning them we turned running and went to the railroad east from there, and the white people tried to cut us off. They were shooting at us all the time . . . By 5 o'clock that evening, there was near 300 more white people coming on with guns, shooting and killing men, women and children. So I took the children and women and went to the woods and stayed until the next morning when the soldiers' train came. I took the children and women and made it to the soldier men; then they took us and carried us to Elaine village and put us in the white school-house and I was there five days." Moore concluded that the "white people want to say that union was the cause of the trouble. It's not so; the white people were threatening to run us away from our crops before this trouble started. The Phillips County people know they started this trouble and they only got the army there to cover what they had done." The white men took his family's cotton and corn crops, as well as his household goods.[65]

The mob exhibited the most gruesome kinds of behavior as it indiscriminately killed women, children, and old people. The mob seized Lula Black and her four children from their house, demanding if Mrs. Black belonged to the union. She responded that she had joined the union because "it would better the condition of the colored people; when they worked it would help them to get what they worked for." When the mob heard her response, they knocked her down, pistol whipped and kicked her, and then took her to jail. The posse then moved on to Frank Hall's house, where twelve men from Mississippi carrying an axe along with their guns killed an elderly woman, Frances Hall, and in a final gesture of disrespect tied her clothes over her head and threw her body in the road to lay exposed for several days. Ed Coleman, seventy-nine years old, had been at home asleep during the Hoop Spur meeting. People fleeing from the church shooting came to his house to warn him and his wife to leave. When they started to run from the posse, they saw Jim Miller's family burned alive. They hid in the woods for two days until Coleman decided to return to his home. As he approached his house, he found that the white men had shot and killed some of the women and children.[66]

The reportage of White and Wells-Barnett produced overwhelming evidence to counter the planters' narrative. But it would take the intervention of the federal government to bring the truth of Elaine to national attention. In 1923, the U.S. Supreme Court, in *Moore v. Dempsey*, overturned the convictions of six of the black men accused of murdering Clinton Lee. The NAACP agreed to defend the twelve sharecroppers accused of murder. Scipio Africanus Jones, a prominent African American attorney from Little Rock, represented the defendants in the various state appeals cases, and remained on the case when it went to the Supreme Court. Two separate cases existed. One, for the murders of Adkins and Tappan, bore the name of Ed Ware, and carried with it the cases of William Wardlow, Albert Giles, Joe Fox, Alfred Banks, and John Martin. The second case led with Frank Moore, who was accused of murdering Clinton Lee, and the cases of his accomplices—the brothers Frank and Ed Hicks, J. E. Knox, Ed Coleman, and Paul Hall. The Arkansas Supreme Court overturned the convictions in the case that bore Ed Ware's name, arguing that the Phillips County jury had failed to state that the men had been convicted of first-degree murder (a state law required both the judge and the jury to state whether the defendant was charged with first- or second-degree murder). The Ware cases then wound their way through the state court system until 1923, ending with the freeing of the men. The Moore case went to the U.S. Supreme Court, which overturned the conviction in 1923 in *Moore v. Dempsey*. Justice Oliver Wendell Holmes argued that before the trial had begun, the Committee of Seven had promised the public that the defendants would be executed if they were spared a lynching. He also noted that the defendants' testimonies had been secured through torture and that the trial had occurred in a setting dominated by a mob spirit, consequently violating the men's right to due process of the law. The court remanded the case to the federal district court. After a year of political dealing, the final six men were freed.[67]

The NAACP's victory in the Supreme Court was made possible by the affidavit of two white men, T. K. Jones and H. F. Smiddy, who had been involved in the massacre and who reversed their testimonies. Jones, a special agent for the Missouri Pacific Railroad, corroborated the version of the black community. On the night of September 30, according to Jones, Deputy Sheriff Dick Dazell requested that he allow two of his employees, special officers Smiddy and W. A. Adkins, to ride with Charles Pratt to Elaine to arrest a bootlegger named Clem. Smiddy was too tired, but Adkins went along. Leaving around 9:00 P.M., they dropped by E. J. Weyeth's house for liquor. At 2:00 A.M. Dazell called Smiddy and Jones, saying Adkins and Pratt had encountered trouble and insisting that they drive down to Hoop Spur. Arriving at Hoop Spur around 3:30 A.M., Smiddy and Jones found the dead body of Adkins about fifty feet north of the Hoop Spur Church. Jones went into the church and found the benches turned over, and a horse and wagon hitched north of the building to a fence. From the church, the men drove to Elaine, where Dazell had phoned Sheriff Kitchens in Helena for help. Later in the day at Elaine, Jones overheard planters discussing how a number of them had gone to the Hoop Spur Church the night before to break up the union meeting. They acknowledged that the white people had started the shooting by firing into the church. One of the men said to another that he knew his "negroes don't belong to that blankety blank union." The other said, "How in the hell do you know they don't?" He answered, "I told my negroes about two weeks ago that if they joined that blankety blank union I would kill every one of them."[68]

Jones did not witness the shooting of Clinton Lee, but he said that "automobiles were running up and down that road continuously and if negroes wanted to kill any white men they had ample opportunity to do it." The Missouri Pacific had run a caboose through the area loaded with men several times a day, yet black people had not fired at them. Jones never saw a single black person with a gun or weapon during the entire day. When he rode the train back into Helena, he noticed as it passed through Hoop Spur that the church had burned down. "From the information I gathered while I was down there the whole trouble started because the white folks objected to the negroes having this union; that the negroes were organizing to employ counsel to represent them in getting settlements from their white landlords."[69]

Smiddy provided a similar account. He testified that at Hoop Spur he had found "a condition that showed that the last people who had been in the church had left there hurriedly. Benches were turned over, window lights broken out on all sides of the church, glass scattered all over the floor and every evidence of a stampede was in the church house. We also found some literature of the Farmers and Laborers Household Union of America. We found nothing in the literature to indicate a criminal or unlawful purpose on the part of the organization." Ed Collins had told him that they had come to the church to break up the meeting and that Adkins had fired into the church first. Collins insisted he had killed one of the men, but that the others had picked him up. Collins then ran to Wabash and woke up a deputy sheriff who refused to help him, slamming the door in his face. After talking with Collins, Smiddy and others arrested several men, women, and children who were picking cotton and brought them into the church.

By the following morning, continued Smiddy, several hundred people from all over Phillips County had arrived and began to "hunt negroes and shooting and killing them as they came to them." Smiddy and a posse of fifty to sixty men marched down a slough leading off from the church, with some on one side and some on the other. "We began firing into the thicket from both sides thinking possibly there were negroes in the thicket and we could run them out and kill them. As we marched down the thicket to the southwest I saw some of them running and trying to get away. They were shot down and killed by members of the posse. I didn't see a single negro during all the man hunt that was armed, and I didn't see a single negro fire a shot." Smiddy saw the murders of Jim Miller and Arthur Washington, and he shot Milliken Giles, who was on the edge of the thicket trying to hide. "He didn't have a gun and was not trying to shoot anybody." After Arthur Washington was killed while running away from his house, "we marched down to the thicket where the road crosses. The thicket ran out at this road and we were going to march up the thicket firing into the thicket from both sides. As we were marching back from the thicket, Tappan was killed. He had gone down that side of the thicket and when we came to the point we turned around and were going back on the same side of the thicket. Tappan was killed where the thicket was about 30ft wide." Smiddy insisted that there were "no negroes in the thicket at that point as we searched it thoroughly after the shooting of Tappan."

Smiddy did not know who had killed Tappan, but since he had been shot on the left side of his face, and the posse had been going north on the east side, Smiddy insisted that "I feel perfectly sure he was accidentally killed by a member of our posse on the other side of the thicket. Substantiating Joe Fox's and Gilbert Giles's account of the event, Smiddy said that he had heard someone shout, "Look out we are shooting our own men." Indeed, one of the men had also wounded Smiddy and Dazell. "When we started down that thicket it was the understanding with all of us that we would shoot the negroes as we came to them, which we did." Smiddy, in the car with Clinton Lee when he was shot, insisted that the gunman had not been a black person.

At Elaine, Smiddy "found the people there expecting an attack from the negroes on the town," and a number of them had gotten "on top of the stores and houses." Upon searching the surrounding fields, however, the posse found no black people. He also described a crowd of men who had come into the vicinity of Elaine from Mississippi and had hunted down, shot, and killed men, women, and children without even knowing whether they had belonged to the union. Negroes, he recounted, were killed "time and time again" while out in the fields picking cotton, harming nobody. On October 2, the soldiers arrived and placed the town of Elaine under martial law, and swept the surrounding countryside, arresting and bringing black families into the Elaine schoolhouse. Smiddy then returned to Helena and noticed on the way that the Hoop Spur Church had burned. He then learned that white men had burned the church on October 1 to destroy the evidence of those who had fired into the meeting.[70]

Smiddy and Jones both established that Phillips County officials had tortured the twelve men, as well as others who had confessed to the murders of Lee and Tappan. According to Smiddy, the Committee of Seven brought the sharecroppers before them and tried to secure confessions from them or encourage them to name other sharecroppers as instigators of the insurrection. When the persons refused to provide the information the committee wanted, members took turns abusing them, eventually sending them up to the third floor to the "whipping room" and the "electric chair," where the men were stripped naked and whipped with a seven-pound leather strap. "The Negroes were whipped unmercifully. Every time the strap was applied it would bring blood." Smiddy said that he "had personally applied the lash to a great number of these Negroes. We whipped them to make them tell what we wanted them to tell. We wanted them to tell facts that would convict themselves and others under arrest."

Some men received such severe beatings that officers had to drag them to their cells and place them on their beds, where they remained for several days without any medical attention. Later, the men received a second lashing on their sores, usually bringing a confession. Some, like Frank Moore, after receiving three such whippings, said he would rather die than confess to a crime he did not commit. Officials also administered formaldehyde to the noses of some during their whippings. Others were placed in the electric chair and shocked until they confessed or blamed others.

Smiddy insisted that "no Negro freely and voluntarily testified in these cases. They were either whipped and compelled to testified [*sic*], or tortured in the other ways herein stated." Dick Dazell, Louis Anselman, and Charley Gist were among those who administered the torture. The Committee of Seven's claim that the union sought to murder planters, testified Smiddy, had never been substantiated except through torture. He had heard some of the black people say when confronted with the electric chair, "White folks, what do you want me to say, I will tell you anything you want." While Smiddy did not know how many people had been killed at Elaine, he insisted that he had seen "with my own eyes" between two and three hundred black people killed, while he knew of only five white men who had died.[71]

In light of the Supreme Court decision, one might have expected the planter class of Phillips County to hide its face. Planters and their partners in local law enforcement had obviously been accused of torture, indicating at the very least the limits of their version of the massacre. Yet they held to their story, indeed until this very day. The actual number of deaths in the Elaine Massacre will never be known. Federal troops and vigilantes combed a wide area that came to include other counties, and people continued to die after the troops had left. Estimates of the dead ranged from five to twenty-five white men and up to 856 black people. The NAACP's official publication, the *Crisis,* estimated that from twenty-five to fifty black people were killed, while only five white men had died, and claimed that the "stench of dead bodies could be smelled for two miles." Walter White amended that estimate in 1920 to around two hundred black people. Ulysess S. Bratton insisted that at least two hundred men, women, and children had been killed, while, as previously discussed, Smiddy testified that he personally witnessed the killing of two to three hundred people. NAACP Attorney Moorefield Storey, in his argument to the U.S. Supreme Court in the *Moore* case, said that from two to three hundred black people had died.[72] Unfortunately, the claim by L. S. Dunaway that 856 black people had been killed is impossible to verify because he failed to cite his source. It seems safe to assume, however, that at least two hundred black people died.

An accurate account of the massacre would require the skills of forensic archaeologists, much like those used near the end of the twentieth century to find and identify the bodies of torture victims in Chile and Argentina, or those of ethnic cleansing in the former Yugoslavia. Regardless of official investigations, black people persisted in remembering and testifying to the slaughter. For example, Mrs. Ruth Jackson of Snow Lake recalled that two years after Elaine, people continued to find skeletons all over the area, while planters continued to take everything people had. John Morrow, who was a teenager at the time and whose grandfather had been in the union, recounted how the dead bodies of black people were stacked in boxcars and hauled out of the region. Robert Miller, the grand nephew of Dr. D. A. E. Johnston who was murdered along with his three brothers in the massacre and whose grandmother had driven out from Helena to re-cover the bodies, said that his family never discussed Elaine, and thus to this day he never knew what had really happened. Immediately following the massacre, his grandparents sent his father to school in Boston.[73]

For black people all over the Delta, Elaine remained known as a place where African Americans were not safe. When Mrs. Gladys Hammond moved as a young girl to Elaine in 1932, she feared that white people would kill her upon her arrival. Stella Seals, who grew up in Wilson, Ar-kansas, over one hundred miles north of Elaine, recalled how her mother had always told her never to go to Elaine because white people would kill her.[74]

Although Frank Moore and all of the other defendants were freed after the Supreme Court upheld their appeals, sharecroppers and tenant farmers in the Elaine area and throughout the Delta remained wary. Terror still reigned. In November following the massacre, Obie Carroll, an eighty-four-year-old former slave, came to the law offices of Bratton to report how the chief of police in Pine Bluff had beaten him without provocation. This was also the town where veteran Flinton Briggs had been lynched in 1919. In addition, according to an anonymous letter from Wabash in No-vember of 1919, the slaughter of black people continued long after the troops had left. Addressed to "Uncle Sam," the writer commented that "we as colored people of the south is having a dreadful time down here. All of the men are being taken away and lynched . . . and we wemon [*sic*] are left in a suffering condition being treated awful cruel." She concluded that her people "are begging for mercy."[75] One can only imagine what "awful cruel" entailed for these women. The letter suggested that while men may have gone to prison, women who escaped arrest still suffered punishment on the farms.

The families of the union members found no welcome when they returned to their homes. Mrs. Frank Moore had managed to escape the massacre and to hide for four weeks. After she read in the newspaper that the trouble had ended, she returned to the Archdale farm to pay what she owed and to get her furniture and clothes. Mrs. Archdale told her that she had nothing, although Mrs. Moore saw her furniture in the Archdale house. When Mrs. Moore asked the whereabouts of her husband, Frank, Mrs. Archdale replied that he was in the Helena jail. "Did he kill anybody?" queried Mrs. Moore. "No," she said, "but he had just come from the army and he was too bigoted" against white people. Billy Archdale then appeared and told Mrs. Moore that if she did not leave, he would "kill her, burn her up, and no one would know where she was." When she left, another landlord who was considered a leader of the mob arrested her and took her to the Helena jail. She remained there for eight days where she worked with fifteen other black women from three o'clock in the morning until ten at night.[76]

Mrs. Ed Ware and her daughter spent one month in prison at hard labor, sleeping on concrete floors. Officials told them when they were discharged to go back home, go to work, and "never join nothing more unless they got their lawyers' or landlord's consent." When Mrs. Ware returned, she had nothing, though she saw some of her belongings in white people's homes.[77]

The fate of the Elaine Twelve, whose cases the Supreme Court had overturned, remains largely unknown. In 1936, two were reported still living in Arkansas and two others in Chicago. It is difficult to imagine that any returned to Phillips County. The fate of the white people involved was much brighter. E. M. Allen left the region after 1919 and became president of the National Surety Company in New York City. Phillips County prosecuting attorney John E. Miller was elected to the U.S. Congress in 1931, and served in the U.S. Senate from 1937 until President Franklin Roosevelt appointed him as U.S. district judge for the western district of Arkansas. He presided over the implementation of the U.S. Supreme Court's rulings on desegregation, which he continued to oppose. Both Allen and Miller held to their accounts of the Elaine Massacre as late as the 1960s.[78]

Black men and women joined the Progressive Farmers and Household Union because it promised to aid them in improving their lives. The union members had exercised a most basic right of citizenship when they secured a lawyer to represent them in court and when they later demanded a fair trial by a jury of their peers. Black people in Phillips County knew their rights and they acted accordingly. Their brave actions also inspired other people in the region, as black Arkansans mobilized to fight for the release of those convicted of murder. By organizing the Citizens Defense Fund Commission, black people raised at least ten thousand dollars for the defense in the *Moore* case. Many others, like a group of forty ministers from Pine Bluff, visited Governor Thomas McRae to press him into staying the executions of the twelve men sentenced to death. The victory secured in the Supreme Court's decision belonged first to the black people of Arkansas.[79]

The NAACP's support and extensive publicity of the trials indicated a significant change from the prewar years, for now an outside agency existed to hold the planters accountable. For those who searched for the truth in the Elaine Massacre, the NAACP had provided the information for all of the world to see. In cities like Harlem, the Elaine defendants became a cause célèbre as groups raised money for their defense. Delta black people now had allies outside the region.

The confrontation between planters and the PFHUA also demonstrated the tradition of armed self-defense in the rural black community. Guns were central to rural life for both black and white southerners. Even during slavery, some slaves had carried guns for hunting game. But guns carried a different weight for black people. Born and raised in the violent world of sharecropping and Jim Crow, black people also armed themselves for self-defense. Sharecroppers in Elaine knew that their efforts to form a union would not be met with kindness. Like their forebears and later descendants, the sharecropping families in southern Phillips County armed themselves and prepared for the worst. The *Helena World* reported that the troops had confiscated large quantities of rifles, shotguns, pistols, and ammunition, some of which were "of the latest model and very expensive."[80] Evidence indicated that veterans such as Frank Moore had organized the men into squads. The guards at the Hoop Spur Church carried guns and were prepared to defend themselves. Indeed, the lore among many black people in the Elaine region to this day holds that more white people were killed than has ever been recognized.

Regardless of how well armed black people might have been, they were no match for the machine guns that the troops unleashed on them. Thus, while the people surrounding Elaine aimed to hire a lawyer and to work through the legal process, as citizens normally do in a democratic society, they were also prepared for a different scenario. It was said that the women in the Hoop Spur Church carried automatic pistols concealed in their stockings, and that soldiers found guns hidden on many of the women they captured. Surely others carried pistols concealed in their food buckets when they went to pick cotton in the fields—as did freedom fighter Fannie Lou Hamer's mother across the river in Mississippi.[81]

The wholesale massacre in Phillips County indicated how fearful planters and their allies had become of the changes the war had brought, and it revealed their determination to destroy the aspirations of Delta black people. White leaders did not have to worry about federal intervention to end segregation and disfranchisement. It was clear by 1919 that President Woodrow Wilson would not bring his fight for democracy back home to America. But planters could not erase African Americans' growing expectations generated by the wartime mobilization. Wilson might turn his back on democracy, but less certain were the intentions of Delta plantation laborers. By requesting and receiving federal troops, planters signaled to African Americans throughout the alluvial empire that any assertions of these rights would be met with the utmost force. By burning the Hoop Spur Church and black men, women, and children, planters sought to destroy any trace of black demands for economic justice. And by indicting Ulysses Bratton for barratry (for encouraging unwarranted complaints and lawsuits from the sharecroppers), officials made it difficult for others to provide legal representation for the croppers. But planters could not make the NAACP or the hated *Chicago Defender* disappear. They could not suppress their reports of the events nor the Supreme Court's decision.

Rumors spread of potential revolts in other parts of the Delta. In January 1920, 130 troops were called into Dumas, a town of five hundred people located on the Mississippi River several miles south of Elaine, where black people outnumbered whites by thirty to one. The white people were mostly planters, with a few others working in the sawmills. While the details have remained sketchy, one account held that many black people had been run out of their community near Dumas for organizing black mill workers. Apparently, armed black people in the settlement had attacked deputies when they approached the village to arrest Doc Hayes for stealing hogs from a nearby plantation. It seems unlikely that Governor Brough would have sent 122 troops to protect those trying to arrest a man for stealing hogs. Another account held that white mill workers had captured

Hayes for stealing hogs on a plantation, and then he escaped and returned to the Burrus mill with a rifle and drove the men into the woods. The sheriff and two deputies then arrested Hayes. When the federal troops arrived in Dumas, they were supposedly met by the returning posse who assured them that everything had been settled. As in Elaine, the phone wires between Dumas and outside regions had been cut as soon as the trouble started, suggesting that planters did not want anyone, including the military, to know the true version of events. The incident revealed the anxiety felt by planters in other regions of the Delta following the Elaine Massacre. It may also have indicated the persistent efforts of black workers to secure decent wages and conditions. Perhaps the IWW had been active in the region; reports placed them in the counties surrounding and including Phillips at about that time.[82]

Black people witnessed efforts to circumscribe their access to guns and outside information. Planters sought to disarm black people in the Arkansas Delta by banning the sale of firearms and ammunition to African Americans. And the Committee of Seven requested from the federal government more than one hundred regulation army rifles and twenty-five thousand rounds of ammunition, as well as six Browning rifles with five thousand rounds of ammunition, to help preserve order.[83] Measures were also taken throughout the region to outlaw the distribution of the *Crisis* and the *Chicago Defender.* Mississippi passed a law in 1920 making it a misdemeanor to "print or publish or circulate" literature favoring social equality.[84] In Arkansas, Governor Brough also moved to ban the *Defender.* In Pine Bluff, eighteen black leaders, including two ministers, were named in a suit filed by city officials who sought an injunction against the distribution of the *Defender* on the grounds that it incited black people. One week earlier, news dealers in the town had been banned from selling the paper, which had published an account of the murder of George Vick, "a negro who had recently slain a city detective, which is alleged to have been false and intended to stir up strife between the races." In Holmes County, Mississippi, E. R. Franklin received six months imprisonment and a four-hundred-dollar fine for selling the *Crisis.* Local leaders claimed that an editorial in the January issue had demanded "too many rights for the negroes, and would only serve to swell their heads."[85]

Civic leaders became especially concerned with banning fraternal orders, often referred to as secret societies. Fraternal lodges alarmed planters because they had become, as they had in Elaine, a locus for political activity. As affiliates of national organizations, lodges served as conveyers of outside information, while the Masons stressed self-improvement and good citizenship. Many had organized entire communities for the migration northward and some had contributed the first members to local NAACP chapters and to labor unions. Their secretive nature fueled planter anxieties in the wake of the Elaine Massacre.[86] Indeed, a man whose work involved calling on funeral homes in several southern states had written to the Department of Justice in April 1919 regarding the forming of secret African American societies in Arkansas and Mississippi. He had predicted at the time "that there would be a race war in the States within six months . . . That race war has happened," he continued, "only it happened in Arkansas in place of Mississippi where I thought the outbreak would occur." The writer urged the department to send investigators to determine how extensive these organizations had become.[87] Fears of fraternal lodges continued among the planter society throughout the 1920s. The sheriff of Pine Bluff, Arkansas, reported in 1920 that he watched black people closely in anticipation of an uprising. Another officer reported that "negro lodges at Pine Bluff were very strong and their leaders were known to advocate equal wages, political offices and social equality for the colored people."[88]

When the National Baptist Sunday School Association met in Little Rock in 1921, many white Arkansans were certain the meeting had come to the city because of the Elaine Massacre. While an FBI agent found no basis for "these wild rumors," he reported that his confidential sources indicated "the negro ministers of this place have in the past attempted to arouse feeling among the negroes by pressing social equality and advising the negroes of their equal rights, and if unable to obtain them through peaceable means, then resort to violence. It is a well known fact," he concluded, "that the majority of the negroes are well armed with high powered guns and ammunition."[89]

World War I tore the seams of class and racial relations in Delta society. The aftermath of that war—in particular, the Elaine Massacre—left no doubt of black people's determination to secure justice in their economic dealings with the planter class. It also left no doubt that planters would draw on the full force at their disposal to prevent black people from achieving their goals. The Elaine Massacre cast a long shadow over the following decades. The planters had realized their worst fears—that black people would act not in the stereotypical ways, but as people making their rightful claims for the fruits of their own labor and the liberties guaranteed them under the Constitution. As the preamble of the charter of the

Progressive Farmers and Household Union claimed, "We Battle for Our Rights." The Elaine sharecroppers had exposed the intransigent racism and barbarism behind the scientific progress of the New South, while demonstrating to everyone the NAACP's ability to fight Jim Crow justice in the courts. Even though planters in the following years initiated a new reign of terror that sought to destroy black institutions like the churches, lodges, and locals of the NAACP, black people showed remarkable resilience. In the face of the horrors that marked the next decade, black people still found ways of fighting back.

4 | The Black People's Burden

Henry Lowry crossed the Mississippi River in 1918 with his wife, Callie, and their four-year-old daughter to live and work on O. T. Craig's plantation in Nodena, Arkansas. Like other Mississippi farm laborers during World War I, he hoped to find opportunity in the rapidly expanding plantation economy in neighboring Mississippi County, across the river from Memphis. Instead, Lowry encountered a landowner who was as oppressive as any he had known in Mississippi. Craig ruled his alluvial empire as a separate colony within the broader polity known as the State of Arkansas, drawing few distinctions between the power of the state, civil society, and his own personal power. He owned everything from the tools used to work the land to the clothes worn on the backs of his sharecroppers. Like other planters, he made his workers trade at his commissary, ensuring their continued indebtedness to him. Craig was known as someone who never settled with his tenants; he simply worked them from year to year without any acknowledgment that he owed them anything. His son, Richard, served as a postmaster and clerk of court, further collapsing the line between the supposedly independent power of the federal and local governments and that of Craig. The planter saw himself as the only "government" when dealing with his black tenants. As one of his sharecroppers, Mrs. Lucy Oliver, recalled, Craig was "mean to black people," and he "beat black folks who would let him."[1]

Lowry was not afraid of Craig. About forty years old, he was a big man, who stood well over six feet tall. A thirty-third-degree Mason (the highest level within the Masonic order, awarded only to men of outstanding character and leadership qualities), Lowry commanded the respect of his fellow sharecroppers and was known as someone who "stood up for his people" as well as for himself. Yet "Mr. Henry," as Lowry was known in the black community, "didn't take nothing off of nobody," including the Craigs.[2]

110

Tired of working hard only to grow deeper in debt, Lowry decided in December of 1920 to move his family and look elsewhere for work. With this in mind, he figured his own wages and expenses for the past two years that he had worked for Craig and demanded a settlement. Lowry knew that if he moved without obtaining written evidence that he was debt-free, Craig could "attach" his family and their belongings. Because he controlled the mail, the landowner probably knew that Lowry aimed to move elsewhere, and he refused to issue a settlement. Lowry, however, was determined to obtain a clean slate and move his family from the Craigs. Armed, Lowry went to Craig's house on Christmas Day and demanded a settlement. Craig came out and threw a stick at him. Lowry then fired his gun, killing Craig and his daughter, Maybell. As the two sons came out of the door, Lowry shot them as well, wounding both.[3]

Lowry then hid among friends and family, many of whom belonged to the Masons and Odd Fellows. Meanwhile, a posse formed to search for Lowry and bring him to justice. They searched all of the houses on the plantation, but never found him. As Mrs. Oliver recalled, Lowry was in the home of her friend Julie and her husband when the posse came. He hid in a room and waited for them to leave, then asked for turpentine to put on his feet so that the dogs could not pick up his scent. According to Mrs. Oliver, Lowry stayed near Nodena for several days until he decided to leave. He could have killed the posse at anytime, she insisted, but he knew that many black people would die if he did.[4] Lowry finally fled to El Paso, Texas, with the help of his fraternal brothers.

Nodena newspapers sensationalized the worker's murder of his employer and demanded a lynching, but attempts to locate the suspect failed until a local postmaster, in a routine practice for the Delta, opened Lowry's mail. The fugitive had written to a lodge member, asking that he find his family and send them to El Paso. The sheriff immediately detached twelve deputies to Texas, men who also collected a one thousand dollar reward for returning the fugitive. When they found Lowry, he begged the posse to kill him rather than return him to the mob that he knew awaited in Nodena.

For a moment it appeared as if Lowry would deny the crowd in Nodena its execution. While in El Paso, he had contacted the president of the local NAACP, L. W. Washington, who visited him in jail. Lowry had agreed to return to Arkansas and stand trial if his safety could be guaranteed. The NAACP hired a lawyer who contacted Arkansas Governor Thomas McRae, requesting that he ensure Lowry's safety. The governor agreed.[5] McRae ordered the deputies to bring Lowry straight to Little Rock and he reportedly phoned Mississippi County sheriff Dwight H. Blackwood several times, though he never reached him. The deputies instead took Lowry by train to Sardis, Mississippi. A mob of fifteen unmasked men, after receiving a call from a deputy who informed them of Lowry's trip, arrived in Sardis, took Lowry, and announced their intentions to parade him through the Memphis streets before crossing the river to carry out the actual lynching. Authorities in Memphis blocked the roads into the city, forcing the mob to disband. Five men then drove Lowry by car to Nodena, while the remainder went to the Peabody Hotel for dinner. The Peabody was a major gathering place for Delta planters, lawyers, and others who had business in Memphis.

Six hundred people watched on January 25, 1921, as the mob burned Henry Lowry on Craig's plantation. In an effort to torture him as much as possible, the lynchers roasted Lowry slowly for roughly an hour by sprinkling dry leaves on the fire around his feet. Finally, they poured gasoline on his upper body to create a dramatic ending. As his wife and daughter watched, Lowry reached for and swallowed hot coals, depriving his executioners of witnessing longer suffering. After the victim had died, the leaders turned to the black people in the crowd and ordered them to cut him down and bury him. The people replied, "You can cut him down yourself!"[6]

The NAACP used the brutal affair as further proof that conditions were so horrible in the South that black people had no choice but to leave for points North. Lowry's life and death provided evidence of the persistence of the "shadow of slavery"—of debt peonage and the oppressive sharecropping system. Native Arkansan William Pickens, field secretary for the NAACP, immediately traveled to the Delta and investigated the murder. He found that the "rural districts of Arkansas are more unsafe for colored people to-day than they were thirty-odd years ago; perhaps more than they have ever before been."[7] The Mississippi River Valley, he concluded, was the "Congo of America" where "labor is forced, and the laborer is a slave," though the form of slavery "is a cunningly contrived debt-slavery, to give the appearance of civilization and the sanction of law." He blamed the sharecropping system for all of the lynchings and burnings that had occurred around that time in the Delta.[8] Pickens correctly saw the persistence of sharecropping as the root cause of much of the postwar violence that swept the Delta, yet he failed to see the other side of the issue—the growing postwar militancy of rural Delta peoples that had grown out of wartime changes.

Lowry's execution, occurring one year after the Elaine Massacre, provides an entry point into the American Congo of the postwar years—a region that resembled its African namesake in that democracy and the law did not function for black workers. The events leading up to his murder shared similarities with the Elaine Massacre and demonstrated the changes that World War I had brought to rural black political culture. Like many of the members of the Progressive Farmers and Household Union, Lowry was a Mason. The war had strengthened the role of fraternal lodges as sources of information regarding northward migration and as centers of black civic life. Masonic symbols—and the role of black fraternal associations—were an important part of the Lowry lynching. The mob was sending a message in its choice of execution site: in front of the home of J. T. Williams, one of the fraternal brothers who had hidden Lowry. Also, just before he swallowed the coals, Lowry turned to a mob leader and whispered, "Have you no cure for the widow's son?"[9] As a thirty-third-degree Mason—the highest level of that society—Lowry knew the secret code to convey his status and to supposedly protect him from harm. Although in this case it did not help him, the mob leaders would have understood this statement as confirmation that the Masonic order was active among black people in the area and was helping the fight against white supremacy.[10]

The mob intended to lynch several other members of the fraternal orders, especially J. T. Williams, who had hidden Lowry for two days. Five members of the nearby village of Turrell Odd Fellows Lodge who had helped Lowry escape were taken to the Marion jail: Morris Jenkins and his wife, Jennie, were held under a five-thousand-dollar bond for having loaned Lowry money to get to El Paso, as were Mott Orr, John Radditt, and Walter Johnson. The governor sent telegrams to the American Legion posts in Blytheville and Wilson requesting that they prevent any additional lynchings. Henry Corbin and J. T. Williams were moved to a jail in Caruthersville, Missouri, for safekeeping. Fortunately, muddy roads prevented the mob from traveling any further.[11]

Planters feared the fraternal orders and rightly saw them as sources for black political activity and independence. They recalled Elaine, where sharecroppers had fused their fraternal associations with a labor union, and they knew of the role the lodges played—and continued to play—in migration. Thus, white people gathered after the lynching in Blytheville, the county seat of northern Mississippi County, to discuss ways of destroying the black fraternal orders in Arkansas. Many white people blamed the deaths of the Craigs on these lodges because Lowry had been a prominent member of several secret orders and because his fraternal brothers had aided in his escape. "A majority of the lodges," according to the paper, "are said to have been organized by smart eastern negroes for the double purpose of inciting the southern negro and for getting what money they can out of him."[12]

Lowry's murder illustrated another change that had occurred as a result of World War I: the growing importance of the NAACP to southern black people. Lowry knew to contact the NAACP in El Paso for legal help. The organization's role in securing the release of the men who had been convicted of murder in the Elaine Massacre signaled to Delta black people that an organization outside of the region had the resources to defend them from Jim Crow justice. And while the NAACP may not always have answered their pleas for help, black people nevertheless continued to call on them in the 1920s.

Aided by the forces unleashed by World War I and the Elaine Massacre, a rural black political culture emerged that was based on fraternal orders, the churches, and chapters of the NAACP and Marcus Garvey's Universal Negro Improvement Association (UNIA). While planters had destroyed the Progressive Farmers and Household Union by murdering hundreds of its members and forcing others to leave the region, rural black people found other ways of fighting back. Labor unions were not part of their strategy in the 1920s. Instead, they turned to their organizations and institutions to keep the planters off balance and to challenge white supremacy where they could. Planters knew as much, which explains in part their horrific response to Lowry's murder of the Craigs. Lowry's refusal to bend to planter demands and his willingness to challenge Craig while armed terrified the planters and revealed the limits of their authority to control black civic life on the plantations. Through Lowry, and those who helped him, planters saw the relationship of fraternal societies and the NAACP to growing black challenges to white supremacy. By lynching Lowry, planters sought to rein black people in, but the workers followed their own course. It was said that the Craigs had serious difficulty finding labor after the lynching.[13]

World War I, then, launched a crisis for planters in the alluvial empire from which they would not escape until mechanization was completed in the 1960s, ending the need for black sharecropping. From World War I on, planters confronted an increasingly assertive and restless working class that responded to the terrors of sharecropping by migrating to cities and factories, by forming local chapters of the NAACP and the UNIA, and by challenging planter authority through daily defiance. On one level the crisis was economic, for after the war planters faced a cotton market of low prices and overproduction. As wartime demand for cotton ended, cotton prices fell from a wartime high of 43 cents per hundred pounds to 13 and 15 cents in 1920. Planters never recovered, and by 1930, cotton was bringing in only 9 to 10 cents. Low cotton prices led to the collapse of the rural credit structure as planters were unable to make their mortgage payments, while others, unable to pay their taxes, lost their lands to foreclosures. And the 1927 Mississippi River flood, followed by a major drought in 1930–1931, pushed planters deeper into debt. Depression struck the Delta well before the 1930s, rendering a fatal blow to the labor-intensive plantation system of sharecropping.[14]

Planters also confronted, on another level, a social crisis that questioned their ability to rule and dominate their black workers. They desperately needed labor, yet they continued to oppress the workers they had. And they constantly struggled to control a marginal white working class of tenant farmers, lumber workers, and aspiring landowners who engaged in whitecapping and nightriding—forcefully intimidating sharecroppers and landowners—and Klan activities designed to drive black people from the land. Some planters, especially on the Mississippi side, claimed that they had reformed the plantation system and that conditions were good for black people; they blamed harsh conditions on the marginal, smaller, and less powerful planters who lacked the sophisticated methods of labor control. But large landowners like Lee Wilson engaged in some of the harshest practices, as did his counterparts in Mississippi. Above all, World War I had emboldened Delta black people, and as horrible and terrifying as the Elaine Massacre had been, on some level it strengthened people's will to fight on, even in the remotest places.

Indeed, black people in Mississippi and Arkansas continued their migration in the 1920s, though not as many left as during the war. For example, three of ten Arkansas Delta counties lost a little over 11 percent of their black population during the 1920s, while the remainder lost from 3 to 6.9 percent. The Mississippi Delta saw one county lose 13.3 percent of its black population, with the remaining counties losing less than 9 percent.[15] Those who remained behind persisted in defying their oppression. And the planters countered with a fiercer clamp on their workers. Historians have yet to adequately record the extent of violence and theft that occurred following World War I in order to destroy the "New Negro" in the Delta.

In their attempts to tighten controls on a recalcitrant workforce, planters moved more strongly to reassert their dominance over civil society that the war had weakened. For this effort, they employed three strategies that repeated prior patterns but with much greater intensity. One involved the sharecropping system itself, which became even more oppressive and damaging to families. A second line of controls involved law and government, both used traditionally by white people in the American Congo to deny black people their rights and restrict their mobility—through controlling the mail system, overseeing contractual arrangements, enforcing convict labor, and denying them justice in the courts. Finally, they cemented this rule with outright terrorism, through lynching, daily violence, and the resurgence of the Ku Klux Klan. Remarkably, these measures failed to quash black resistance. And as more African Americans either fought back personally or left the Delta for the North, planters had to employ more than violence, eventually turning to forms of welfare capitalism to try to entice workers to remain in the South. But everyone knew that the soft glove of this new paternalism barely covered a hand of iron.

In the face of the persistent terror that marked the postwar decades, rural people continued to organize NAACP branches all over the Delta, most often in remote plantations or villages. The letters they wrote to the national office revealed the issues on their minds and also indicated their growing determination to fight for justice. Not for nothing had their people sacrificed and died in both the war and in the struggles at home in places like Elaine. These letters show that planters took seriously the threat posed by this organization and the kind of conflicts that made life on the plantations increasingly more difficult.

The local chapters linked rural people to events outside the region by providing them with information regarding the fate of people of color all over the world. And the national office created a venue for rural black peoples' political aspirations, making them part of national political campaigns. Thus, Delta chapters raised money to aid in the passage of the Dyer antilynching bill that floated in the U.S. Congress throughout the decade, and they helped to raise money for the defense of the nine young black men accused in the early 1930s of raping two white women in Scottsboro, Alabama. Delta branches wrote to the national office asking for copies of the *Crisis* in order to obtain lynching statistics and to report murders, rapes, peonage, and other injustices in their communities.

Delta black people also formed chapters of Marcus Garvey's Universal Negro Improvement Association. This was not surprising, since in the latter decades of the nineteenth century, rural black people in both Arkansas and Mississippi had formed a major part of an emigration movement to Africa. Followers of Bishop Henry M. Turner, for example, sought to escape the hard economic times of the 1880s and 1890s, as well as the rise of disfranchisement and segregation. Thus, when Marcus Garvey arrived in New York City during the World War I, many rural black people looked to him for a solution to the postwar hard times. Many of them may have drawn from the earlier "nationalist" sentiment in the region that looked for the roots of an African American culture and identity in Africa. In the 1920s, Arkansas claimed forty-three UNIA chapters while Mississippi had fifty-six. The majority of these chapters were in the Delta. Through the association's official publication, the *Negro World*, black people learned of events in the African Diaspora and of the emerging anticolonial struggles.[16]

It is difficult to tell how many Delta black people actually joined the NAACP or the UNIA. The realities of rural life limited from the very beginning the success of these organizations. Poverty prevented many from paying their monthly dues, while planter terror kept others from holding their meetings. Local NAACP charters seemed to have come and gone as people struggled to pay the dues that kept the organizations running. Some locals had as few as five members; others had more. The UNIA kept poorer records than the NAACP, making it difficult to determine the nature and scope of its locals. But obtaining an accurate membership list, or measuring the significance and success of these organizations by their members, whether many or few, misses the point of their existence. That people sought to form NAACP chapters following the horrors of the Elaine Massacre was a stunning event in and of itself. Mere correspondence with a civil rights organization, or the possession of literature from any such group, threatened a sharecropper family's very existence.

Even though members often could not sustain their chapters, they still found ways of remaining connected to the broader freedom struggle. For example, most people belonged simultaneously to fraternal orders, churches, and to either or both the NAACP and the UNIA. The church was the meeting place for all of these groups, and often ministers led the organizational drives. While the chapters may have folded only to begin again at some later time, people took to heart what they had learned as members. And people could belong to the NAACP whether or not a local chapter existed. Even if one person in a community or church received the *Crisis, Negro World*, or *Chicago Defender*, many others had access to the publications. For subscribers passed the publications among their fellow lodge and church members, while the literate read to the illiterate. Thus rural black people, like industrial workers of an earlier time, had ways of transmitting information they deemed relevant to their community's survival.[17]

Far from being ignorant peasants living on isolated plantations, then, rural people hungered for information about their "race." Some in Jericho, Arkansas, who had read about an upcoming NAACP convention in Garvey's *Negro World,* wanted the organization to send them information because "we can't get any facts on our people." A. T. Cunningham wrote that he had read and heard much about the NAACP and "its great work for the good of our race and desiring to become a factor in everything for the advancement and uplift of our people." His community, "largely populated by our people, progressive in many ways," was eager to form a chapter that "would mean much to us as a race unit." In Lake, Mississippi, Madison Price wrote that the "Colored People are stirred up as never before" over the issues of disfranchisement and segregation, despite the terrorizing activities of the Klan in their communities.[18]

The NAACP also interfered with planters' controls by encouraging other means of escaping oppression. Migration to northern cities continued in the 1920s as a means to improve southern black peoples' lives, and many, like Mrs. Roberta Johnson in Clarksdale, Mississippi, wrote to the organization asking for help in moving to Chicago. Some even looked beyond the borders of the United States; J. F. Griffin in Marianna, Arkansas, for example, wanted assistance in moving to Brazil. W. H. Wyatt asked for aid in getting out of Arkansas and moving to California where "there is millions of opportunities of all kind [for] both men and women." He saw conditions "growing bad in the South land for the Race people."[19] Rural people also knew about the NAACP's campaign against lynching, an issue that directly affected their lives in the Delta. Reverend Thomas Jordan wrote from Waynesboro, Mississippi, declaring that if the Dyer antilynching bill did not pass, he wanted to move to Mexico, Africa, or England. According to Jordan, local white citizens had complained that black people intended to rule the Delta. In his view, if the bill ever passed, the entire Congress would have to come South to enforce it.[20] Still others wrote to the NAACP and asked for help with the marketing of crops. During the 1920s the cotton market collapsed, and black Delta farmers sought any outside help they could. For example, Mrs. B. B. Johnson in Shelby, Mississippi, and her sister each owned eighty acres with tenants and had not made any money in 1920 because of bad market conditions. Aiming to avoid southern white cotton factors, or marketing agents, she asked the NAACP to send her the names of northern cotton firms to which she could sell her tenants' cotton.[21]

NAACP field secretary and native Arkansan William Pickens wanted to

Fig. 3. The American Congo

organize at least one thousand of Phillips County's 36,000 African Americans. Recalling the Elaine Massacre, Pickens urged members in the county not to distribute antilynching literature, and to advertise his forthcoming visit as one where he was to speak on the friendly cooperation between black and white people in the community. Attempts to arrange Pickens's visit reflected the problems of organizing in the Delta, for according to Miss Frankella Jackson, recent floods had left the roads in bad shape for traveling, and the chapters held meetings only on Sundays since the members worked for long hours during the week and were unable to attend at any other time. "There is no place in the United States," wrote Miss Jackson, "where colored people need to understand the use of the ballot and the protection of the law as they do around this part of the country." She urged Pickens to come for at least two or three days because she hoped to "arouse" people from a thirty-mile radius.

Pickens's visit to Phillips County never materialized, but Miss Jackson's chapter in Southland, in spite of the difficult conditions, had fifty-three members in 1929. In the early 1930s, the chapter managed to raise twenty dollars for the Scottsboro Trial. The group had also sought more information on the murder of Charles Shepard, who had been burned in Mississippi on New Year's Day in 1929. In nearby Marvell, education dominated the minds of organizers. In their community, white people completely controlled the schools, and black people could not vote in the school board elections. Some communities had no schools at all.[22] The rural branches also knew about the activities of the larger urban chapters, especially the one in Little Rock where attorney Scipio Jones, the successful defender of the Elaine cases, was a major leader. Jones organized a protest in 1927 to prevent Wallace Townsend from becoming the federal judge for the eastern district of Arkansas. As chairman of the Pulaski County Republican Committee, Townsend had been successful in using the police to keep black people out of the Republican primary. Jones insisted that Townsend's appointment would further peonage in the Delta.[23]

NAACP members wrote describing the terrible conditions under which they lived and sought to organize. In Pine Bluff, Mary Branch went to jail for refusing to sign away to a white person the deed to her property. Another member wrote that organizational efforts fared okay in the town, given "we live in a city where it tries men's souls to live." He insisted that the NAACP had "given the Negro race its second emancipation."[24]

While helping in this second emancipation, the NAACP's activity, and black resistance in general, provoked greater tensions within the sharecropping system. Letters to the organization revealed the harsh conditions and the terror that people experienced as part of their daily lives on the plantations. H. L. Henderson and other members of the local chapter in Proctor, in Crittenden County, Arkansas, had walked forty miles in an effort to secure a settlement from their landlord. The planter had stolen people's crops, hogs, chickens, and labor, and had "barred" Henderson from going to where his wife and children lived. The planter, H. L. Slaton, was "an old convict driver and murderer" who read every sharecropper's mail and threw what he allowed them to read on the side of the road. "He has taken peoples' bed clothes, they are naked and barefoot," said Henderson. He insisted that the workers "is mad" and feared there may be another "uprising."

Henderson described the condition of other sharecroppers in his area. Mr. Crosby "beat a colored man half to death and run him off . . . In June Mr. Johnson take an Iron Single Tree [the crossbar to a draft harness] and beat a man and taken his mule and hogs and chickens and household goods that he brought from Miss. And he claimed that he was in his debt and Mr. E. Williams he has got all of his people starving and in his debt to his day hands and won't pay them off and there is no work else where they can get to help themselves. They all stand together," he continued, "Now they want to run the hands off from their crops and take them. He did not pay them last year for picken cotton, some he owed $75 Dollars. They had to go away without their money and now they are having high power rifles shipped out here and is trying to find out" when they held their NAACP meetings. "They are aiming to du us as it was dun in Elaine."[25]

The white people, Henderson said, "Have a mob in every county and when they want to kill the Negro, they ring each other up." Henderson reported that the white men in his area had gone to Grenada, Mississippi, where they had joined a mob, lynched a man, and hung him on a highway. "We are looking to be swept off the face of the earth anytime." Henderson believed that "We are on new ground here" and requested that the NAACP contact Little Rock for help. He noted that the previous week a black man had been killed in Helena for insulting a white woman. A mob doused him with gasoline and burned him, but the rain had washed out the fire.[26]

The conditions of terror under which people lived in Democrat, located in St. Francis County, created problems for the local NAACP chapter. According to Josie Coleman, the chapter could not send a delegate to the national convention in 1922 because members had no money to pay their dues. The chapter had also held a rally to raise funds for the antilynching bill currently before Congress, when a black preacher, Reverend Mitchell, "carried their business to the sheriff." Consequently, the branch president had to flee town. "The white people here have got some of our members under slavery," she wrote, "yet telling them they got to chop their crops until they open ready to pick drives an curses our members like dogs. You all don't know what we have to undergo with here in this cummunity," she continued. "The white people are getting worse on us instead of better here in this place. White man carry his pistol over our members do the women like he do the men, drives the women to work with out they cooking any dinner. Some days they got to go that field the white agent behind them running them." The white people in the villages of Hughes and Heth "has ordered a car load of guns and ammunition, so we are informed and the people are all uneasy about it, so will you all kindly see after it please for us . . . We don't know what they are doing this far. We down here are in a critical fix, no guns to protect ourselves at all."[27]

Black people saw that one important means of fighting back came through using the black press to publicize the terrible instances of peonage on the plantations. Reading the *Crisis* prompted Jim McHerring from Democrat to write to the magazine, and the NAACP published his and other letters from the town. "We are treated like dogs," with "no regard for the law," wrote McHerring. "In every county of the South these southern pecker woods is mad with the colored people and they are doing every mean thing they can to them." He told of various beatings and practices of peonage. "Whites are threatening to destroy our organization," he reported, and they threatened "to make another Elaine scrape out of it." He agreed to clear land for his landlord, Beverly Turner, for fifteen dollars per acre. After clearing the land, the man insisted on paying in the form of a cow and heifer. At the end of the year, the landlord "fixed it" so that he got them back for McHerring's debts. He asked the NAACP to contact the Department of Labor and report these conditions. Noting that peonage existed all over Arkansas, McHerring wrote that white people had caused workers to run away by night, riding and hunting them down like they "were bears." He concluded: "The truth is the colored people have never been free since they were said to be emancipated." Southern white people had set out with the intention to "run a general slave law." McHerring proposed that he attend the Detroit NAACP National Convention to present his plan to secure federal loans of one thousand dollars to place people on "Uncle Sam's" land.[28]

J. C. Coleman of Democrat described his plantation manager as being the same as a convict farm agent, for "he don't allow people to go to church, no burying or nothing like that. He drives the women to work like he do the men. They have to go at the tap of the bell before daylight every day. If this aint peonage I don't know what is and a lot of this is going around this branch." Planters forced sharecroppers to move constantly from one place to the next, scattering Coleman's members all over the area. People wanted to rent land, but the planters refused. People lived in a "piece" of houses, "want let us make a living, make us sharecrop . . . If this ain't mobbing and lynching I would like to know what is."[29] Lucious Holiday on B. C. Puncy's place wrote, "I am reporting on the suffering condition of a few of us in the colored race just how we are fairing. We are just slaves here. He furnishes groceries every Friday night just what he want us to have and when they give out we do without until the next Friday night but the work have to go on. He furnishes a 2 pound bucket of lard to a family and he charges 75c for it. A 12 pound sack of flour he charges $1.25 for it. It's time to lay by the crop and go to work to make support for ourselves."[30]

Peonage persisted in the Yazoo-Mississippi Delta as well. When plantation workers escaped during the 1920s and migrated to cities outside of the South, they wrote to the NAACP on behalf of those left behind. One man left the Charlie Johnson plantation near Minoler and headed to California, where he described conditions on the farm to the president of an NAACP chapter. The president wrote to the national office that people on the plantation were "drove, wiped [sic], and striped [sic] both men and women. If it is as bad as it is pictured it is just the same as our forefathers suffered." Miss Mary Williams wrote from Chicago on behalf of her sixteen-year-old sister and her twenty-one-year-old brother who were held on a plantation at Filter, forced to work without pay, and unable to receive their mail. She listed eleven other relatives who worked for "charity" on the plantation. And in Glenora, James Walker fled a plantation and demanded that the planter send his sixteen-year-old son to him. The landowner threatened to kill the son if the son tried to leave.[31]

Peonage and coercion helped control the ability of black people to move. Benjamin Franklin Underwood held Ethel and George Johnson in debt servitude on his plantation in Scott County, threatening to kill them whenever they tried to leave. When Underwood's cousin paid a forty-dollar "debt," he took Ethel as his cook. According to the Johnson's African American lawyer, Robert L. McLendon, Underwood "buys and sells negroes." He claimed that peonage existed all over the Delta. McLendon also reported that Nick Lang held a sixteen-year-old boy who lived in a barn on his plantation, beating him every time the young man sought to escape.[32] Arthur Jackson wrote from Sidson, Mississippi, in a letter whose legibility reflected a struggle to write that mirrored his life, asking if it was "the law for your Bost man to whip you." One Sunday in June, when his landowner whipped him, he ran away, but the owner "come and got me after the fourth Sunday in August," whipped him again, and worked him through the fall, in the rain and mud, without pay. The landlord also "werk my wife from June up to until dec and did not give her a pany." To prevent Jackson from moving, the landlord "put a $4.42 [debt] on me to keep me on his place he werked me and my wife and did not give us no cloth he werk us necki . . . on the top of that he put us out on the highway on the gravel road. White and Black seen my thangs out on the road and took 5 cow from my farther. He has a half Bail of cotton that he ant seddle for yet."[33]

Black laborers were not the only ones who complained. Planters had hired several thousand Mexican workers to harvest the 1925 cotton crop, and the Mexican embassy received reports that the powerful Lee Wilson Company in Mississippi County had abused more than five thousand workers in Arkansas and Mississippi. An agent of the company had hired the workers in El Paso, offering them $1.50 for picking cotton. When they arrived, however, the price had fallen to one dollar and eventually to sixty cents. The workers did not have a written contract because they had mistakenly thought that a circular printed on official paper of the U.S. Employment Service represented a contract. The Wilson Company forced its terms and conditions on the workers in Arkansas, knowing they had no written contract and that the workers had no way of returning to Texas. Above all, these men spoke no English and were not citizens of the United States, so they had no access to the local authorities or courts. When the workers protested, Wilson's minions threatened them with guns and imprisonment. Planters in both Mississippi and Arkansas had refused to send the men back to Texas once their work was completed.[34]

A peonage case actually went to trial in Memphis against the Lee Wilson Company. The plantation manager, a deputy sheriff, and two other men were charged for following a cotton picker, Bud Powell, to Memphis after he had left the plantation. They claimed he had driven off in an automobile owing Wilson money. They arrested him in Memphis, took him to jail in Mississippi County, and held him until he agreed to pick cotton on the Wilson plantation. Powell had escaped to Memphis and reported the abuse, though the outcome of the case is unclear. Other peonage reports came from the town of Cotton Plant in nearby Woodruff County.[35]

The weight of the sharecropping system bore down on the entire family. By watching the mail, stopping people without cause to check for their membership pins, and forcefully moving families from house to house on their plantations, landowners and managers tried to control the behavior of their workers. The lives of women deteriorated when managers drove them to the fields early in the morning, keeping them there for the entire day. Unable to prepare the family's meals in the morning or after lunch as was their custom, women returned after sunset to prepare the meals, wash the clothes, and conduct the other chores associated with the care of the household. Men and children bore their responsibilities as well, chopping wood, maintaining a garden, feeding the livestock if they had any, and pitching in with other household chores. According to J. C. Coleman, the managers had "got us now drifting from pillar to post now so if we ever needed any help it is right now," for the planters "got all we made last year and are ill treating us now." The chapter also wrote to the postmaster general, complaining that they did not receive their mail. When their letter arrived in Washington, the seal on the envelope had been broken. Yet in the face of this terror, croppers continued to organize. Coleman collected $52.50 from his members by "hard scuffing, while another member reported that people had sold their chickens to pay for their chapter dues."[36]

The case of Lucinda Holman illustrated how little power parents often had over their children's welfare. When she became ill, Holman's planter, William Lawler in Coahoma County, sent her to live on a relative's plantation in Sunflower County. She took her fourteen-year-old daughter, twelve-year-old son, and her four-year-old boy, along with her furniture, clothes, and chickens. As her illness worsened, Holman moved to a charity hospital in Jackson for a year, leaving her children and belongings under the supervision of the black manager, Charles Nathan. When she returned, Nathan and the planter, Mims Wilson, refused to release the children, even though Holman had offered to pay for their food and housing. Wilson claimed that he needed their labor. Mrs. Holman's church paid for her to escape to Oxford, Mississippi, where she filed a complaint with the U.S. attorney.[37]

This powerlessness meant that decisions about flight and protest often were made collectively by members of a family who all benefited and suffered from the consequences of certain acts. The family nature of sharecropping was illustrated by a man who had decided to leave the plantation of J. W. G. Ratterree for that of a Mr. Brannon. The sharecropper received an advance and moved his furniture over to Brannon's farm, but his family refused to follow. Brannon had him arrested and jailed in Greenville for violation of his contract, because he had not provided the labor he had promised. While Ratterree saw this as peonage, the more important factor centered on the refusal of the family to follow the father.[38]

Robert Harris of Vincent, in Crittenden County, wrote of two widowed women, Mrs. Ellen Harris and Mrs. Ida Miller, who had moved onto a farm belonging to Will Hill, who lived in Memphis. When the farm manager, Frank Nabor, moved them to Hill's farm, the women owed nothing but moving costs. In the spring, however, Nabor took all of their household goods, foodstuffs, cattle, and hogs to his house. He then presented them with a lien at gunpoint, forcing one of their sons to sign it, and on the same day that Ellen Harris's daughter was to give birth to her child. Consequently, Ida Miller had to carry her niece to another place for her confinement. Harris described his region as "a pure district of nothing but slavery. The agents whips the field hand and nothing said or done about it." Mrs. Harris's son had been killed there a year ago, yet there had been no investigation and no arrests. The Harris's had hired a lawyer, but to no avail. Mr. Harris wrote to the NAACP and pleaded for help and an investigation, asking them to send their answer in a plain envelope so as not to attract attention.[39]

Some workers sought the protection of the U.S. government, with less than auspicious results. Several from Joiner in Mississippi County wrote to the "department bureau of protection" that "We as negroes here at this place need protection and must have it. Now listen, we have a man here in our community that I think is treating the negro real brutish and there is no help for it. He is just a renter and have [day] hands with him. And whip them same time unmerciful, without a cause. He had a widow woman with him this year and whipped her until she was sent to the asylum now whipping her children unconscious at times, without a cause. He and the other two men whipped a negro this summer until he died the next day taken their knife and castrated him this was don in the presents of a white lady, and his wife. We as negroes," they insisted, "cant help our selves, the white people don't seem to be very much interested about it. Will you send a man for him or to take care of the situation for us, or shall we continier to beg for mercy. Is it possible that we must continure to cry for help and can't get it." The man, Will Slaten, was "a heaven [*sic*] set man with red face, five feet, seven inches, weighs about 175–180 pounds, big nose."[40] In Mississippi a sharecropper named Henry Evans appealed to the Department of Justice on behalf of his son, who was held in peonage at R. T. Clark's levee camp in Jeffrie. The young man apparently owed seventy-five dollars. Evans returned to his own planter in Arkansas and asked him to send ninety dollars for the debt and for a train ticket home, which he did, but Clark returned the money.[41]

Those who remained on Delta farms continued to fight on their own behalf, reporting cases of peonage and demanding that the Justice Department investigate. In Drew, Sunflower County, Richard Dunbar was shot when he sought to leave the James Mild plantation. The Justice Department sent an investigator to the plantation, but Mild had so terrorized his workers that no one, including Dunbar, spoke with him. In McComb, W. D. Moore pled guilty to taking a black man from the Delta, placing him in chains, and making him work out a debt. And Perry W. Howard and W. L. Moon successfully filed a petition for a writ of habeas corpus to rescue Dock Holloway from a Delta planter who had him arrested for jumping a contract, and had similarly placed him in chains and made him work out his debt. In a rare instance, Holloway's planter was arrested for this peonage.[42]

The isolation and terror that reigned on most plantations made it difficult, as the Mild case illustrated, for the Justice Department to investigate or to make arrests. Nor is it clear how widespread peonage was in the Delta in the 1920s. As the leading scholar of peonage noted, the South registered fewer peonage complaints than it had twenty years before, yet those who investigated cases said that it was widespread. "Community support of the planters, both in keeping the abuses quiet and in forming sympathetic juries, continued to hinder prosecution."[43] Nevertheless, southern black people continued to write to the NAACP and the Justice Department hoping to secure justice. How they felt about the meager outcomes remains unknown.

One of the more telling cases about the limits of federal intervention occurred when Sam Edwards, a black man, decided to visit his home in Greenwood. Edwards had joined the Coast Guard in 1929 as a mess attendant first class. While stationed in St. Petersburg, Florida, he received word that his mother was ill and went home to visit her on an eighteen-day leave. While waiting for a bus in Tchula, Frank Gwin approached him, wanting to know what business he had in the town. Edwards produced his Coast Guard papers, but Gwin refused to accept them, accusing him of having robbed someone to obtain the papers. Gwin then arrested him for trespassing without money, even though Edwards had eight dollars and another twenty hidden in his vest. Edwards was taken to a grocery store where Gwin presented the coast guardsman to Judge Wallace, saying he "had another victim for you." After a search that uncovered the eight dollars and a gold watch, the judge charged Edwards with vagrancy. When Edwards told the judge that he did not pick cotton, the justice found it strange that a Negro born in Mississippi could not pick cotton, sending him to work out a twenty-dollar fine and thirty days on a farm owned by Gwin's son. The judge refused to call Edward's father at the Delta Feed Company to verify the validity of his credentials. Edwards worked on the farm from November 10 to December 16, 1931.

After the first three days on the farm, he wrote a letter to his commanding officer explaining what had happened. When he tried to mail the letter, "Captain" Brown, a black man, threatened to whip everybody until he found out who had sent it. When Edwards confessed, he received twenty-seven lashes from a seven-pound strap. On several other occasions he received whippings for failing to pick less than one hundred pounds of cotton a day, for drinking two cups of water rather than one, and for breaking a hoe handle while chopping weeds. Edwards worked with seventeen other men who were held on the farm. After his thirty days had ended, Brown offered to release Edwards if he would sell his gold watch to him for seven dollars rather than the twenty Edwards had requested. After his release, Edwards took a train to Greenwood and notified his commanding officer of his experiences, who then reported the case to the Justice Department. But the department's investigator deemed that no federal law had been violated.[44]

That local law dominated in the American Congo and kept federal authority at a distance was no accident. Planters and their supporters shaped the law in order to dominate black people socially, politically, and economically. They did this in a variety of ways that included the convict lease system and a process of supposed law and order that prevented African Americans from finding justice in the courts.

In the 1920s, the convict lease system was still alive and well in Arkansas, supported by a web of familial relationships that spanned from the local to sometimes the national level. While Arkansas had banned convict leasing in 1913, it remained possible for city and county jails to lease prisoners until 1939.[45] One example involved the Driver family of Mississippi County, which had relatives serving as justice of the peace, a U.S. Congressman, and manager of a plantation that used convict labor. G. C. Driver and his brother C. S. had a contract with a county judge to take all of the prisoners convicted of misdemeanors from the county jail to their farm. Their father, John B. Driver, was one of four justices of the peace in Blytheville who heard and ruled on misdemeanor charges. Every Monday, the Drivers made a trip to Blytheville, the county seat, to secure new prisoners convicted over the weekend. The needs of the plantation drove the structure for legal fines. The Drivers opposed setting fines too low, which would allow convict workers to pay them off too quickly. This caused John Driver to assess unusually high fines for offenses such as gaming, bootlegging, and riding a train without a ticket. The system drew some opposition within the court itself, but the other justices could not break the hold of the family, which had national clout: U.S. Congressman William Driver had signed off on the arrangement. An FBI agent investigated conditions at the Driver farm for the Justice Department and found that workers had adequate living quarters and decent food, and that they worked without wearing shackles. The U.S. District Attorney argued that the statutes of Arkansas allowed county judges to lease county prisoners, thereby letting the Drivers conduct their business.[46]

In Hughes, located in St. Francis County, Charley Hulett ran a convict farm for black people, arresting them under false pretenses such as bootlegging and carrying them to the Forrest City jail, which then released the prisoners to his farm. Hulett, according to NAACP member Jim Coleman, "hunts up things like this to keep us stired up scared all the time. An so he will kill a colored man if he looks too straight and so my members has a hard way to go." According to another chapter member, John Callie, Hulett "catches strangers passing through," forcing them to work on the convict farm. In James Dunlap's case, Hulett stopped him on the way home from work, found a NAACP membership pin, and then shot him. Hulett and his men then took Dunlap's pistol and money, carried him to the farm, and never told his pregnant wife where he was.[47]

Reverend W. H. Booker described conditions in Peace, Arkansas, in Cleveland County: "We have no law to protect us. The system of debt slavery rules in this county. If a negro is arrested, he is taken to jail and kept there a while then he is taken to a big man's farm and put to work with out any trial whatever. Whenever a white man kills a negro he [the black man] is taken buried and that is all there is to it." But "if a negro commits a crime against the state [and] if he promises the white man that he will work for him in the cotton field that settles the case. One big white man rules the eastern half of the country and what he says go law or no law. I am writing what I know not what I think. I was raised around here. I could name one deed after another," he concluded, "but space will not allow me to do so. I am willing to testify to these things any where if it cost my life for I know the miserable condition of my people here."[48]

Local authorities also waived respect for proper procedures and protection of civil rights when it came to "investigating" crimes. In Pinckney, S. B. Argain provided a vivid account of police procedures in the robbery of a peddler. Authorities beat a man named Slim on 96 Plantation to secure a confession. When that did not work, men tied the hands and feet of the accused and dumped him into the Mississippi River. Eventually the man confessed and was taken to jail.[49]

Besides regulating mobility and wage relationships, the law also continued to constrain black people's ability to market their crops. When planters refused to offer a decent price on the cotton, some tenants "stole" the bales and sought to sell them on their own. In Ruleville, B. C. Taylor, Marcus Brown, Annie Hardison, George Edwards, and Buddy Ross took the cotton from their landowner J. W. Cook's plantation and sold it to another white man who had offered to buy it for a good price. All five were tried for taking and selling their cotton "between suns." The buyer received a fine of five hundred dollars for buying cotton at night. On a nearby plantation, Henry Clay stole nineteen sacks of nitrate and sold them to a merchant. And in Leland, Mississippi, Will Johnston received a one-hundred-dollar fine for stealing chickens, though a white man who attended court on the same day as Powell received a five-dollar fine for assault. The law was weighted against black people making money on their own.[50]

Planters resorted to other measures to control their laborers' options. They set voluntary wage ceilings and vowed to utilize the traditional method of invoking vagrancy laws. Coahoma County threatened to use anti-enticement laws against labor recruiters, or, as one planter put it, "If they cannot be handled through legal channels there are other methods that will prove effective." J. W. McNair said that planters in the county had become the "laughing stock" of negroes who hold out for the "highest wages," refusing to sign sharecropping contracts knowing they can make more as wage laborers.[51]

Vagrancy laws, as always, were invoked, though the blatant arrogance of the *Sunflower Tocsin* surely set a new standard, even for the Delta, when it urged, "We would like to see every vagrant taken up. They are too impudent and trifling to work if you ask them to and gardening is being kept back on their account. If they won't work for wages arrest them and put them on the streets where they can work for glory awhile." A month later the *Tocsin* crowed, "The town authorities have been after the vagrants this week and they have effected a good moral cleansing in the city as well as assisted the home keepers in securing needed help." In spite of these worries, the newspaper noted in the late fall that planters had enjoyed a prosperous year. In 1925, a similar tale of woe appeared, as the paper insisted that "vagrants, white and black, should be forced to work or made to move. There is plenty of work to do but this class of humans seems to think the world owes him a living without work and his natural tendency is to hang around crap games, boot-leggers and negro dives. The servant problem would easily be solved if vagrants were forced to work." And again, in 1926: "Now is the time to enforce vagrant laws and get cooks, maids, and cotton choppers back to work." Yet the *Tocsin*, in the contradictory voice of the planters, also noted that Sunflower County had always enjoyed plenty of labor since tenants received such a good deal. One could only wonder why black people would refuse to work under such fine terms.[52]

But when push came to shove, white people in the American Congo used terrorism to drive black people from their land or out of their businesses and jobs. Nightriders, the Ku Klux Klan, and local mobs burned homes and businesses, seizing property all over the Delta. During the early 1920s there was a rise in Klan membership that mirrored that in the rest of the country. Surely the increase in violence in the region derived from the gains that some black people had made during the war and the collapse of the agricultural market immediately following the war. The Delta experienced the further consolidation of landownership, a decline in both white and black landownership, and a rise in tenancy. These changes, combined with continued black migration, created greater concern among planters over retaining and controlling a black labor force. But nightriders and the Klan employed contradictory tactics that defy full explanation. For example, as white men lost their small farms during the depression of the 1920s, many resorted to forcefully driving black families from the land, whether they were sharecroppers or landowners. Yet planters also used Klan members to frighten the nightriders who were driving their black laborers away. Planters belonged to the Klan and used it as a tool for maintaining white supremacy. Yet they also worried about landless whites, who posed a threat to their black workers. How these relationships played out in the Delta is difficult to determine and beyond the scope of this study. Delta black people had suffered from nightriding and whitecapping since the region had been developed. But the war had unleashed a renewed fury among landless white people, as well as other kinds of workers threatened by economic decline.

Indeed, agents of several northern banks after a tour in 1921 of the Gulf and lower Mississippi Valley regions, reported a rapid spread of "voluntary" peonage in the cotton, sugar, and tobacco regions. Employers no longer even promised wages; instead they simply worked people for a ration of food. In their view, this "return to serfdom" had resulted from the collapse of the cotton market and the planters' deployment of the Klan to terrorize black people.[53]

The revival of the Klan in the 1920s was part of the growing nativism, racism, and antiradicalism that swept the country—indeed, the world— following World War I. As the historian Eric Hobsbawm has noted, this was "an age of extremes," when the forces of democracy and decency struggled against the counterrevolutionary movement of fascism. The American South did not escape this global trend. If anything, the American Congo was more at home with the terror of fascism than with the ideals of democracy.[54] In 1923, in a lengthy article on the revival of the KKK in America, a New York City newspaper estimated the Arkansas membership at 50,000, and claimed that the Little Rock membership included almost every Protestant minister in the city. The Arkansas Klan was "thriving" in both urban and rural areas, continued the article, with "farmers and planters in the more populous counties" reported as active members.[55]

Klansmen and nightriders sought to drive black sharecroppers from the fields and black landowners from their property in the rapidly expanding Delta sections of Arkansas, where for many white people, it became increasingly difficult to be a small landowner. Northeastern Arkansas was especially susceptible, for this region since its inception had been viewed as white man's country. In Mississippi County, for example, white tenancy had climbed from 30.5 percent in 1920 to 43.3 percent in 1930, and in Craighead County from 55.9 to 66.5 percent. In those same counties, white landownership had declined from 16.8 to 9.4 percent and from 51.3 to 32.1 percent, respectively. Especially telling, Craighead saw white landownership decline by 20 percent between 1920 and 1925.[56] While these two counties experienced the most dramatic rise in white tenancy and decline in landownership, others saw similar trends.

The collapse of the cotton economy following World War I thus led to increasing acts of violence against black people, especially during the first half of the decade. For example, in 1921, thirty-one men were tried in Jonesboro, Arkansas, located in Craighead County, for burning barns and gins, and for threatening farmers who sold their cotton for a low price. The violence that swept the Delta reflected the hard economic times that followed the war.

Terror swept other regions of the state as well. For example, six prominent white men were wanted for terrorizing black people in a township known as "Little Georgia" outside of Hot Springs. The white men had burned the home of wealthy planter Jefferson Hollis, who among other black people owned some of the richest land in the Ouachita Valley, where black landowners had repeatedly refused to sell their land to white bidders. In 1926, one night after Thanksgiving, two farmers and a sales manager for the Chicago Mill and Lumber Company drove into McClellan, in Woodruff County, and told all black people to leave within ten days. Chicago Mill and Lumber Company owned thousands of acres in northeastern Arkansas and aimed its land sales solely at white people.[57]

Nightriders continued to drive black sharecroppers and wage hands from the fields. In 1920, three Klansmen in Marion received a five-hundred-dollar fine and twelve months in prison for threatening three black families in Crittenden County with death unless they stopped picking cotton. The stiff sentence indicated planters' determination in protecting their labor force against whitecappers and nightriders. But landlords continued to abuse their own croppers. When Isaiah Moore and his brother made a crop in Ruleville, Mississippi, and refused to sell it to the landlord's brother, seventeen whitecaps broke into Moore's home, ripped open Mrs. Moore's nightgown and fondled her, then beat her with a Winchester rifle. The terrorists then took all of the Moore's chickens, crops, mules, corn, and hogs.[58]

Middle-class black people and those with sources of independent incomes, such as disability payments, presented particularly important targets for white terror. This group represented dangerous independence and success in a white supremacist society. In Jackson, Mississippi, prominent attorney S. D. Redmond received a letter from the KKK warning him to leave town. "You niggers are getting too much foothold in Jackson . . . you have entirely too many niggers hanging around your store . . . and you are too near Capitol St." In Brinkley, Arkansas, nightriders ran Dr. B. L. Underwood from the town, and in Malvern, Klansmen sent a letter to a black jitney driver, who had driven his bus for three years, saying that he must leave town. In Meridian, Mississippi, townspeople had repeatedly warned Dr. Charles Smith to leave. When he refused, a group of men shot him and his fiancée, a teacher at Tougaloo College, while they were driving in their new automobile.[59]

Professor J. W. Gibson of Helena was "one of the well respected citizens" of his community, being "identified with everything for the advancement of the community and for the race," and standing "high in all kinds of lodges being a Mason with all of the degrees from the first to the thirty-third." Unfortunately, his outstanding credentials did not protect him from local harassment and abuse. Gibson arrived in Helena one evening on a train from Cotton Plant where he had farming interests. Upon exiting the train, he stood on a downtown street corner waiting for a streetcar to take him home. He carried a shotgun with him for protection, and a night watchman appeared and asked for the gun. Gibson, seeking to allay any fears, informed the man that he had no shells for his gun because he did not think he needed them. The watchman then asked to see the Doctor's black bag and found that it was full of books and papers. Asking him what kind of "nigger are you," Dr. Gibson replied he was a "man," just like the watchman. Furious, the watchman took Gibson to jail and murdered him.[60]

Nightriders and klansmen also aimed their force at skilled black workers in various sectors of the economy in and around the Delta. In 1921 in Texarkana, white men drove bell hops and porters from their hotel jobs, while residents in Benton interrupted work on a section of the Little Rock–Hot Springs highway because the construction company had employed twenty-five black workers. In the early 1920s, Mississippi white workers launched a concerted effort to force black fireman, porters, and flagmen from the Illinois Central Railroad. While some of the worst offenses occurred in areas outside the Delta, such as in Tishomingo County, West Point, and Brookhaven (the home of racial demagogue James K. Vardaman), the Delta did not escape violence of this sort. In Water Valley, white workers offered a reward of three hundred dollars for each black trainman murdered. After the murder of three trainmen, Governor Lee Russell, prompted by the Department of Labor and the railroad management, issued instructions to all Mississippi county sheriffs to protect black railroad workers. In 1923 in northeastern Arkansas, a mob threatened one hundred black men who had been brought to Paragould to repair Missouri Pacific railroad tracks damaged by a recent overflow. Four shop men on strike at the Rock Island Rail Road in Crittenden County murdered two black strikebreakers, while in Phillip, Mississippi, a black brakeman was shot while he repaired a freight train. In Minter City, a mob beat two railroad hands for alleged offenses against two white women, though one of the apparent offenses involved one of the men sitting in a car with a white woman and refusing to leave when threatened.[61]

For some white men, shooting black workers was a sport, like shooting deer or quail. In 1923, the Louisiana governor had to ask the governor of neighboring Mississippi to stop his citizens from shooting their squirrel guns at black men who worked on the Louisiana-Mississippi Highway.[62]

Klansmen, probably in support of planters' need for labor, also sought to prevent blacks from migrating North. Because many African Americans gave as reasons for leaving their inability to find a job, Klansmen paraded through every black section of Abbott Field carrying signs that read "Farm hands are needed, get on the job or get out," "Negroes, stick to your jobs or watch out," and "White blood and black must not and SHALL NOT mix." Black people had left this city in large numbers, in part because of the Klan.[63] Yet this goal of keeping workers also prompted the Klan to clarify when it had not performed acts of terrorism, to reassure African Americans that they could remain in the South. When a black man, Howard Flowtow, was lynched on an "aristocratic golf course" in Panola County, Mississippi, thousands of black people left within ten days. The Klan quickly went to black churches in the town of Sardis without their masks and insisted they had not murdered the man, offering a reward of five hundred dollars to anyone who could tie the Klan to any murders or threats to black people in the community. The spokesman, allegedly one of the members in the mob who lynched Flowtow, denounced northern labor agents for luring workers away, calling them scalawags and frauds. The Klansmen begged the congregants not to "listen to the voice of the agitators who were attempting to lure them from their friends, the Southerners." To prove that black people were not safe in the North, they then read an article from the *Memphis Commercial Appeal* describing twenty-five black people whom officials in Milwaukee, Wisconsin, had sent to the county farm.[64]

Not surprisingly, such acts of terror contributed to black migration. As one citizen noted in a letter to the Helena newspaper, "Through innate fear, negroes are leaving Helena and Phillips County by the hundreds and already there exists a very great labor shortage which will become more acute as time passes." He acknowledged that the Klan existed to regulate a "certain class" of white folks—nightriders—but he suggested that black people saw things differently. African Americans did see the Klan differently, for while planters may have hired the Klan to protect their black workers from nightriders who sought to drive them from the land, black people also knew that those same Klansmen were equally capable of torturing them. In any case, the writer's concern went unheeded. In 1923, over ten thousand people attended a Klan rally in Helena, with members coming from Arkansas, Mississippi, and Tennessee. Dr. Moore, a leading national spokesman for the Klan from nearby Pine Bluff, was the key speaker.[65]

Another incident in Osceola, Arkansas, near the site of the Lowry lynching in Mississippi County, further illustrated the inability of planters to control the actions of local white men. In 1920, Lewis Ward and his wife were driving in a car with a white woman, Mrs. Henry Gifford, to find labor in nearby Bassett, when they stopped to fill up the automobile with gasoline. While there, three white men who had been drinking drove up beside them, telling them to fill up their tank also. Ward replied that an attendant would assist them and then drove off. The men followed the car, pulled it over, and beat up Ward. According to the *Memphis Commercial Appeal*, "While mob violence is not unheard of in this county in cases of extreme heinous crimes, a situation similar to this one where the cause was apparently trifling, is unusual and has excited no small interests."[66]

In the 1920s, lynchings, murders, and torture continued as factors in black peoples' lives in the American Congo. Arkansas alone had twenty-eight lynchings in the 1920s. The more common beatings, humiliations, and murders were more likely to affect the daily lives of black people than the dramatic lynchings, however. In fact, acts of humiliation may have increased in the 1920s as planters increasingly lost control over their workers. For example, D. M. Peak, an "aged tenant" on the Fletcher plantation in Lonoke County, filed a $10,000 suit against Tom and Burel Fletcher for forcing him to get down on his knees and submit to a pistol whipping. They then forced him and his family to load their goods on a wagon and leave. It was rarely enough for a planter or one of his henchmen to simply fire someone; they often resorted to beating and humiliating the cropper, whether a man or a woman. Humiliation formed an important part of southern domination.[67]

Yet Henry Lowry was not the only African American in the early 1920s to meet violence with violence. Black people with guns had always posed the greatest threat to planter authority, especially when disputes arose over crop contracts or merchant bills. When in 1921 a sharecropper cursed and struck landowner M. F. Humphreys in Stoneville, Mississippi, he shot and killed the tenant. Another sharecropper, Aubrey Delap of Diaz, Arkansas, fired twenty-four shots into his planter's leg over a crop dispute, but the planter then killed Delap in return. "Delap bore a bad reputation," noted a Memphis newspaper, "being of an impudent and overbearing disposition." In Winona, Mississippi, seventeen-year-old John Noey Brewer worked on Mrs. W. C. Brooks's plantation. Mrs. Brooks considered Brewer a "good negro" who had for ten days "been moody and subject to fits of anger when reprimanded." One Saturday she asked him to pick up the mail in town and he refused; in turn, she threw him off the farm. He returned that night and shot her, then threatened her daughter and shot himself. While the Memphis newspaper insisted that Brewer was insane, one wondered how many reprimands it took before he decided he could or would not take the abuse any longer. And in Camden, Arkansas, officials displayed the bodies of four men after they had been executed at the state penitentiary for killing a local merchant. More than one thousand people viewed the bodies.[68]

Despite the terror and threats, black workers continued to fight back when their lives were threatened, even if such actions led to their deaths. And while rural black people had always carried guns for hunting and self-protection, the frequency of armed confrontations between planters and croppers, based on the frequency of reporting, may have increased in the decade following World War I. For example, Less Smith shot a deputy sheriff in 1927 in Morrillton, Arkansas, for trying to arrest him. The act resulted in his lynching. In Pine Bluff, Bud Nelsen was found dead with his body riddled with bullets after he had allegedly killed the son of a planter in Pine Bluff. An unnamed man was lynched in Jonesboro because he supposedly had led an organization of young men who refused to work for planters at starvation wages. Across the river in Greenwood, Mississippi, Hal Winters and George Blakely were lynched in 1927 for killing a plantation manager, Wisley P. Martin. While they were working in the fields of the J. P. Jones plantation, Winters heard his daughter scream from their cabin. He and Blakely ran to find Martin trying to rape his daughter. Winters shot Martin and fled with Blakely. A posse composed of clergymen and businessmen chased the men to the Leflore County line. In another case, a mob fired two hundred shots into the body of Dan Anderson for killing a planter in Noxubee County. The planter had heard that Anderson was leaving without paying his debts. When he went to Anderson's house, the tenant shot him. D. O. Alexander, owner of a large plantation near Itta Bena, shot and killed Sam Jefferson over a crop dispute after he had heard that Jefferson and his father, heavily armed, had been looking for him. And in Brandon, Mississippi, Sandy Thompson killed his landlord and paid for it with a hanging. White merchants also incurred the wrath of angry sharecroppers, as did one leading merchant and postmaster found hacked to death in Sunflower County. Two black men and a black woman were arrested for the crime.[69]

Several murders of defiant tenants occurred in Clarksdale during the middle of the decade. A mob killed Lindley Coleman after a jury had just acquitted him of murdering a plantation manager. In another incident, four black men were tried for killing a plantation manager, though one of them, John Fisher, had the mentality of a ten-year-old and never understood why he was on trial. All four received a death sentence. And E. J. Mullens, Sr., shot Louis Roberts for trying to jump his contract and go to Vicksburg. Mullens had helped to get him acquitted for murder and arson and wanted him to stay on his Clarksdale plantation. In Money, site of the Emmet Till murder three decades later, a sharecropper shot the manager of the livestock department on a plantation.[70]

Few acts of defiance matched that of Joe Pullen, a tenant on W. T. Sanders's plantation in Drew, in Sunflower County. In 1923, Sanders had offered Pullen $150 to recruit families to work on the plantation. Instead, Pullen took the money and repaired his house and purchased other necessities that he believed the planter owed him for work he had performed and never been paid for. When Sanders and John Manning approached him and demanded he turn over the money, the six-foot-tall Pullen shot and killed Sanders with a .38-caliber pistol. As a posse gathered, Pullen seized his shotgun and ran for a ditch. He ambushed the posse, killing one with a shot to the face, hitting another in the head, and striking a third in the side. Although the posse used eight to ten boxes of shells in response, none of them hit Pullen. Posse members then poured a gallon of gasoline into the ditch and started a fire. The posse fired into the flames, but Pullen shot back, hitting another man. They brought in more gasoline while a party from Clarksdale arrived with two automatic rifles and a Browning machine gun. It took a third gallon of gas to reach Pullen. When he finally ran out, they shot and killed him. The posse then tied Pullen's feet to a car and dragged the body into Drew where people came from all over the region to view it. They also displayed Pullen's shotgun. Someone cut off his ear and placed it in a jar to be viewed along with the body. According to freedom fighter Mrs. Fannie Lou Hamer, a child at the time, after the Pullen murder "Mississippi was a quiet place for a long time." While the newspapers claimed that four white men had died "in defense of law and order," Mrs. Hamer recalled that Pullen had killed thirteen white men and wounded twenty-six others before dying.[71]

African Americans' constant challenges to the structures of white supremacy kept the dominant class off balance in the 1920s. Black people tested the limits of white supremacy not simply by carrying guns and defying planter authority on a daily basis, but also by pressing the limits of segregation—such as when B. Fowler refused in 1921 to leave a white waiting room in a train station in Brinkley. Or when a black man in Pine Bluff sought to purchase a ticket to a local circus intended only for white spectators. Or when the Civil War veteran Richard Fletcher refused to give his landowner in Edmundson, Arkansas, two bales of cotton for a thirty-dollar debt. After the planter murdered Fletcher, his family hired a lawyer in Memphis to help bring the planter to justice.[72] Many white people must have felt as Judge Walter White of Harrison County, Mississippi, did when he sentenced two black men for killing a white man who had stopped them on the road, cursing and striking them, and charging that their automobile had splashed mud on his car. According to the judge, "The negroes of this State go looking for trouble. They carry arms, the men revolvers, the women razors. When one commits a crime, the whole negro community protects him."[73] After World War I and the Elaine Massacre, white people had been put on notice that their abusive actions would not go unchallenged.

Instead of direct confrontation, a more common response to the increasing violence and persistent oppression was to leave the region to find jobs in the North or West. Wartime migration had halted somewhat, but black people continued to leave throughout the following decade. In 1920, a report from Helena noted, "Ever since the Arkansas massacre, colored people have been quietly leaving Elaine, and other sections of Arkansas, going to Chicago, Michigan, Ohio and other points in the North and East. Whites who are greatly in need of labor are assuring the people that they will be protected if they remain, but the feeling of unrest cannot be quieted." A report by an agent for the Bureau of Agricultural Economics who traveled throughout the Arkansas Delta to investigate the reasons for and the extent of the migration in 1923 showed even greater losses. While men formed most of the stream northward, many women were going to join their families. The greatest labor shortage existed in Lee and Phillips counties. Black people had left, the agent wrote, because of the four- and five-dollar-a-day wages for unskilled workers and the ten-dollar wage for skilled labor being offered in northern cities. The agent estimated that 15,000 had left Arkansas over the last six to eight months, out of a state-wide black population of 400,000.[74] Indeed, the southeastern Arkansas Delta counties lost a greater proportion of their black people than did any of the other counties. For example, from 1920 to 1930 Chicot lost 11.3 percent of its black people, while Desha lost 11.5 percent; Lee, 11.9 percent; and Phillips, 6.9 percent.[75]

An investigation in Vicksburg in the summer of 1920 indicated that more than ten thousand had left the area in the last three months. And in Memphis, "The through trains passing via this city on the way to northern communities for more than four months, have been crowded with men, women, and children forming part of another exodus to the North which is due to lynchings and a general state of unrest among the people."[76] The U.S. Department of Labor estimated that nine thousand black people, mostly single men and women or young married couples, had left the Yazoo Delta between the fall of 1922 and May of 1923.[77] By 1930, Bolivar County had lost 8.4 percent, Coahoma, 7.4 percent; Humphreys, 13.3 percent; Leflore, 1.6 percent; and Sunflower, 3.9 percent of its black population.[78]

Reports regarding the labor situation in the Delta sounded like those of the war years. From Coahoma County, Mississippi, came complaints of a "general unrest among its negro laborers, evidenced both in the negroes moving about from one plantation to another and in their leaving the state . . . It is said that in one day during the season of contracting for labor, 80 persons departed for Arkansas and Louisiana." On another day in Clarksdale, black families shipped seven carloads of household goods to destinations outside the region. In the lower section of the Yazoo Delta, "there has been noticed an unrest evidenced in the moving of the labor from one plantation to another, and in the great amount of travel among the negroes. All have money. This fact has been clearly demonstrated," continued the report, "in the inability of those who have work to be done to secure laborers, and in the buying they did at Christmas time."[79]

An Associated Negro Press survey indicated that, unlike the war when people had left for economic reasons, the migration of the 1920s occurred because of intimidation and lynchings. The survey revealed that in 1920 the astounding number of lynchings had driven people out of the region. According to the *Memphis Times,* black people had left at the rate of a hundred a day, although a "leading race man" who had arrived in Chicago from Mississippi estimated a daily exodus of 1,500. By the end of 1922, local sources reported that 3,500 had left the Delta during the past sixty days. Yet the reporter saw that fear was not the only factor that drove black people north. "Lured from their homes by promises of better living, sometimes social equality in northern cities, hundreds of negroes are leaving old friends and homes in Mississippi for the great manufacturing districts of the north."[80]

Letters from the northern migrants to those left behind praised the living conditions and the lack of Jim Crow laws in the North. "Numerous presents have been scattered among their friends back home as proof of the money flowing into their pockets." The Delta, "where more cotton is grown per acre than in any place in the world, has been flooded with these letters during the past six months. They started coming through the mails last winter. Negroes who have grown up on plantations have been induced to pack up and leave." While the lure of northern riches drew people to the North, just as many left for the reason given by a man from Jackson, Mississippi: "that ex-Senator James K. Vardaman and a Colored Man could not live together in the same state."[81]

As the sociologist T. J. Woofter noted at the time, the mass exodus from the South signaled "a strike against the plantation regime." Black people, as they had during World War I, stated clearly their reasons for leaving. In 1923, a mass meeting of black people in Jackson, Mississippi, led by S. D. Redmond cited the numerous reasons for fleeing. As "property holders" and "citizens ourselves," they insisted that the "Negro feels that life is not safe in Mississippi, and his life may be taken with impunity at any time upon the slightest pretext or provocation, by a white man." The group saw the recent defeat in Congress of the Dyer antilynching bill as an indication of the white South's determination to continue to rule through mob violence. In their view, the "Negro has generally despaired of obtaining his rights as a citizen in this section. He has lost faith."

The list of grievances indicated how little had been achieved since World War I, despite the promises of prominent white people. For every dollar spent on a black child's education in Mississippi, twenty was spent on each white child. Black students had only one high school in the state, while whites had one thousand high schools. White schools received funding from the state's white and black taxpayers, while black students relied on charity. The state had spent more than $1 million for a white reformatory for youthful offenders, while black children went to prison with hardened criminals. Black people had no tuberculosis hospital, no institution for the blind, and no state normal colleges. Though the meeting occurred in a city, the attendees stressed the importance of sharecroppers' and tenants' having the right to sell their own crops without mediation by the land-lord.[82]

The group concluded, "The State of Mississippi sent more Negro soldiers to the World War than whites, but the Negro boys on their return home found themselves with no more voice in the state and government which they fought to defend, than the German enemy whom they helped stay from American soil." The black person "generally finds himself excluded from all jury service" and from all participation in the government "under which he lives." Drawing the connection between the vote and representation, the people insisted that lack of participation in the government had led to "many inequalities and injustices under the law," and demanded that black people secure the right to vote.[83]

Planters heard what they wanted to hear regarding black people's reasons for leaving and their stated conditions for remaining in the South. In 1923, the Mississippi State Chamber of Commerce, in the tradition of the Welfare League that was formed during World War I, met and appointed a committee to deal with the exodus. Like the Welfare League, the committee acknowledged the need to improve education, health, and living conditions, yet urged that "any and all discussion of the social and political phases of this situation be avoided as having nothing whatever to do with the solution of this purely economic question, and that inter-racial committees composed of both negroes and whites be formed in every community so that each race may be informed of the viewpoint of the other so that dangerous incidents may be handled by legal means."[84]

White northern reports tended to favor the planters' perspective. A reporter for the *New York Post* found in 1920 that

> there is little heard of social equality in Mississippi, for the trend of teaching there from leaders of both races is altogether away from this. Both races try to teach pride of race—a separate and distinct development side by side and without intermingling. Political matters are of relatively small interest to the average negro, although what the future will hold in this respect and how the white South will meet its

problems cannot be forecast at present . . . At any rate in Mississippi today the lot of the negro is a happier one than at any period in the history of the race, and the attitude of the better class of white persons is more tolerant, more actively helpful and more sympathetic.[85]

An investigator from Chicago who visited the Delta in 1923 supported the planter's view that the urge for the exodus was economic, not political. "The ballot as a motive seems negligible, except in the case of the educated Negro. The plantation hands are not moving north because they want a chance to vote, although the colored politicians insist suffrage privileges are a chief reason for the population shift." The reporter found instead that a "desire for better education, fairer treatment in the courts and a square deal at settlement propels them north." He insisted that the migration had produced noticeable differences in Delta society. Invoking the notion of equal suffering, a Greenville planter insisted that "whites and blacks have exploited each other. The unprincipled planters stole from the plantation negro in settling at Christmas, and the negroes stole all they could lay hands on. It's changing. The best planters had no trouble keeping their hands, but the bad ones found their fields deserted, and they have had to mend their ways." He continued that the "great majority of the planters now give settlements instead of handing the tenants what they feel like at Christmas time. But get this straight. Whatever stealing has been done, both sides have played to an even break."[86]

The reporter found the traditional "recognized Negro leader," selected by the planters to speak for black people, who observed that "brutal treatment has been the fundamental cause of the exodus; the labor demand in the North was just an opportunity to escape. But a change has come. The white folks have become a wondrous kind. It means, I believe, the giving of opportunities for advancement long denied to the Negro." Another planter said that "undoubtedly many planters treated their negroes unfairly, just as the unprincipled exploit the ignorant and helpless everywhere. But they've stopped it. Sentiment is strongly against it, and if they kept it up they couldn't get labor for their fields. The old Simon Legree stuff went out long ago," he insisted, and "doubtless in districts remote from the cities there have been rough ones who bullied their Negroes and sometimes treated them with violence. But it's too easy for the Negro to get away for that to prevail any longer. There are too many roads and too many flivvers on the pike. Legree is as out of date as is old Uncle Tom himself."[87] The "leader" used the distinctions that large Delta planters often made between themselves and smaller landowners, who they claimed were the real abusers of black workers. Yet the evidence has consistently demonstrated that both large and small planters oppressed their workers and participated in maintaining white supremacy.

Officials in Arkansas pursued more desperate measures. Colonel H. L. Remmel, collector of revenue for the state, asked President Calvin Coolidge in 1923 to appoint a commission to stop the black migration. The migration had crippled the cotton industry, he argued, and the landowners "cannot get along without the negro." Remmel wanted Coolidge to appoint five southern black people to a commission, headquartered in Tuskegee, that would tour the South, hold mass meetings, teach agricultural diversification, and inform people why they must remain in the South. While the president apparently liked the plan, the Colored Chamber of Commerce in Little Rock condemned it.[88]

Planters responded to the migration as they had to the labor shortage at the turn of the century, by insisting that white labor replace black workers. In 1923, the Southern Alluvial Land Association saw the attraction of northern European farmers from the northern states as the solution to the labor problem. According to W. R. Satterfield, vice president of the Chicago Mill and Lumber Company and chairman of immigration for the association, the northern white farmer "can come in with nothing more than his bare hands, start as a share-cropper, a tenant, or a farm laborer, with the usual furnishing seen after by the planter and landowner. In a few years he is a substantial citizen, provided of course, he is a selected or hand picked immigrant to begin with."[89] Mrs. Walter Sillers, Sr., wrote an essay for the Bolivar County Daughters of the American Revolution entitled "Community Farms for Americans Proposed," calling for the creation of model farms to settle colonial descendants on thirty-acre farms. Such a project, Sillers insisted, was essential in order that "this fine race of people may be kept in ascendancy in this nation." The homes were to be located on a highway with an artesian well to prevent farm women from suffering the drudgery and boredom of farm life. The exodus of black people raised the labor issue, and Sillers wanted planters to recruit "Anglo Saxon stock from the hill sections," noting that "those who own land own the country."[90]

Planters met all over the Delta to discuss plans for recruiting white workers. Clarksdale planters hoped in 1923 to increase the white population in Coahoma County from 3 percent to 20 percent within a year, aiming for a 50 percent white labor force in twenty years. In their view, black people for the first time had competition, and if they expected to succeed, must "stir" themselves and provide better labor. In the opinion of one planter, white labor was reliable: "They will not jump you overnight, but if they see that they are going to have a loss, they will stick by their crop until it is made, take their loss and then, if they still so desire, leave the place." He expected to work the whole plantation with white people whom he furnished with money instead of supplies. "If they own their own teams they get two-thirds of the crop and if we have to furnish them with teams they get one-half. They handle their own share of the crop, selling where they please. They don't tear down plantations: they build them up. They take pride in the appearance of their homes and they not only keep up improvements that have been made but lend individual efforts to the new improvement work."[91]

The Burke Planting Company was purchased for the express purpose of recruiting white labor, and it brought farmers from Grenada, Leflore, and Yalabousha counties to farm exclusively with them. The company promised to build a new schoolhouse and a water pump. Many others wanted to use white labor, but did not have the proper facilities for them and could not have them living next to their black workers. To woo white farmers, Clarksdale built a new consolidated school system at a cost of $225,000, with paved roads for the buses.[92] And in Greenville, a committee of planters led by W. T. Wynn and LeRoy Percy met to discuss dividing up some of the larger plantations for sale to white farmers.[93]

Fears over securing enough labor also drove Arkansas and Mississippi planters to recruit Mexican workers in the 1920s. Sunflower County planters recruited several hundred in 1925, treating them not much better than black workers. According to the *Sunflower Tocsin*, "The greasers may remain here to make next years crop," but conceded that the "'African Machine' is the best picker we know." Apparently landowners were not satisfied with the Mexican laborers, and did not want them to return. "We believe they will create dissension among our negro labor," observed the *Tocsin*, "which is the best labor in the world for the Delta." Even more important, Mexican workers violated the racial boundaries of the Delta. "If the Mexican cotton pickers are ever needed here again," insisted the *Tocsin*, "it will mean the beginning of another race problem. These fellows butt into exclusive white places and make themselves at home in negro places. They marry negro women and try to marry among the lower class of whites. We hope they will all leave this part of the Delta and never come back here."[94]

While planters devised plans to create an alluvial empire worked by white labor—a design that if successfully implemented would have truly distinguished Delta plantations from similar operations the world over—they persisted in their usual efforts to recruit and retain black workers. As they had during World War I, planters sought to bring black migrants back. Delta newspapers were flooded with articles describing the return of happy migrants. In 1923, when two trainloads of former plantation laborers arrived in Indianola from Chicago, the *Memphis Commercial Appeal* described the people as being in bad shape, needing clothing, money, and health care. "Accustomed to being taken care of by the white folks, they quickly found that they must depend wholly upon themselves. Food must be paid for, clothing must be paid for, rent must be paid, and it took cash to buy coal. Furnishing they found to be an unknown term."[95]

Newspaper editors reveled in describing the trainloads of eager and grateful black people taking advantage of the excursion fares railway companies offered to returning migrants. But black people occasionally turned the excursions and the furor over their return to their advantage, as did a group who arrived in 1925 in Clarksdale from Chicago and St. Louis. According to the *Commercial Appeal,* "The negroes apparently had not come to the south to pick cotton, but rather to avail themselves of excursion rates to visit relatives . . . Scores of planters and several hundred spectators were at the station when the trains pulled in. Most of those who accosted the negroes were met with the remark that they would 'look around a little' before engaging in picking cotton." The planters found the majority of the arrivals well dressed; they did not "look like cotton pickers."[96]

At the same time, planters continued to trumpet their reform efforts, which included building more schools for black children and stepping up public health campaigns for smallpox and typhoid vaccinations. Red Cross and social workers joined county farm and home demonstration agents to bring public health issues and better dietary plans to sharecroppers. As one observer noted, however, while black people "eagerly" embraced these health forays into their communities, the efforts had proven "equally to the interests of the white land owners, in that it makes for an efficient, steady, dependable producing class who will not only prosper themselves, but will be an asset to the whole community."[97]

Delta newspapers frequently reported the barbeques that planters gave their workers during the summer lay-by season. Reminiscent of similar efforts of factory owners of the decade to retain workers and prevent them from joining unions, planters threw picnics and offered incentives for good cotton growing. On the Robert Shaw plantation, "Old time negro singing was enjoyed after which the old pastor of the place offered up a real stirring prayer." Rev. Walker of a Baptist church in Greenville "made the negroes a splendid and effective address in which the outstanding idea was 'tote fair.'" Rev. Walker "is the kind that makes Christianity popular, right living the only kind of life and the brotherhood of man the ideal earthly existence." The planters of Doddsville decided to give a barbeque on the Fourth of July for all of the black people in the Delta. The event included races for boys and girls, jumping, mule races, baseball, speaking, and greasy pole climbing. Two thousand pounds of barbeque and a thousand loaves of bread fed four thousand black people. The Yancey Company in Marianna, Arkansas, handed out cash prizes while the county agent gave a Booker T. Washington–style talk on why local workers should put down their buckets and remain in Lee County.[98]

Planters continued to display their capacity for self-deception by portraying themselves as benevolent managers and reformers. When Mr. and Mrs. John Bell Hood held a grand opening for a community center they had erected on their Matagorda plantation outside of Clarksdale, the *Memphis Commercial Appeal* reported on the affair. With a tone that blended elements of Old South paternalism and New South management, the newspaper described Mrs. Hood as "a lady of rare culture who has traveled every continent, regards every worker, white or colored, on this vast plantation as the special wards of the owners, who have a grave responsibility for the social and spiritual uplift of their charges. Not content to give a 100 percent square deal to every employee of the plantation and do full duty in the ordinary methods of human interest, Mrs. Hood has gone the limit for catering to the social needs and general betterment of the several hundred souls dependent on Matagorda." The Hoods had built at a cost of five thousand dollars a building to serve as a recreational, social, and educational center. The facility had a stage and galleries (segregated, of course) for black and white viewers, as well as an auditorium for motion picture watching equipped with an expensive radio set so that "the happy colored folks when entertained by the silver screen, may be regaled and astounded with the mysterious music and voices" they heard beamed not only from New York, Memphis, and New Orleans, but also from Cuba and Canada. In addition, the Hoods organized a six-piece plantation orchestra. "The entire scheme and every program is under the supervision of the owners, who, with commendable foresight, nevertheless leave the actual running of the community center in the hands of the colored people to encourage them and develop in them a sense of responsibility." The plantation minister, Rev. McMillan, thanked the Hoods for setting such a fine example. "It would keep the negro in the south, where he naturally belongs, away from gambling haunts and evenings of dangerous idleness," claimed the preacher. The newspaper noted, "A very touching expression of gratitude was made by this colored preacher in the fervid oratory and unique English of the dark race." At the conclusion of the dedication of the center, the Hoods served refreshments and received applause, while "many a moist eyed old darkey called a fervent god bless you both."[99]

Planters delivered on some of their promises to improve education for black people, recognizing that their own futures were at stake. In 1923 the Delta Industrial Institute became the first black agricultural high school in Mississippi, with its own agricultural chemist, Professor J. R. Pendleton, who held a degree from Tuskegee, and with W. F. Reden as the director. Reden's biography represented the sort of rags to riches story that Delta planters hoped to promote. Left an orphan when he was eight years old in Iowa, Reden sold newspapers, shined shoes, and learned the painter's trade. He completed high school in Iowa, then received a degree from Iowa State with honors in 1908 and moved to Mississippi in 1910, where he started the Industrial Institute in 1912.[100] In 1925 Reden asked black people to send their children to school if they were "interested in educating your children in fair treatment by the planter and in farming the best land in the world." Appealing to the xenophobia of the times, Reden insisted that the "need for education among the negro is more so now than ever before. If the citizens of the U.S. are to become 100 percent Americans, it must come through the public school room. Secret orders and the church will not solve the problem."[101]

The gem of the scientifically managed plantations, the Delta and Pine Land Company, came under the management of Oscar Johnston, a planter and businessman, in the 1920s. Known as the "syndicate," the plantation had its own black newspaper, the *Cotton Farmer,* that sought to persuade black people to stay on the farm. While the paper featured the usual fare of letters from black people describing why they should remain, other letters used scare tactics, as the one E. E. Elsworth wrote describing the plan of one planter to bring five thousand Hungarians to work in the Delta. Elsworth urged the workers on the plantation to be diligent and to inform on those who were not in an effort to prevent white workers from taking their jobs.[102]

Johnston and the Delta and Pine Land Company continued to boast the finest schools and hospital in the region. The *Manufacturer's Record* described the company in 1923 as "an outstanding example of the opportunities that can be available for the negroes of the South," an almost "Utopian dream being brought into an actual, practical reality, and one which enabled thousands of the negro race to grow cotton under conditions which mean comfort, success and happiness for them." By this time, Delta and Pine Land Company owned 60,000 acres organized into eighteen plantations with eight thousand black workers. Accompanying photographs revealed black people's "happiness, contentment and satisfaction."[103]

Planters still tried to influence their workers' consumption habits, as did those in Washington County who complained that town "sharpers" in Leland had fleeced black croppers on Saturdays. Leland "seems to have a lot of well dressed negroes who strut around in fine clothes with plenty of money and no job," whined the *Leland Enterprise*, "No town is big enough for that kind of negro."[104] Yet many Mississippi Delta planters had, as a consequence of the war and the continued migration, given in to sharecropper demands for greater freedom in shopping—paying them in cash that allowed workers to shop wherever they wanted. Thus commissary managers found themselves stocking their shelves with meats, cheeses, crackers, cakes, candies, preserves, and soft drinks, as opposed to the traditional fat back, meal, lard, and molasses.[105] Despite the celebration of opportunity and contentment, workers still left the Delta and Pine plantations. Perhaps as a result, Johnston was moved to publish in the plantation newspaper a copy of the company's enticement policy, although with the caveat that when enticing servants, consent for a person to work off the plantation must be given in writing for both adults and their children.[106]

For all of their claims of improvement and reform, planters continued to oppress their workers. LeRoy Percy, one of the most revered of the large "reform" planters, illustrated the limits of the more enlightened landowners. Edgar Webster, a manager on Percy's Ackelena Land Company plantation, informed Percy that, because of the boll weevil, black tenants had not made enough cotton to pay their rent. The tenants thus had requested a rent reduction. Webster suggested as one option that Percy "attach" their agricultural products, though this would strip them of everything, compelling them to leave. "Shall I collect as much as possible without process of court," he asked, "or go to the limit and collect as much as possible?" Percy replied: "Take as much as you can get from the negroes without process of law where they are willing to remain on the place. If they are going to move anyway, it seems to me you might as well clean them up."[107] Large planters, not simply the smaller ones, continued to engage in the practices that drove black people northward.

Planters used their friendships and political connections to mediate their relations with workers. In one instance, Betty Simms had been working on Walter Sillers, Sr.'s Evelyn plantation for two years when she married an old man on the Bruce place and moved there to live with him. She made no contract and was thus not bound by her husband's contract, because a wife's rights and property were entirely separate from her husband's. According to Sillers, she was "boss of herself and as my experience is, she is boss of him too." She soon tired of her new husband and wanted to move back and live with her son at Evelyn. Sillers insisted that she was too old to work, and urged Judge Robert Arnold to write the manager, asking him to allow her to leave with her belongings without any trouble. Sillers did not want to "disturb their labor relations" by issuing a writ of reprieve for her things.[108]

Delta planters in the 1920s struggled with the issue of retaining a cheap and reliable labor force in the face of a bad cotton market. Their remedies ran the gamut, from a greater reliance on scientific management and corporate welfare incentives to coercion and terror. Even when planters conceded that black people's concerns had some foundation, they were unable to address the economic conditions that influenced them. Many probably felt as Walter Sillers did when he acknowledged, "We feel ashamed of the habitations we furnish our tenants, yet the man who seeks to better conditions goes in debt, mortgages his property and is finally foreclosed." Yet it was clear that changes were in order. Noting that the cultural methods on cotton plantations had remained the same as in slavery days, Sillers wrote, "Think of a great industry standing still for a hundred years." After describing the labor-intensive process of growing cotton, he understood why labor had left. He called, like many of the larger planters, for a greater use of tractors, insisting, "We must have intelligent and scientific methods on the farms as well as the factories."[109]

Yet planters still could not admit to the underlying reality of class relations in the Delta. Sillers continued to insist that black people were better off and did not leave from fears of violence: "No law-abiding negro fears mob violence because he knows his planter will protect him. He not only knows he is valuable to the white man, more so than his mules and fine horses, but he also relies upon the kindly feeling and sense of justice of the white man." He recalled the Reconstruction era in Bolivar County when black people served on juries, a black man was elected to sheriff, and Blanche K. Bruce, a black man, became the U.S. senator. Even then the county had a Ku Klux Klan, but black people did not leave. Sillers blamed the current exodus of black people not on mob violence, but on the labor agents who wanted cheap labor and servants.[110]

Sillers was not alone: other planters remained blinded by their racist assumptions and oblivious to their own contradictory responses to their workers. John Sharp Williams, a U.S. senator from Mississippi and a planter, when complaining that he could not raise anything in the Delta anymore, blamed his problems on black workers. The trouble, he wrote to Florence Sillers Ogden, was "the negro in the woodpile," who was "one of the best plantation hands in the world and about the poorest farmer that God ever made. He doesn't know anything about cotton, and won't learn anything but cotton." Ogden's husband, Harry, responded even more dramatically to the labor problem. According to his wife, he had "not only gotten to be a typical southern planter, but I strongly suspect him of being a cyclops in the KKK and if the exodus of negroes continues, he will fire on Ft. Sumpter [*sic*] and secede from the union."[111]

Unlike during the Civil War, southern planters did not need to secede from the Union to retain their way of life. What Sillers could not foresee was a Great Depression that would call forth federal remedies to restructure the collapsed southern cotton economy through parity payments and mechanization—methods that increased planter fortunes and eventually rendered obsolete an African American labor force. This process would not go unchallenged by the black people whose lives would be transformed yet again.

5 | Revolt against Mean Things

During the two decades following World War I, the world suffered a deep depression, the rise of fascism, and a second world war. During the Depression, rural and industrial workers formed unions, staged strikes, and fought for their livelihood. War and depression broke the back of European imperialism, paving the way for the peasant revolutions in the former colonies of the last half of the twentieth century. The United States did not escape these vast changes. It did not experience a major political shift, either from the right or the left, but during the 1930s the nation experienced the rise of organized labor and a limited welfare state.

For the Delta, the 1930s represented a major turning point, as it did for the rest of the South. New Deal agricultural policies restructured the plantation economy, leading to further land consolidation and mechanization. As the old labor-intensive sharecropping system gave way to the capital-intensive, mechanized production of cotton, thousands of black and white rural families found themselves without a job or a place to live. Displaced from the land and with no place to go in a depressed economy, sharecroppers and tenant farmers fought back. Unlike in Elaine, rural workers in the 1930s organized interracially, and they had help from more outside organizations than the NAACP: outside supporters, writers, and journalists publicized life in the American Congo for all of the world to see.[1]

In the 1920s, the Delta had more in common with other parts of the world than it did with the "New Prosperity" that more generally defined American society. The region continued to register one of the highest rates in the United States of illiteracy, poverty, malnutrition, infant mortality, and death from preventable diseases. Both black and white sharecroppers and tenants eked out a bare subsistence as cotton prices fell. Still, hard times worsened on the plantations in the early 1930s, as more people found themselves in the ranks of tenancy and sharecropping. Cotton

152

prices fell in June 1932 to 4.6 cents per pound, causing the meager incomes of black sharecroppers to decline even more. In 1932, sharecroppers in the Yazoo-Mississippi Delta made $129, down from the $333 they had earned in 1913. One study determined that sharecroppers in this region earned forty-five cents a day. Conditions were not much better across the river in eastern Arkansas, where wage hands in 1936 netted an annual income of $203.[2]

In addition to declining incomes, the region suffered two major natural disasters in the postwar years when the Mississippi River and its tributaries flooded the plantation region in 1927, followed by a severe drought in 1930–1931. In both instances, the American Red Cross provided relief, though not without problems. During the flood, Delta planters used the relief to retain control over their labor, forcing black people to remain on their land and to work for their rations, in some cases engaging in peonage. Relief workers encountered similar problems during the drought—which hit the hardest in the Arkansas Delta—despite a Red Cross policy that prohibited making clients work for their rations. In Marked Tree, Arkansas, for example, croppers worked for their landowners for one dollar a day, which was then applied to their commissary accounts while the Red Cross fed them. Indeed, planters still shaped the Red Cross program through their control of the local relief committees. Many landowners refused to allow their workers to receive Red Cross aid during harvest time, forcing people to pick for lower wages. After the cotton had been gathered, however, planters cut off supplies to croppers at the commissaries, allowing the Red Cross to feed their workers. And the Red Cross discovered that merchants in Jefferson County had made a 30 to 40 percent profit from processing the agency's food orders intended for relief clients.[3]

Planter control of drought relief meant that untold numbers of families went hungry, with some succumbing to disease and death. In particular, planters denied workers food until December and January, when winter had set in. By then, the Red Cross faced a gigantic relief program. On January 19, 1931, the agency had fed 23,000 of Phillips County's 44,350 residents, and 12,838 of St. Francis County's 33,000 residents. Lee County predicted that 20,000 of its 28,000 people needed relief. In Marked Tree, relief workers had to work for one dollar a day in order to receive aid.[4]

The Depression and drought, coming on the heels of the 1920s, wore sharecropper families down. Many continued to write letters to the NAACP, as they had done in the previous decade, to describe their plight and to appeal for help. One black cropper wrote in September of 1930 from Round Pond, Arkansas, to "inform you that the people . . . is in a suffering condition and are greatly in need of government assistance and we need the aid" from the NAACP "in getting help from the government." The "people here is catching fish out of these mud holes and boiling them and eating them. The water is about 8 inches deep and there is about as many dead fish in the holes as there are live ones." He added that the "people are afraid to write. They are afraid that they will get killed." Planters, he said, forced croppers to work more acreage for less cash furnishings at the commissary, where they charged a 20 percent interest for what they bought. "It is a shame before the Lord how the colored people are being treated here." This "is not one-third but I will quit writing."

Pressing the NAACP for help, the author asserted his citizenship rights. "And we as colored people citizens of the United States and Republicans we feel that President Hoover should help us. We helped him to take his seat and we feel that he should help us as we are greatly in need of the government." He asked for a northern man to come and investigate the conditions. Lawyer J. R. Booker, in passing this letter on to the national organizational office, noted that his office in Little Rock had received "day after day" complaints "as to the actions of these landowners and their treatment toward our people." Booker insisted that the letter from Round Pond "reflects the true situation," for "we find that large numbers of our people are being duped by even the landowners who are taking their crops and permitting the tenants to suffer terribly."[5]

Sharecroppers did more than write letters. They watched as planters used the expanding labor surplus, which the Depression fueled, to maintain their practices of peonage, murder, and theft of people's crops and labor. The planters' ability to deny them Red Cross food when their families starved, even died, angered them. After a decade of oppressive life in the American Congo, black people fought back. In counties all over the Arkansas Delta, flyers appeared in cotton fields urging people not to pick cotton at the prevalent wage. In Phillips County, black people refused to go to the fields and pick cotton for twenty-five to forty cents per hundred pound, forcing planters to import five hundred Mexican pickers. County sheriffs attributed the labor problems to Communist agitators and rumors that the Red Cross would feed them.[6]

In England, Arkansas, black and white sharecroppers and tenant farmers followed H. C. Coney, a white tenant farmer, into town and demanded Red Cross relief that had been slowly administered. When the relief committee told them the agency was out of forms, five hundred angry black and white men and women, tenants and sharecroppers, demanded food immediately. They then got their rations. Similar demands for food were reported in Lepanto, Crawfordsville, and Monet.[7] These collective efforts to demand relief contrasted with the more personal confrontations of the previous decade. Planters must have worried when they saw both black and white families join in Coney's protest.

Mississippi Delta planters also had trouble getting their cotton picked during the Red Cross relief program. In Holmes County, ninety-three sharecroppers and their families walked off a plantation in 1932 when their landlord refused to pay them a cash settlement. They set up camp and lived in tents scattered around the yard of Old Jerusalem Church. Unable to force the workers back on his plantation, the landowner instead persuaded the county health department to declare the tent colony a health hazard. According to the *Daily Worker*, a sharecroppers' union had recently organized in nearby Charlotte. Reports from other sources also noted the refusal of Delta croppers to work for their Red Cross rations.[8] These reports from both Arkansas and Mississippi suggest that the Communist Party may have been active in the Delta in the early thirties, since it was organizing at this time a sharecroppers' union in the Alabama Blackbelt. Indeed, Lement Harris and Harold Ware, members of the Communist Party, had traveled through the Delta in 1931, gathering information for a farm survey that the party had sponsored and then published. Harris actually interviewed H. C. Coney from England, publishing an article in the *New Republic*.[9]

In the early years of the Depression, then, Delta black people fought their growing impoverishment and planter efforts to deny them relief, whether it came from the Red Cross or the Communist Party. And outside agencies, like the NAACP, the Federation of Colored Farmers, and the National Negro Business League continued to press the Red Cross and President Herbert Hoover to provide adequate relief for Delta black people. Hoover turned a deaf ear to their pleas for help, but a new president arrived in 1933 who favored the poor far more than his predecessor.

Federal relief came to the Delta with the election of Franklin D. Roosevelt and the implementation of New Deal relief policies starting in 1933. The programs had a mixed effect on Delta society. Planters and other employers in business controlled the local relief committees, as they had during the Red Cross program, continuing to utilize relief for their own ends and forcing black people to work on their terms. The legislation passed during the first New Deal in 1933 illustrated the limits of decentralized relief. For example, the National Recovery Act (NRA) established voluntary codes for businessmen to abide by, including payment of minimum wages and equal wages for black and white workers. Most southern employers fired their black workers rather than pay them equal wages, however, leading black people to refer to the NRA as the "Negro Removal Act." The work relief programs also discriminated against black people. Both the Works Projects Administration (WPA) and the Civil Works Administration (CWA) hired fewer black than white workers, discriminated against them according to skill, and paid black people less than their white counterparts.[10]

Delta black people's experiences with New Deal relief mirrored those of other black southern workers. In Forrest City, Arkansas, attorneys Scipio Jones and John Booker filed a complaint with the NRA for one hundred black women workers against the Maid-Well Garment Company for having hired and worked them under code wages, then laying them off without pay. The lawyers sought six thousand dollars in back pay. In Greenville, Mississippi, the Workingmen's Association complained that local businesses did not pay code wages and had decreased the labor force by consolidating their operations. A similar report in Memphis found that the NRA had led to the displacement of hundreds of black workers.[11]

Black people also complained of discrimination within the WPA and the CWA. African Americans in Mississippi had hired a secret investigator to travel around the state and study relief administration. He found that in Jackson, Meridian, and Vicksburg, black people had not been hired for skilled jobs, and that hundreds had been arrested for vagrancy. Further, no CWA projects existed in black communities to build libraries, parks, and schools. The report also noted that black women especially suffered: although 25 percent of them were self-supporting, the CWA had made no provisions for them nor had it created any jobs for them. Most CWA teaching positions in black schools had gone to white people.[12]

Relatives of the planter class, if not the planters themselves, often administered the relief programs. For example, in Tunica, Mississippi, the wife of one of the largest planters supervised the WPA program. When cotton-picking time came, thousands of the twenty thousand black residents of Tunica County were dropped from the WPA relief rolls for refusing to pick cotton. Mrs. Mary Jane Harris, for instance, eighty-five years old, had to care for two invalid daughters and she herself suffered from high blood pressure. She picked cotton for one month, but because of health reasons and the need to care for her daughters, left the fields. She lost her monthly WPA relief check. In nearby, Memphis, CWA administrators sent black women to clean the administrators' friends' houses in return for a ration of groceries. Indeed, Walter White of the NAACP reported that in Delta cities and towns black people had lost their federal relief for refusing to pick cotton at low wages, creating a condition, he said, that "savors of peonage."[13]

The precipitating factor that produced an actual organized challenge to planter authority in the Delta came from New Deal agricultural policies, specifically the Agricultural Adjustment Act of 1933 (AAA). Large-scale farmers, led by the American Farm Bureau Federation, had pushed in the 1920s for a federal crop reduction program that would also raise farm prices. The AAA achieved this by paying farmers a parity for voluntarily reducing their production. This measure represented the triumph of agribusiness over smaller family farmers, and offered very little for farm workers. Delta planters welcomed the program, for it boosted their profits and allowed them to move faster toward mechanization. Their interests were directly represented in the AAA Cotton Section, which was headed by Mississippian Cully Cobb, and in the Cotton Pool Section, headed by Oscar Johnston, president of Delta and Pine Land Company.[14]

Delta planters controlled the application of the AAA, creating a nightmare for the destitute sharecroppers. Local committees, consisting of large landowners, county officials, and agricultural extension agents, administered the program. These committees determined who received the AAA allotments and designated the percentage of acreage to be plowed. Delta planters then plowed one-third of their allotted cotton in return for a parity payment. Planters, however, were required by Section 7 of the AAA—written by Oscar Johnston—to split the parity payments with their tenants according to their rental arrangement, 50–50 in the case of sharecroppers, and 75–25 in favor of third and fourth tenants. Landowners welcomed the parity payments, but did not want to share them with their workers—they wanted more of their tenants' subsidy payments, and thus resorted to various schemes. They forced or persuaded illiterate tenants to place their mark at the end of a long, legal form whereby they unknowingly signed over their portions of federal payments to the landlord. Or they cashed AAA checks payable to both landlord and tenant and kept the money. Sometimes landlords, when signing their annual contracts, did not mention they had tenants. With the passage in 1934 of the Bankhead Cotton Control Act, which limited the amount of cotton one planter could market by issuing bale tags for the legal amount of cotton to be produced, planters simply took the tenants' tags, or they demanded payment of past debts in the form of tags.[15]

Black sharecropper Deacy Real's experience with the AAA on a plantation in St. Francis County illustrated the consequences for workers. When her husband received a small AAA check, his landlord took it from him. "My husband couldn't read or write. I tried to teach him, but he just couldn't learn." Mrs. Real told her husband not to place an X on the next check. When the next check arrived, Mr. Real went to the county agent's office, which was crowded with riding bosses from all of the plantations, and requested his parity check. A man then snatched the check and told him to sign it over to his planter.[16]

In the end, the AAA made it advantageous for landowners to simply plow under all of their sharecroppers' land, using the full subsidy payments to hire them back as wage workers at low costs. It did not require planters to pay a share of the crop to wage workers, but it prohibited them from starting persons out as croppers and then firing them so they could avoid sharing the parity payment. With the aid of cooperative county agents, however, most landowners got around this ruling. The result was a dramatic decline in the Delta in sharecropping and tenant farming. The actual numbers of displaced are hard to determine, but estimates range from 20 to 40 percent. The results for planters are easier to assess. A U.S. Senate committee in 1936 revealed that Oscar Johnston's Delta and Pine Land Company received over $318,000 in parity payments between 1933 and 1935. In Washington County, Mississippi, ten plantations received $148,022 in 1933, five got $86,707 in 1934, and four received $68,202 in 1935. Overall, from 1933 to 1936, Arkansas planters received $2.1 million and Mississippi planters, $2.5 million.[17]

In some ways planters in the 1930s used the AAA to legitimize actions they had always engaged in, such as driving sharecroppers from the land after they had planted the cotton, then hiring day labor to pick it. Under this arrangement, the planter received free labor for planting the crops and secured all of the profits from the sale of the cotton. (These actions had occurred earlier, in Elaine, precipitating the organization of sharecroppers.) Planters continued to evict workers in the 1930s, but with the aid of the federal government. In other cases, croppers were not evicted, but instead suffered crop reductions without receiving the benefit of parity payments. As one sharecropper from Shaw, Mississippi, complained to the AAA, "The Southern People do not pay [*sic*] fair."[18] By 1934, thousands of sharecroppers had found themselves without a crop to plant or a contract to hold them over between the seasonal cycles of the crop when no wage work existed.

The AAA also allowed planters to use some of their parity money to purchase tractors, further displacing sharecroppers. Mechanization of cotton occurred first in the Arkansas and Mississippi Delta, in part because large plantations had more capital to expend on technology. But because mechanization occurred in stages, beginning first in the 1920s with tractors used for cultivation, and expanding in the 1950s to include the actual picking and weeding of cotton, the social consequences of the process were spread across three decades. Full mechanization did not occur until the 1960s. For example, two studies of the Arkansas Delta in 1938 revealed that displacement of sharecroppers had occurred in two stages, first in 1933 and 1934 because of AAA policies, and second in 1937 and 1938, when more planters had purchased tractors. Chicot and Mississippi counties thus saw a 12 percent decline in resident cropper families. Yet although tractors were used for plowing, they were not used for picking or weeding the cotton. Planters needed wage labor for these tasks. Thus many displaced sharecroppers were rehired as wage laborers, or received smaller acreage allotments as croppers.[19] The combination of the AAA plow-up program, with its increased mechanization, undoubtedly worsened the lives of the drought- and Depression-weary sharecroppers.

The massive evictions of sharecroppers led two small-town white socialists from Tyronza to organize the Southern Tenant Farmers' Union (STFU) in 1934. H. L. Mitchell owned a dry cleaning store that serviced the plantations surrounding Tyronza; Clay East, who came from a landowning family, was township constable, the leading law officer in town, and owned a gas station. In 1932, both men became interested in Socialist Party head Norman Thomas's campaign for the U.S. presidency. After hearing Thomas speak in Memphis, they returned to Tyronza and founded a local of the Socialist Party. Mitchell and East drew from a socialist tradition in the region dating back to the early twentieth century and to the formation of the Homesteaders' Union a decade earlier, which had united small white farmers against planters.

Their first project centered on securing relief for local applicants. The CWA had come to town offering jobs for twenty hours a week at twenty-five cents an hour. Planters controlled the program and hired their favorite sharecroppers to clean ditches and build roads on their plantations, excluding many black and white people in need of the five-dollar-a-week jobs. Mitchell and East organized in 1933 the Tyronza Unemployment

League at the local Odd Fellows Lodge hall to demand jobs for the needy. The league lasted only a couple of months, but during that time, it was able to persuade the state CWA representative to prevent planters from using the agency for their own ends. Consequently, the Socialist Party grew in the area, attracting black and white members such as the Reverend E. B. "Britt" McKinney, a prominent circuit-riding minister in the area's black communities.[20]

The STFU was formed in July of 1934 when Hiram Norcross, a St. Louis financier who owned the Fairview plantation in Poinsett County, evicted twenty-three sharecropper families. Next door to his farm, eleven white and seven black men gathered at the Sunnyside schoolhouse to form the union. Among them were several of the evicted croppers. The union had several goals, among them farm labor representation on agricultural boards and the enforcement of section 7 of the AAA contracts, which provided for rental and parity payments to be made directly to the sharecroppers. The same section required planters "insofar as possible" to maintain on their farms "the normal number of tenants and other employees"; to permit "all tenants to continue in the occupancy of their houses on this farm, rent free, for the years 1934 and 1935"; to provide tenants with access to wood lands for fuel; and to allow the use of adequate acreage to grow feed and food crops as well as the "reasonable" use of work animals and equipment in exchange for labor. The union also wanted an end to the evictions. Acknowledging that sharecropping would continue as a way of life and work for many, the STFU proposed a model contract that included an adequate cash furnishing at the commissary during the farm season at a legal rate of interest and with the right to trade anywhere; pay at prevailing wages for all improvements made on the landowner's property; decent houses for each family with the use of an adequate portion of land rent-free for growing food and feed crops; access to woodlands for fuel, and to a wagon and team to haul the wood; and the right to sell cotton at the market price to the person of choice.[21]

In the early stages of the union's development, Mitchell and East drew support from their white socialist allies. Locally, Uncle Charley McCoy, a former machinist from Truman, organized white tenants, while J. R. Butler, a sawmill worker from White County and a "self-educated country schoolteacher" employed a "mish-mash of ideas drawn from Populist, Wobbly, and other Midwestern radical sources." Butler's influence appeared in the union's constitution in the call for "one big union of all agricultural workers" and for the creation of a "cooperative order of society."[22]

The STFU also attracted organizers and supporters from an indigenous radical movement of southern white liberation clergymen who were educated at Vanderbilt's School of Religion and fired by a radical social gospel that drew from the New Testament and Karl Marx. Howard "Buck" Kester, who belonged to the Fellowship of Reconciliation (FOR) founded by theologian Reinhold Niebuhr, was deeply committed to combating the Jim Crow system and had investigated lynchings for the NAACP. Presbyterian minister Claude Williams, a native Tennesseean, had been driven from his pulpit in northwestern Arkansas for working with striking miners. Ward Rodgers, a Texas-born Methodist minister, had also been with Kester and Williams at Vanderbilt and was considered the best white organizer and speaker in the region. The STFU also enjoyed the support of William Amberson, a socialist who served on the faculty of the University of Tennessee Medical School and wrote articles and pamphlets describing the sharecroppers' plight.[23]

In the early months of the union, Mitchell and William Amberson focused on collecting evidence for a pamphlet funded by the Socialist Party describing the effect of the evictions on sharecroppers. The findings were published in 1934 as *The Plight of the Sharecropper*, authored by Norman Thomas. The report shocked even members of the AAA. Landowners, outraged over the growing publicity of the evictions, requested their own AAA investigation. Cully Cobb, after being told incorrectly that Amberson was a communist, sent one of his aides, E. A. Miller, to interview planters. Miller refused to review the union's survey of displaced sharecroppers; instead he visited planters and adopted their view that no eviction problem existed. He informed the landowners that although they must retain the same number of tenants each year, they did not have to keep the exact families, which paved the way for landowners to continue evicting the union members and others.[24]

The Miller investigation in 1934 was so outrageously biased in favor of the planters that H. L. Mitchell, E. B. McKinney, and others drove to Washington to place their case directly before Secretary of Agriculture Henry A. Wallace, who promised another investigation. Jerome Frank, one of the union's allies in the AAA, secured the appointment of Mary Connor Meyers to conduct another investigation, resulting in a report so damaging that the head of the AAA, agribusinessman Chester Davis, destroyed it. The interpretation of section 7 and whether planters had to retain the same number of tenants each year—even if not the same ones—provoked a fight within the AAA between the pro-planter forces, led by Davis, Cobb, and Johnston, and those like Jerome Frank and Rexford

Tugwell who sympathized with the sharecroppers. Davis and his group won. Oscar Johnston, the author of section 7, insisted that it was only "a proviso morally obligating landowners," and not intended to be legally enforceable.[25]

The sharecroppers and their allies were no match for the power of agri-business—the Farm Bureau, as well as large growers in both the South and the West—and of southern conservatives in general. The majority leader of the U.S. Senate, Arkansan Joseph P. Robinson, was not about to let his planter friends down, nor to allow the sharecroppers to embarrass him in front of Roosevelt during the president's visit to Little Rock. Nor was Roosevelt about to compromise his New Deal coalition by alienating the powerful southern conservative wing of the Democratic Party. The AAA thus became the primary relief source for planters while helping to destroy the lives of thousands of sharecroppers, who in the midst of a depression had few places to go.[26] The failure of the union and its allies to secure justice from the AAA and U.S. Department of Agriculture did not bode well for their organizing efforts. If the federal government supported the planters, to whom were the sharecroppers to look for protection from planter violence? As the union stepped up its organizing in 1935 and 1936, planters fought back with their traditional weapons of murder, beatings, and evictions.

Mitchell and East had begun to organize locals of the union in 1934, a process that accelerated in 1935. Together with E. B. McKinney, they agreed that the organization must be based on a sharecropper leadership, though illiteracy—which was highest among white people—created obstacles. Black women were most likely to be literate within black families, and often served as secretaries of their locals. Organizing locals meant finding ways to circumvent the riding bosses and plantation managers. Most of the black union meetings occurred in churches. On Sundays, a union member might tell the congregation about the organization, usually without any help from an organizer. Dues ranged from ten to twenty-five cents per month. According to Mitchell, the union never had a large number of paying members. Most sharecroppers simply did not have the cash. Mitchell claimed in 1934 to have two thousand men and women members, largely in Poinsett County. One year later, the organization had expanded into Mississippi, Crittenden, Cross, and St. Francis counties, where the union drew its strength. By 1935, Mitchell claimed twenty-five thousand members in Arkansas, Oklahoma, Texas, Tennessee, Mississippi, Missouri, and Alabama. But the organization never had an accurate account of its membership. According to Mitchell, "If one member of a family signed up, I counted three more also as members." He estimated that for every ten who actually enrolled, there were probably a hundred others who participated in the union. The number of locals fluctuated also, making it difficult to achieve an accurate count, though one estimate listed two hundred locals of the union.[27]

The most difficult issue immediately confronting the organizers was the albatross of southern working-class movements: race. The eighteen black and white men who gathered in July to form the union had confronted head-on the question of interracial unionism. Burt Williams, a sixty-five-year-old white man, told of how his father had ridden with the Ku Klux Klan to drive the last of the Republicans out of Crittenden County. In spite of this history, Williams advocated the formation of an interracial union. An African American, Isaac Shaw, agreed, noting that he had been a member of the all-black union in Elaine that had been destroyed. He insisted that black and white sharecroppers and tenant farmers had to fight together if they were going to defeat planter oppression.[28]

The commitment of the founders to interracial unity proved difficult and was not always honored when locals were organized. When one of the early locals organized in Marked Tree, in Poinsett County, union leaders compromised and allowed two segregated locals to form. Black and white people did not work together on plantations in this region and refused to join an integrated local. McKinney became the president of the black local, and held the meetings of both groups in the black lodge hall, the only place large enough to hold all of the members. Walter Moskop, a former bootlegger, headed the white local. Mitchell justified his support of separate locals by saying, "Of course it is quite all right for the two races to organize into separate locals just so long as they are all in the same union and fighting for the same things." Class would supposedly trump race in the union.[29]

The resort to a segregated union policy was partly influenced by the original settlement patterns of the Arkansas Delta. Several northeastern counties had been settled almost exclusively by white people. For example, whites in 1920 formed 57.3 percent of Cross County's population, 57.9 percent of Mississippi County's, and 80.4 percent of Poinsett County's. Those percentages increased slightly in 1930.[30] As we have seen, the promotional efforts of the Southern Alluvial Land Association during and after World War I had sought to sell and settle the cut-over lands with white farmers, large and small, southern and nonsouthern. Thus, in some counties, plantations operated either with an all-white labor force of sharecroppers and tenant farmers, or with a strictly segregated labor force. As black union organizer George Stith recalled, a large percentage of northeastern Woodruff County was white, which yielded a large proportion of the white membership. (Poinsett County had a population that was around 40 percent white and 60 percent black.) At one time, Stith remembered, the "whole section north of McCrory, around South Bend, over as far as Martin, until you get up near Wynn, was mostly white. At one time Negroes wasn't allowed to go through these places north of McCrory unless they was a white person with them."

Because of these settlement patterns, Stith said that "the racial makeup of a local depended a lot upon the area where you organized. Agricultural labor, especially in the cotton fields, at that time was about 85 or 90 percent black so your membership normally ran just like your area. In Arkansas in the early days of the union, I think our white support was an over-average percentage compared to their population at large. Our white membership at one time ran higher than 15 percent whites, much higher, especially in certain areas." The make-up of the locals, according to Stith, "was a community thing. Naturally the communities were segregated. That's why we had segregated locals, because whites and blacks usually don't live on the farm together. There were locals that were integrated though."[31] Unfortunately, no accurate account exists of the numbers of segregated and integrated locals or of black and white membership. One historian has estimated, however, that from half to two-thirds were exclusively African American.[32]

Given the history of northeastern Arkansas, where nightriders employed violence to drive out black sharecroppers and landowners in the 1920s, invoking terror all over the region, the interracial union had a hard row to hoe. And it was in these counties that white landownership in the 1920s had declined and tenancy had risen, leading one historian to suggest that, at least in Poinsett County, the declining status of white farmers and tenants, and their evictions, made them more likely to join an interracial union.[33] While some white people were sharecroppers, however, most had other backgrounds that prevented them from finding common ground with black people. Most were some variation of renters or even landowners. Alex East, brother of Clay, had lost his land to the Hiram Norcross plantation and then became the manager on land he had once owned. It may be that some of those who had lost their land or who had been evicted became more sympathetic to black people. Yet when white people had organized in the immediate past, as with the Homesteaders' Union, they had formed a segregated organization. Indeed, these members had even blamed black people for taking their land. As farm owners or as aspiring landowners, they stood to become employers of black workers. Placing these people in a union with black sharecroppers who had struggled alone against the terror of the plantation system made the future of the union precarious at best. Nor would black people necessarily trust a union that contained former nightriders or members of the KKK.

Segregation's mores affected how and where union locals conducted their meetings, and how white and black people understood their religious traditions as they related to class struggle. For example, black people held their meetings in their churches and schools. White workers could not do that since all white people—owners and tenants alike—went to the same churches and schools. As Stith observed, "Where they [white members] belonged to a church, the higher ups also belonged, and they couldn't get the church to have a meeting."[34] Further, white southern Protestants, especially poor ones, were not as fortunate as their black counterparts in the form of evangelicalism they inherited. Black religion, growing out of slavery, celebrated humanity and forgiveness, insisted on the power of redemption, believed deeply in justice and freedom, and hoped for deliverance from oppression. White southerners' religion cursed their poverty as part of an unworthiness before the eyes of a vengeful and unforgiving God. Innate sinfulness, not redemption, formed the contours of southern white religion. Rare was the southern white preacher who dared to suggest from a pulpit the inhumanity of the class relations of the Jim Crow South that condemned both black and white people to poverty and ignorance.[35]

While the STFU's initial founders and leaders were white southern radicals with both socialist and communist affiliations, the union membership and the locals grew out of and drew from the institutional structures already present in the black community. Union meetings were held in black churches and organizers of the locals were often preachers. The union locals of the 1930s came from the counties and villages that had organized NAACP chapters and locals of the Garveyite UNIA in the 1920s. In fact, some of those who joined the union also belonged to a local of the NAACP. Many of the complaints of peonage and murder in the 1920s had come from St. Francis County, where a number of NAACP chapters had existed. With an African American population in 1930 of 67.3 percent, St. Francis County became a center for black STFU activity.

Like the Farmers and Laborers Household Union in Elaine, the STFU employed Masonic-like rituals and passwords. The terror of the plantation required black people to employ secrets and passwords to conduct their daily affairs; labor organizing made these skills crucial to the success of the union. Sharecropper and organizer Mrs. Carrie Dilworth remembered the secret signs used when traveling: "When we first opened up to try to build an organization, you'd have to go to different towns and different places. We would have signs when we'd get off the bus or off the train or out of the car, so you could get to see if there was any members there. Just rub your right hand across your face this away [back of right hand across forehead from left to right]. We also had something to say to get into the union hall."[36]

The largely African American membership thus drew from its own traditions rooted in the churches and in a notion of collective suffering and injustice. For example, one of the union's rituals included the "Ceremony of the Land," written by Howard Kester. The text of the ceremony involved a call and response, blending notions of godly and Marxist justice based in part on scriptures. The beginning of the ritual, however, left no doubt as to the class dimensions of a struggle infused with black religious fervor:

> *Reader:* Bowed by the weight of centuries he leans
>   Upon his hoe and gazes on the ground
>   The emptiness of ages in his face
>   And on his back the burden of the world
> *Audience:* Who made him dead to rapture and despair . . .
>   Stolid and stunned, a brother to the ox?
> *Reader:* The status of tenancy demands complete dependence. The
>   landlord assumes the prerogative of direction in the choice of crop,
>   the method by which it shall be cultivated, and how and when and
>   where it shall be sold. He keeps the records and determines the
>   earnings. Through the commissary or credit merchant, even the
>   choice of diet is determined. The landlord can determine the kind
>   and amount of schooling for the children, the extent to which they
>   may share benefits intended for all the people. He may even
>   determine the relief they receive in the extremity of their distress. He
>   controls the courts, the agencies of law enforcement and as in the
>   case of the sharecroppers in eastern Arkansas attempts to thwart any
>   efforts at organization to protect their meager rights.

Audience: It is you who have eaten up the land: the spoil of the poor is in your houses; what mean ye that you crush my people and grind the face of the poor.[37]

Other scriptures also drew from the Old Testament, appealing to the long-standing sense of justice that black people had derived from the Bible since slavery days. The passage from chapter 23 of the Book of Jeremiah described the consequences that fell on those who oppressed the poor: "Woe unto him that buildeth his house by unrighteousness and his chambers by unjustice; that useth his neighbors' service without wages and giveth him not his hire." Nor did the passage from chapter 2 in Amos: "They have sold the righteous for silver and the needy for a pair of shoes; they pant after the dust on the head of the poor." The ritual concluded with a prayer written by the Social Gospel minister Walter Rauschenbush: "Speed now the day when the plains and the hills and the wealth thereof shall be the people's own, and thy freemen shall not live as tenants of men on the earth which thou has given to all."[38]

While Kester blended the Ceremony of the Land into his own theological background, the union clearly drew its strength from the black church. Most meetings took place in this center of black cultural and political life. Black organizers such as Reverend E. B. "Britt" McKinney meshed their union organizing skills with the oratorical power drawn from the pulpit. McKinney personified the institutional connections present in the STFU, for he was a circuit-riding preacher and a member of the UNIA. Eventually, he was drawn as well to the Communist Party. Music also played a major role in the unionizing process. John L. Handcox, born and raised a sharecropper on a plantation in St. Francis County, wrote union songs, some based on spirituals. One of Handcox's most famous songs was entitled "There Are Mean Things Happening in This Land," which describes the strikes, and evictions and terror that followed.[39]

As with the collective notions of politics in the earlier Progressive Farmers and Household Union, the STFU included in its membership entire families. As black organizer George Stith noted, "Where there was a widow involved, she was the head of the family, so she took out a legal membership. But where there was a man and wife involved, she was a member too. She had a voice when it come down to talking or voting on." Indeed, there were some black locals that had all-women memberships, as in Round Pond, and in many locals women held the position of secretary. More women than men were literate and thus their role became especially significant for the success of the union. According to Stith, "Women were

very active and made a lot of the decisions. Women decided to do things
that men felt like they couldn't do. We had several locals around Cotton
Plant and I believe in one of the locals all of the officers were women. This
was because men were afraid. Owners never bothered women." Usually,
continued Stith, "they would pick up the men. They was a little bit slow
about bothering women. They might go up to her and talk to her. And
women look like always were apt to move out. They would walk up and
say to the plantation owner, look, that is what I ain't gonna do. In this case
usually men took the first step. You'd always find somebody who felt it was
not a woman's job. Its all right if we gonna use some women for help. And
even though he might have been afraid, somebody always stepped forward. There are cases where women said, 'I will' first and a man would say,
'I'll do it, you don't have to.'" He remembered a woman named Henrietta Green as being very outspoken in the Howell local. They had worked
on a large rented plantation that the manager had rented from a widow.
The contract stipulated that the croppers receive one-half of the corn they
planted, but the manager gave them only one-third. Green and Stith's father, who were both older, approached the manager and demanded one-
half. He refused and they said they would no longer plant the corn. The
manager agreed to give them half.[40] Thus, black men and women drew
from their collective political tradition both to organize the STFU and to
fight planter terror and injustice.

The union members realized that fighting the evictions meant combating the terror and torture that were entrenched in plantation life. It was
difficult to fight one aspect of the system without also attacking others.
Planters and their riding bosses had retained their workers for decades
through terror and violence. In the plantation region, state and civil society were one, and both sustained sharecropping and peonage through disfranchisement, segregation, lynching, beatings, and theft. Law enforcement existed to support white supremacy. George Stith recalled how large
plantations had their own money, courts, and laws. "The plantation,"
Stith shrewdly noted, "was actually like a state. It had its own government,
and the plantation owner actually appointed the justice of the peace . . .
back in those days Negroes didn't vote too much, and the justice of the
peace was elected by very few people." Landowners told their agents and
all of the white people whom to vote for. Many plantations had their own
courts with a judge and a justice of the peace. Stith recalled that many
"times the agent on the place where I worked went to trial for me. I didn't
go; he was my representative." These large plantations, like Wilson's, had

their own penal farms. He added: "They really didn't want you to go to work off the plantation unless you got permission from them. They wanted to keep you busy, and you didn't get any money out of it." If anybody needed a "little grocery money," they received it in coupon books. These coupon books were the only money on plantations. One planter named Cole had a mint of his own currency called "brozeen." Stith said that Lee Wilson had about five plantations, each having its own brozeen, good only at a Wilson store.[41]

In August of 1935, the large planters announced that they had reduced cotton picking wages from the 60 cents they had paid in the previous fall to 40 cents per hundred pounds picked. Since the average picker gathered around 200 pounds per day, this represented a daily decline for the workers from $1.20 to 80 cents. According to Mitchell, he decided that the union should call a wage conference and set its own wage standard. He and Howard Kester got in their car and rode at night all over the Arkansas Delta, spreading the word among union members to attend a wage conference that would meet in a farmhouse outside of Memphis. All of the locals held meetings and discussed the strike, taking a vote on whether to support it. Each local then sent a representative to the conference, where they voted as a body. At the meeting, Mitchell wanted all members to refuse to pick for less than the union wage. But the majority decided to have workers pick for whatever wage they could get, build up their family supplies, and then call a strike for a $1.00 per hundred pounds wage at the peak of the harvest in September. Union members were then polled, and according to Mitchell, voted 11,186 for and 450 against the strike, though Mitchell admitted exaggerating the numbers for publicity purposes. The members then formed local wage committees, with a key person appointed for each county to coordinate the strike with other counties and the main office in Memphis. The strike occurred mainly in Crittenden, Cross, Mississippi, Poinsett, and St. Francis counties.[42]

Black union organizer Mrs. Carrie Dilworth recounted how members prepared for the strike. The locals distributed fliers calling for the strike starting at precisely eleven o'clock the evening before the stoppage was to begin. Dilworth collected the fliers on a Sunday night and distributed them in her region. "I was riding in my car," she recalled. "Marie Pierce, a student from Memphis, was riding in the back seat with Mr. Bolden. Mrs. Burton and I sat in the front. I was laying down on my stomach holding the door cracked open, and I'd push the leaflets through the crack and spread them out in the street. You pick up speed and that'd just make them things go flying all over the yards . . . Then this car came swooping by us. I said, 'Cut the lights off and let's go right into these woods.' We got down in a little curl and cut the motor off. If they had caught us," she continued, "I don't know what they would've done to us. But they couldn't tell where we was. They went out there where they was fixing the levee and got stuck in the mud. Water was up to our knees in the car. It was three o'clock that next morning when we got home and it was still raining. It wasn't no easy job. White folks thought it was a plane that distributed fliers."[43]

White union members Walter Moskop and Ed Pickering did more than distribute fliers. In an effort to ensure that pickers, whether union members or not, obeyed the strike, they spread a rumor that several scabs had been killed for breaking the strike and picking cotton. In Cross County, the county sheriff reportedly went in search for the alleged dead who were killed by the strikers, though he never found them. Mitchell and Kester claimed that they had met a poor worker heading for Tennessee to find work. The picker supposedly reported that "They's a strike on over heah and 25 men already been killed for picking cotton."[44]

Initially, planters greeted the strike in early September with self-confidence, insisting that there were plenty of workers despite the strike—"especially," as the *Arkansas Gazette* observed, "in view of Federal relief regulations denying relief to those persons refusing jobs." This optimism, however, soon faded into anger as thousands stayed out of the fields. When the Arkansas deputy labor commissioner visited the strike region, he found only five workers picking cotton in three counties, but he saw a lot of people fishing. Planters responded with terror. Two strikers were beaten with axe handles; others were evicted, arrested for vagrancy, and beaten. Still, the strike raised wages to seventy-five cents and the union called it off in early October.[45]

The 1935 strike succeeded in raising wages because the union caught the planters off guard; they simply did not believe the union would succeed. With this victory, however, union membership grew. Mitchell claimed to have organized thirty locals within forty-five days after the strike, while John Handcox organized in early 1936 dozens of locals in Missouri. Mitchell claimed that the membership had risen, as a result of the strike, to 25,000 within a few weeks. The strike also won the support of outside organizations such as Reinhold Niebuhr's Committee on Economic and Racial Justice, various branches of the Socialist Party, and the American Federation of Labor, all of which sent money for strike relief.[46]

The STFU's celebratory moment did not last very long. In early January of 1936, landowner C. H. Dibble in Parkin evicted almost one hundred people. Ironically, Dibble had decided to sign a collective bargaining agreement with the union when planters coerced him into withdrawing his offer. Landowners threatened to have Dibble's bank call in his debts if he proceeded with the agreement. Mitchell decided to use the evictions to publicize the plight of sharecroppers in the Delta. The evicted farmers established a tent colony outside of Parkin near Dibble's plantation. Unfortunately, leading planters responded by blacklisting STFU members all over the Delta and evicting thousands of families. The tent colony in Parkin became a target for violence, too, as planters sought to make the evicted families an example of what others might expect. Dynamite was thrown into the colony, though no one was arrested for the crime.[47]

Despite the planter's campaign of terror against the union, the STFU called a cotton choppers strike in the spring of 1936, demanding an increase from 75 cents per day to $1.25. During this strike, the STFU employed a new tactic. Long lines of men, women, and children marched ten feet apart down the roads along the cotton fields. Many workers in the fields put down their hoes and joined the march. Since planters knew of the strike beforehand, they were prepared to fight the strikers. Violence defined this strike more than the previous one. The marchers faced men who rode beside them with guns and ball bats. Near Earle, deputies Everett Hood and Paul D. Peacher led a mob into a union meeting in St. Peter's Methodist Church. They shot and wounded black union member James Ball, and subsequently sent him to jail. They also wounded two others who ran from the church. After hearing that union member Willie Hurst had witnessed the attack, Peacher and Hood sought to intimidate him into signing a statement exonerating them from any wrongdoing. When Hurst refused, two masked men resembling Peacher and Hood murdered him, and then Ball received seven years in prison. Hood and Peacher also beat black union member Mrs. Eliza Nolden so badly that she later died, murdered black union member Fred Weems, and crippled for life one of the original white union founders, Jim Reese. When Claude Williams went to Earle to preach at Weems funeral, a mob beat him as well as a prominent Memphis woman, Willie Sue Blagden. This beating of a white minister and wealthy southern white woman drew national attention to the union struggle in the American Congo.[48]

The terror continued. Following Ball's arrest, Howard Kester and union lawyer Herman Goldberger met with 450 sharecroppers in the Providence Methodist Church near Earle. As they were meeting, Deputy

Hood led a khaki-clad mob of planters and riding bosses into the church, beating people with axe handles and pistol butts, "guffawing loudly as they cracked the skulls of women and children." Hood pushed Kester out the door, telling him, "There's going to be another Elaine Massacre, only the next time we'll kill the whites as well as the niggers." Threats of another massacre were so widespread that people simply wondered "how soon the slaughter would begin." Terrified, union members went underground.[49]

Supporters of the strike from outside the state also found themselves caught in the dragnet of terror and American Congo–style justice. In Forrest City, a guardsman stopped and arrested Dave Benson, a lawyer from Washington, D.C., who worked with the Socialist Workers' Alliance, for driving with an out-of-state driver's license and car plates, and for interfering with labor. Novelist and Pulitzer Prize–winner Josephine Earle was also arrested for encouraging workers to strike, although she was later released.[50]

Other stories of terror emerged, some from planters who occasionally broke with their class. Charles Flemming was so disturbed by the treatment accorded black workers in Round Pond that he wrote to Governor J. M. Futrell of his concerns. He described deputy sheriffs who had whipped black men and women. "Probably you have heard that we have no law in this county. I'm sorry that I believe that a man can't get justice in any of the courts in St. Francis County, especially where he doesn't vote for the political clique. One of the old negroes that they whipped, Joe Wright, sixty-eight years old, has not been connected, as I have heard, in any strikes or anything that violates the law, was taken out last Friday night, handcuffed, his clothes taken off, was made to lay down on the ground and was whipped with a leather strap. A negro woman," he continued, "was whipped at the same time, then whipped again on the way to Wynne." Joe Wright and the black woman were then brought back to Round Pond and were told by the mob that if they didn't get up the information they wanted within a week they would be whipped again and probably killed." Round Pond was home to several locals of the STFU, one of them consisting only of black women.

Flemming concluded that "if the truth was known, a great many of these strikers have been mistreated by not getting their part of the plow-up checks. I've had no labor trouble anymore than usual and I don't think that my neighbors have. Especially those who have treated their labor right. But," he continued, "we will have labor trouble if the night riding and whipping program is not cut out . . . it is to the interests of every planter that the negroes be protected from night riders and I will personally appreciate it if you will go to the bottom of the whole thing and see that justice prevails."[51] Flemming probably spoke for many planters who saw the brutality of local law enforcement and their fellow landowners as making the labor problem worse. Futrell, however, was not interested in these accounts. As a planter himself, the governor sided with his friends in the Delta by insisting that so long as the agitators remained outside the state line, conditions in eastern Arkansas were fine.

Planters turned to Governor Futrell for help in ending the strike by asking him to send in the National Guard, though by their own admission, they saw no immediate threat of violence: their fears "were for tomorrow."[52] When Futrell sent his National Guardsmen and state troopers to investigate conditions in the Delta, the men basically told him what the planters wanted him to hear. In fact, planters and their extended network of county officials made up the investigative team. A. G. Albright, superintendent of the state police, conducted his investigation with a representative of the guard, a local planter who also belonged to the guard, a county judge, and a sheriff. They reportedly found black sharecroppers who claimed they wanted to work, but feared repercussions from the union. Troopers arrested several organizers and sent them to county farms to work off their fines, then mounted machine guns at key crossroads to protect the workers' "right" to chop cotton. Albright also reported that Clay East, attacked by a plantation manager in St. Francis County, was arrested and placed in the county jail for safekeeping from a mob, then deported to Memphis.[53]

In the end, dry weather ended the strike. Six weeks without rain produced a weedless cotton crop and a need for choppers. Weary of marching, union members called an end to the strike, with wages for plowing and hoeing remaining at $1.00 rather than the demanded $1.50 per day. The members had suffered tremendously during the strike. Several had lost their lives, and the group had little to show for the pain that many had endured.[54]

Occasionally justice did shine on the union. In the summer following the horrors unleashed by Hood and Peacher, Sherwood Eddy, a famous YMCA official, decided to visit Peacher's convict labor farm. Peacher was away and his guards seemed indifferent, allowing Eddy to talk with the thirteen prisoners held on the farm. Eddy's visit led to a nationally covered trial that revealed for the world the extent of planter authority in the

American Congo and its relationship to all of the instruments of local government. His investigation resulted in the trial and conviction in 1936 of Earle's deputy sheriff Paul D. Peacher, on federal peonage charges.

Peacher had arrested eight black men for vagrancy and sent them to his own plantation to work out their fines. At his trial, Peacher insisted that he had gone through the legal system to secure the convictions and had therefore violated no laws. Since he had known black people for years, Peacher was certain that "as a general rule, they were loafers and a honky-tonk bunch." Yet all of the men testified that they supported themselves. Winfield Anderson, for example, was fifty-one years old, owned his own home, and lived on an income received as compensation for an injury. Indeed, Peacher had arrested Anderson in his house. When Peacher presented him along with the others as vagrants, the mayor and justice of the peace also sentenced Anderson. Crittenden County Sheriff Howard Curlin testified that he had conferred with the county judge regarding Peacher's request to work county prisoners and he had responded "it would be all right." The mayor testified that he had sentenced the men based "on Peacher's word" that they were vagrants, leading the presiding district judge to conclude that "Peacher absolutely dominates this man that is Mayor, and this man does what he says."[55]

All eight men were of independent means and did not have to pick cotton. This was their crime. Delta officials and planters never questioned that any men, women, and children not engaged in plantation work, or some other planter-dependent activity, were subjects for vagrancy enforcement. Thus laws, even vagrancy laws, not only served economic ends, but also buttressed white supremacy, reasserting planter authority through law and terror. Indeed, planters raised over five thousand dollars for Peacher's defense.[56] Peacher's trial revealed the interconnectedness of Delta society. A former deputy sheriff, town marshal, and plantation owner, Peacher secured hearings and convictions based simply on his word.

One would expect Futrell and his fellow planters to hide their faces as the horrors of the American Congo were revealed for all of the world to see. Instead they were unbowed, clinging to their views of lazy and inferior black sharecroppers who only sought to take advantage of benevolent landlords. Futrell's inability to acknowledge cropper claims of injustice were illustrated by a trip that he took to the region in early 1936, following the fall strike. Had he actually listened to those he interviewed, he may have learned something of their concerns, because sharecroppers were not shy about telling the governor of their problems or their reasons for joining the union. Black sharecropper Bob Miller explained to Futrell his determination to secure his economic and political rights embedded in citizenship. "We organized this labor union to better our condition as a working class of people. We are trying to educate our children and get better deals. We believe that we ought to have better schools for our children. The negro ought to educate his children; all laboring people ought to. We feel," he continued, "that we are not getting our just dues. We are not getting sufficient schools; we pay taxes and do not get a chance to vote." Miller noted the irony in being denied the right to vote when planters had recently hauled croppers "up there and voted" for the continuation of the Bankhead bill, whether they wanted to or not. Miller said he only wanted to work his crops and pay his union dues. "You would think that you ought to be allowed to sell our cotton, and pay our debts, if we feel that the market is high. Shouldn't I get the market price?" Futrell agreed, and then asked if Miller had a commissary account, noting that many never pay their accounts. Miller replied: that "is what this organization is for—to pay our debts, and raise our children better than in the past. We want to make the future life better than the past."

The governor's questions reflected his views as a planter, indicating that he thought the union had misled and cheated its members. He asked if Moore and others had applied for county relief. They replied that when they had gone to the County Welfare Board, they were told that the office helped only widows and children, and were ordered to go out and find jobs. Yet landowners refused to give them work because of their union membership. As if he had not heard them, Futrell lectured: "I can give you this advice. You had all better go and listen to the white folks, who have never done you any harm. Whether they are right or wrong, they think you are getting up some kind of an organization to do them wrong. They get afraid of you."[57]

Futrell insisted that the violence in the region had resulted from tenants' joining the interracial union, invoking planters' "vivid remembrance" of the "Elaine affair" of 1919. Landowners, he said, recognized the black tenants' right to join a union, but they also knew that the "Negro is easily excited into the most unbridled violence. This has happened in Eastern Arkansas." Apparently forgetting the Supreme Court's decision in the *Moore* case, the governor recounted the planters' story of Elaine. He noted that the "negroes under the guidance of the white men had planned to dispatch several owners of land in that country. A fortunate circumstance prevented the killing of a half dozen landowners within the same few minutes." "You cannot get this fear out of these landowners. They don't want trouble. They don't want agitators around."[58]

His description of H. L. Mitchell resembled the Committee of Seven's depiction of Robert Hill, the founder of the Elaine union. "Through connections which he has, he reaches some rich negro lovers in the North and East and makes collections of money," he wrote to U.S. Senator Joseph P. Robinson. "A negro can be stimulated to the wildest outrages. The Elaine trouble is yet fresh in the minds of the people over there. They know that a negro is a dangerous tool in the hands of an agitator." Mitchell "seeks publicity and has no regard for the truth." Futrell denied the existence of any "trouble" in the Delta, and told Robinson that "you can actually afford to announce Mitchell as a liar in these reports. If the government agents will get the truth and publish it, it will be the end of the matter. If you send an unprincipled agitator down there, a communist, an I.W.W., or something of the kind, you won't get the truth, as they feed and thrive on falsehood."[59] Robinson shared Futrell's concerns and feared that "as a result of advocating social equality these agitators would experience rough dealing which would create further unfavorable reaction on the State's reputation." So concerned was the senator for his state's public image that he stopped the presentation of a play at the Texas centennial celebration that was critical of the tenant problem in Arkansas.[60]

In addition to currying the favor of both the governor and the U.S. senator, planters plied their influence with the press, especially the *Memphis Commercial Appeal*. Yet parts of the northern media served their interests as well, such as Raymond Moley's *Today,* which sent a reporter, Edward Angly, to eastern Arkansas and Mississippi to collect stories that countered attacks from northern liberals and radicals as well as Memphis's own *Press Scimitar.* Angly spoke with planters who gave their traditional version of the plantation system, in which lazy and ungrateful black workers tore up the fine dwellings the landlords had provided for them. These accounts were always mixed with portrayals of loyal black sharecroppers who utilized the abundant sources at hand to create a prosperous life.[61]

Perhaps the most revealing of Angly's interviews with Delta planters was that of W. B. Mann in Marianna, who conveyed his paternalistic sentiments regarding his workers. He drew from his white ancestral myths to explain his current way of life, claiming that he had "known the cropper system since its birth when the defeated and impoverished South began to build anew, after the Civil War." Mann recalled "the day my father assembled all the negroes in our back yard to tell them they were free people and at liberty to move to any farm where they could make satisfactory arrangements. He told them it was his wish and his advice that they continue where they were and work the crop already planted. He said the farmers would have a meeting the following week and establish fair arrangements by which they could work together. These meetings brought the sharecropping system into existence," he explained. "The landlord was to furnish land, houses, all equipment, seed, and everything else necessary to grow and harvest the crop. The cropper was to accomplish all the labor to make and gather the crop." This arrangement, he continued, "was mutually profitable because almost all the supplies sold to the croppers were made or grown on the farm. There was a church and a schoolhouse on the farm. Some of the negroes were real Christians and observed the Sabbath. Many of them belonged to the 'white folks' church while they were slaves." At the present time, lamented Mann, all of "these customs and habits are gone for ever. The confidence and co-operation that existed between the two races has been replaced with distrust and suspicion, until the landlord and cropper now do nothing for each other that the contract does not call for. Such partnership cannot prosper."

Mann explained why, in spite of his disappointment with black labor, he and other planters did not hire white croppers. "I resent everything they do and they feel the same way towards me. If our positions were reversed, and I were the share-cropper, I believe the results would be the same." White people expected black workers to accept close supervision, to act subservient, to work for nothing, and to accept the high interest rates charged by the commissary—this was their "nature."[62]

Mann had summed up the planter class's ruling strategy in the American Congo. White people were not meant to be sharecroppers or wage hands, but to aspire to farm ownership, to become masters of their own fate even if they had begun as tenants. Black people occupied the lowest rung on the tenancy ladder. So long as poor white people accepted this explanation of class relations in the Delta, planters could manage their white supremacist society. But once poor white tenants began to question this scheme of dominance and to see their relationship to poor black croppers, planters could lose their power. Hence the real threat of the STFU and the terror planters employed to combat it.

F. Raymond Daniell, a *New York Times* reporter who visited the area in April of 1935, illustrated planters' fears. He described the bunker mentality of planters besieged by outside agitators. The "average planter and public official is firmly convinced that unless he takes drastic steps, white supremacy, Christianity, the American flag and the sanctity of home and family ties will be overthrown by agents of the Soviet Union." Elizabeth Dilling's *Red Network,* which listed Mayor Fiorella LaGuardia and Jane Addams of Hull House as dangerous radicals, "has become the standard reference work of the locality." He claimed that few planters received outside guests without first looking them up in this handbook.[63]

Planter efforts to portray themselves as benevolent landlords, as legitimate heirs to paternalistic slave masters of the Old South, did not square with the terror, horror, torture, disappearances, murders, and evictions that had occurred in the American Congo since its founding. Ironically, this self-image was based on the southern heritage myth, which was deeply imbedded in upper-class white people's understanding of southern history, but had no immediate roots in the newly formed Arkansas Delta. On some level, Delta planters were enthralled by their own story, if only when talking to newspaper reporters. Their kindness and gentleness existed in the clouded memory of the past, shrouding the brutal reality of the present. But in the 1930s, as the Depression raged, forces beyond their control exposed their true identity to the nation and the world.

While planters presented their case to the public, they continued their efforts to destroy the union. Like their industrial counterparts, planters organized in 1936 a company union in Heth and paid the dues for all of their tenants to join. Two large planters, Carl Morrison and B. Dickey, paid organizers five dollars to sign up members. Similarly, Reverend Abner Sage, an outspoken supporter of the planters, spoke to tenants about the Marked Tree Cooperative Association, whose membership was open to all white men and women and whose sole object "is to do everything possible to find employment for those of our people who need employment." The association claimed to have received eighty-seven applications, and the Chapman and Dewey Lumber Mill had hired twenty-two of them, while the town intended to employ others on work details. A civil engineer, supposedly a former member of the STFU, led the clean-up crew.[64] By limiting the membership of the cooperative association to white people, and by finding employment for the white jobless, planters hoped to destroy the much feared STFU interracial alliance.

In 1936 and 1937, planters continued to arrest the strikers and send them to penal farms to work out their fines. Union attorneys ran up against the plethora of justices of the peace, judges, and county sheriffs who refused to allow prisoners to see their legal representatives or to post bond. In one case, bond was obtained at the exorbitant rate of $2,500.[65] Landowners also continued to hold tenants against their will, to break into their homes illegally, and to murder union organizers and members on their plantations.[66] For example, when a manager on a plantation near Moro in Lee County told a black field hand to get a fresh barrel of water for the other hands, the black worker brought back one that had been filled the night before. The worker was whipped with axe handles for his impudence. Fearing for their lives, workers started to leave until another man urged them to remain, since all of the riders carried guns. Then "some Holiness women started singing church hymns and marched from the field." Consequently, the workers stayed on until the trucks from Brinkley took them back home. A reporter from the *Kansas City Call* wrote that the night of the Joe Louis–Braddock fight, black people in Moro were afraid to go to the local filling station to listen to the fight on the radio. They feared that if Louis won, white people would beat them.[67]

The union called another cotton-picking strike in the fall of 1937, and the planters launched a counteroffensive designed to destroy the STFU once and for all. Mississippi County experienced a greater degree of violence in 1937 as organizing picked up in the plantations surrounding Blytheville. For example, when a local held a meeting in Armoral at the home of Earl Thompson, the manager of the Lee Wilson plantation, Charles Cragery, led about forty planters and riding bosses who broke into the meeting, searched the house, destroyed the furniture, seized the charter, and drove the seventy-five members away. On the same night, a gang of men forced W. B. Moore off of the C. M. and J. R. Whittle plantation. Moore had recruited fifty tenants on the plantation to join the STFU.[68]

The Blytheville Chamber of Commerce endorsed a seventy-five-cent wage instead of the one dollar the STFU demanded, and offered a fifty-dollar reward for the arrest of any labor agitator. The deputy sheriff then told all black people he saw on the streets to either go out into the fields and pick for this wage or go to the county farm. Organizer Sam Barnes found that the members were not yet ready for a strike. "I have been forced to instruct members to pick cotton till 24 September at their price," he told Mitchell. "A number of black and white members have scoffed at us. What are we to do. We look ridiculous." Barnes found that white union members tended to want to strike for more pay per one hundred pounds, but the black majority of the members were in no position to support such a measure. He asked all who could to stay out of the fields, but he insisted that too many were desperate for daily survival. The union, he concluded, was not strong enough to sustain a strike. Barnes later wrote to the Lee Wilson plantation and offered to furnish three hundred pickers a day if the company would stop the Chamber of Commerce's campaign against the union.[69]

Planters had no intention of cooperating with the union, and used their usual resources to combat the strike. For example, when Jesse Rose carried workers to the McFarrin plantation, Charles Cragery of the Lee plantation forced them back, saying he had five pistols to shoot them with unless they left. The manager of the Tri States Lumber Company and Mel Brooks of the Blytheville Chamber of Commerce also threatened workers headed for the McFarrin farm.[70]

Despite the conviction of Paul Peacher for peonage, county judges and justices of the peace continued to arrest labor organizers and send them to convict labor farms. Henrietta McGhee, and Will and Alberta Vaughn, all of the Round Pond local, were arrested in 1937 for intimidating labor when they organized a strike on the Belsha plantation in St. Francis County. Both women prisoners were put in a large cell called the turn-around, which was filled with men. One can only imagine what these women encountered in prison. The court appointed a planter lawyer to represent them, and the county judge levied a $250 fine and sent them immediately to his relative's farm, the Rolfe plantation in Cross County, to work off their sentence. The judge refused to accept the bonds that the union lawyer offered. The lawyer invoked habeas corpus proceedings to obtain the release of the prisoners, but even then the Cross County sheriff refused to release them until he had worked them for another three days. When union lawyer C. A. Stanfield came to defend them, planter and county health officer W. H. Winters struck the lawyer and then hit McGhee twice in the face. The union attorney appealed the case to a higher court, invoking a violation of the peonage laws, but U.S. Assistant Attorney General Brien McMahon replied that no evidence existed of any false charging of the defendants, nor did he find the relationship of Rolfe and the county judge as proof of collusion. Further appeals to U.S. Attorney Fred Isgrig turned up the same results. Peonage was probably not the correct legal venue to pursue for the gross violations of civil and human rights that McGhee and the Vaughns had encountered. But apparently pursuing such cases under the Fourteenth Amendment due process clause was out of the question in the American Congo.[71] County Sheriff J. M. Campbell had warned union members that if black people did not get out of the STFU there would be another "race riot" like the one at Elaine, Arkansas.[72]

In a 1938 picking strike, planters reduced wages even further, from seventy-five to sixty cents per hundred pounds of picked cotton. Beatrice Johnson, the secretary of a black union local in Mississippi County, was arrested with four other members of her family after they had distributed strike leaflets. Ironically, she received a four-year sentence for nightriding—forcibly driving people from the land—while Dan and Henry got a two-year sentence. Both men were near eighty years old. Henry suffered a stroke following his release from prison on bond, and Dan had recently undergone cataract surgery. The union posted four thousand dollars in bonds for them, though Louis Johnson remained in jail and wrote that "this is a hard place here I am a fread all the time that some one is going to hurt me to the laws is so hard on the prisoner Especial the colored one they are beating and lashing all the time I look for them to git me sometime. Mr. Butler I tell you the truth some need to be done with some of the laws thay is killing to memy people here at this jail house an nothing done about it just catching men walking on the road bring them an beating."[73]

In 1936 and 1937, as part of its strategy, the STFU continued to file complaints and bring legal cases challenging planter violations of federal programs and accusing them of engaging in peonage and the general violation of civil rights. Hundreds of cases were filed after 1933 regarding the withholding of the AAA subsidy payments, violations of usury laws, and challenges to the peonage statutes. For example, the union filed a damage suit on behalf of L. C. Washpun, who had been evicted after he had planted a crop on the Bridgeforth plantation in Round Pond. The suit sought to establish the right of a tenant to carry on with a crop until the contract had been completed. And union organizers J. F. Hynds and Melvin Swinea organized relief workers who received only twenty cents an hour on a highway pavement project in Forrest City in 1937.[74]

While the majority of the STFU's membership and its organizational activity centered in the Arkansas Delta, locals did exist across the river in Mississippi. Sharecroppers suffered displacement there as well, and they complained to the AAA about their evictions and failure to receive a share of parity payments. Mississippi planters also responded as harshly as their counterparts in Arkansas. The smaller scale of the union activity, however, drew little press coverage of their actions. For example, Zero Mumford wrote from his local in Stringtown that "these white people is threatin these the Union down here mity bad they askin where we meat at an tellin the hands on there place" not to join the union. The landlords "tell my people it goint be nother ARK scrape i am askin you to dure sothing about it the white tellin negro it ant notin to the Union." His local had fifty-two paid members in 1939.[75]

The case of Claude B. Cistrunk in Mashulaville illustrated the violence that landowners inflicted against union members in Mississippi. Coleman and Kinch Watkins pulled Cistrunk from the milk truck he worked on, threatened him with an axe, and then beat him severely. Cistrunk and his father had worked at the Watkins sawmill prior to 1939. When Cistrunk had tried to pay the men five dollars he had borrowed at Christmas, they refused, saying he must work out the debt. They also claimed that Cistrunk's father owed them and must also come back to work for the company. Finally, Cistrunk secured a lawyer with the help of a white man, who made the Watkins accept payment for the debt. But the brothers told him that if he reported the incident to the STFU they would kill him.[76]

The famous Delta and Pine Land Company, the 38,000-acre plantation run by Oscar Johnston, responded to the union's presence in a self-assured and paternalistic manner. In 1936 Johnston reported to his owners that the company had "not yet been troubled by the 'professional organizers' or the socialist agitators who have been creating more or less disturbance in other sections of the cotton belt." Noting that most of the trouble had occurred in northeastern Arkansas, Johnston attributed the success of the Socialist sharecroppers union to the presence of "a great many white tenant farmers." He assured the British owners that "only in rare instances have the negroes taken any part in this movement. We hear occasionally of sporadic attempts at organizing in sections of the Delta, but to date have had no indication of any disposition on the part of our labor to participate in this movement."[77]

Johnston had also corresponded with Mitchell and East regarding the sharecropping system, insisting that "the half share system of farming is the fairest and most profitable system for the tenant. I know that the laborer who produces a cotton crop does not average more than 125 days of work here. I would gladly exchange the share crop system for a wages system and pay a daily wage," he continued, "but have no work with which to employ the labor during a large part of the time when it is not necessary for him to work in the cotton fields. For this reason, the farm laborer is unable to support himself and family on a wage basis."[78]

Despite Johnston's confidence regarding the superiority of the sharecropping system, he took no chances when it came to the prospect of a union on his plantation. In 1937 the Delta and Pine Land Company organized, under the leadership of Reverend H. H. Humes, a "Pastors' Conference" on all of its plantations with the stated goals of promoting the Christian religion, and social and moral advancement. The conference sought to "cooperate with employers and employees in maintaining true principles of peace and good will, and perpetuating a spirit of true fellowship that has always existed among the white and black races all these years," as well as to "watch for and guard against all agitators or foreign elements who attempt to use the weak of our group as a gateway into this community with far-fetched organizations to unionize our people in such organizations that will disturb the peace and harmony of the two races in this Mississippi Delta." The pastors also insisted that the company "pass upon all periodicals that are thrown out publicly on the plantation among our people, before giving the distributors permission."[79]

Johnston and his managers met the threat of a union with the guiding principle of the company, welfare capitalism—they provided better housing and healthcare, among other things. In spite of this effort, however, when black union organizer F. R. Betton attended a meeting at Scott, the headquarters of the company, two hundred and thirty-five members came, with seventy-five guests from other plantations. Apparently, the plantation workers were not fully convinced by Johnston's affirmation of the sharecropping system, nor by the pastors' efforts to combat the union.[80]

Betton tried to facilitate further organizing at other Mississippi locals as well. He found that the union local at Boyle had 145 members led by Reverend Z. L. Linzy, with 75 percent of them having paid their dues. According to Betton, "These people is real unionized, with much support from the local preachers and teachers." In Beulah, Betton told twenty members how to apply for Farm Security Administration loans. Other locals existed in the Delta villages of Shelby, Duncan, Sunflower, Crueger, Yellow Creek, and Brookville. While the locals were not as numerous as in Arkansas, they were nevertheless active. Part of the problem centered on the inability of the STFU to allocate any funds or staff to Mississippi. When Steve Lucas of Duncan wrote to H. L. Mitchell expressing his discouragement at the lack of STFU support in Mississippi, Mitchell replied, "Eventually we will move into Mississippi with a large organization campaign and will organize the state as we have Arkansas and Oklahoma."[81]

The NAACP succeeded in organizing more locals in Mississippi than did the STFU. Had Mitchell placed more time and effort into Mississippi, there is reason to think that a larger movement would have emerged there. Black people were just as eager as they were in Arkansas to press their demands. As A. J. Hicks from Learned wrote, "I wants to know is there any chance for negro justice in the southern states, if there is let us have it regardless of its costs."[82] But the STFU had its hands full in Arkansas where AAA evictions were greater than in Mississippi, and where the organization had an operating base. Time would tell whether the union would last long enough to extend its base into other regions.

Hampered by the stress of planter violence and a federal government unwilling to intervene to protect the basic human rights of the sharecroppers, Mitchell and the leadership experienced divisions. Part of the conflict emerged over the debate within the union as to whether the STFU should belong to the CIO-affiliated United Cannery, Agricultural, Packing, and Allied Workers (UCAPAWA), which sought to organize all agricultural workers according to tenure. They wanted small landowners in one, and tenant farmers and sharecroppers in another. Mitchell disagreed with this approach, arguing that in the plantation South such tenure distinctions were meaningless, since people moved back and forth across the tenure lines, depending on the economy and the price of cotton. He also knew that the union had to affiliate with the CIO if it was to survive, but he hated the communist leader of UCAPAWA, Donald Henderson. Mitchell wanted to affiliate with the CIO independently. John L. Lewis insisted, however, that the STFU must go with Henderson's union. Thus the STFU became in 1937 part of the CIO, signaling a major defeat for Mitchell.

The marriage was not a happy one. Mitchell fought with Henderson over the control of the STFU, unwilling to concede power to the national union. Struggles emerged immediately over whether the STFU office in Memphis should remain the primary body for dealing with union matters or whether all business should be directed to UCAPAWA's headquarters. Nor did locals know where to send their dues. In 1938, Mitchell sent UCAPAWA organizing materials to 170 locals that he thought had the ability to pay union dues. But Mitchell kept 170 other locals solely as STFU locals because he believed that they could not afford the UCAPAWA dues. In 1938, only 7,389 of the 20,000 members of the merged locals paid their dues.[83]

The merger of the STFU with UCAPAWA also fueled divisions within the STFU between Mitchell and Kester, on the one hand, and the communists E. B. "Britt" McKinney and Claude Williams, who carried a majority of the black members, on the other. McKinney had already threatened to set up a separate black union, because he had decided the black members were the "goat" of the union. (Except for McKinney as vice president, the STFU leadership was white.) McKinney, like the members in SNCC later in the 1960s, had seen too many black people tortured, beaten, and murdered, and had decided that the STFU's commitment to equality was limited. McKinney had also gotten closer to the communists, and was listed in 1936 as a member of the communist-affiliated National Negro Congress executive council. As George Stith remembered, "McKinney was a communist, but I don't think his views were so different than mine when it comes down to the lower class man, the little man, especially the farmer." He differed, said Stith, in where he thought "we should be as a union," agreeing with UCAPAWA that farmers, sharecroppers, and tenants should each be organized into separate unions." Stith, Mitchell, Kester, and others thought that such a policy would only divide the membership. But McKinney "was stubborn about what he believed to be right—about principles."[84]

Mitchell had both McKinney and Williams expelled from the STFU's executive board, but the black members stayed loyal to them and followed their lead regarding the affiliation with the CIO. The fiercest organizers, like Henrietta McGhee, supported the CIO. Apparently, black people believed that their interests would be best represented in the CIO and not in an independent STFU, run by a white socialist leadership. The communists and CIO were also active in Memphis and had organized dock workers in Arkansas river towns, perhaps influencing some of the workers' relatives on the plantations. In any case, when in 1939 Mitchell led his followers out of the CIO-UCAPAWA affiliation, most black members stayed with UCAPAWA.[85]

It is difficult to evaluate fully the conflicts within the STFU. Mitchell later recalled, "We thought, and our people thought, that the CIO was going to sweep the whole country and was going to organize all the unorganized. That's what they talked about; they were going to bring about a complete change in the lives of everybody and make things better. Everybody was enthused about the CIO." The CIO, he said, "was inspiring to people who didn't know any better, who didn't know John L. Lewis, a business trade unionist whose interest was in getting a huge membership that could pay the Union dues." In Mitchell's view, Lewis had no understanding of the STFU, seeing it only as a money-making source for the CIO. "We were naive," said Mitchell. "The ordinary trade unionist never understood the STFU. We were a mass movement, something like the civil rights movement 30 years later. We could have opened the doors in areas where there were farm people," he insisted. "We could have moved into the farming areas around any industrial area. We could have become a great political force, and been a great voice for the CIO in rural America. That's what we thought, that's what we saw in the CIO."[86]

Mitchell saw as a major problem the poverty of the membership and its inability to pay fifty-cent dues to the national office. Sharecroppers simply did not have the money, and most had rarely paid the ten-cent STFU dues. Both John L. Lewis and his CIO wanted a membership that produced revenue to strengthen the power of the national body—not an unreasonable demand at the time, even if a hard one for sharecroppers to meet. But in the end, few union officials were really interested in the plantation workers, for they were the poorest and least powerful of the working class. It was more efficient to organize the workers on the large-scale agribusiness farms of the West Coast and the cannery and processing workers. Perhaps Lewis and other labor leaders knew that the croppers were a doomed group, and that eventually mechanization would drive the plantation workers from the land into the towns and cities. Indeed, starting in the late 1930s, UCAPAWA aimed its efforts at just such workers who had left the countryside and, like Steinbeck's Joads, had headed for California.

Mitchell's use of "we" throughout his recollections is misleading. Indeed, since he collected the STFU papers, his hand dominates the account presented. It was clear that he sought to control the union, regardless of the majority of the members' wishes to join the CIO. In this regard, he resembled the planters in seeing the black members as being misled by Williams and the communists, as if they could not make up their own minds regarding their best interest.

Was Mitchell correct to insist on the meaninglessness of drawing tenure distinctions in the Delta? He was right to argue that people in the Delta moved up and down the tenure ladder. But statistically, black people were the sharecroppers and the day laborers, and tenant farmers were the white people. In northeastern Arkansas, white tenants had become landowners, as the promotional efforts of the alluvial empire had sought to guarantee. From an organizational standpoint in 1934, Mitchell and East probably thought it wise to call the STFU a tenant's organization to appeal to both white and black workers; croppers often referred to themselves as tenants in a broader sense. The settlement and tenure patterns of northeast Arkansas, however, led to segregated locals and probably ones that fell out according to tenure status as well. Still, white tenancy had risen in the 1920s, and more people would become landless in the 1930s because of the AAA's policy that led to larger plantations. As one historian has noted, "Nonwhite farm workers pointed the way to the unionization for whites who had to learn that farm work did not make one a farmer."[87]

White people did join the union, and many undoubtedly became more racially tolerant and more class conscious. The STFU, however, like all previous interracial labor movements in the post–Civil War South, ran up against the power of white supremacy. Given the racism and Klan activity that had dominated the history of these counties following World War I, it was hard to imagine white people placing their hatred of black people aside. And in the 1930s, planter dominance was buttressed more than ever by federal policies that further weakened the ability of black and white workers to fight back. Thus it was all the more remarkable that, given the history of class and racial relations in northeastern Arkansas, an interracial labor union was formed and managed to exist for as long as it did. White workers were not to blame for the limits of the STFU's success in the 1930s.

In the long run, given the acceleration following World War II of land consolidation, labor displacement, mechanization, and crop diversification, black sharecroppers were right to insist that their future lay with a national body like the CIO, one that was committed in principle to interracial equality and one that had the clout to counter the power exercised on the national level by the planters. The STFU had proven no match for the landowners' authority in Washington.

How do we evaluate the success of the STFU? Except for the 1935 strike, it registered few actual gains for the majority of its members. Yet the union did expose the brutality of the planter class and the horrible conditions under which most workers lived. Until this time, the horrors of the American Congo were not part of the national consciousness. In the 1930s, journalists, photographers, artists, and all kinds of activists came to the Delta to witness the plight of the sharecroppers. Producers of the *March of Time* movie series actually made a film of the union that was played in theaters around the country. And magazines and newspapers all over the world saw photographs that depicted the poverty and desperation of many workers. Mitchell also organized speaking engagements for share-croppers like Henrietta McGhee and white union member Myrtle Lawrence, who stirred the interests of reform groups and wealthy donors in northern cities. The Socialist and Communist parties also linked share-croppers to an entire network of legal and civil rights organizations. And the internationalism of both parties drew visitors from Europe, such as the British women trade unionists.

The publicity surrounding the union and its battles with the planters reinforced the STFU's efforts to lobby the federal government to provide assistance for the nation's rural poor, who were being driven from the land by drought, poverty, and increasing mechanization. In some ways, the union placed rural poverty on the nation's agenda. The major result of their lobbying was the creation of the Resettlement Administration and then the Farm Security Administration (FSA), which provided low-interest loans to former sharecroppers and tenants to purchase farms and to form cooperatives, several of which were located in the Delta. From Mitchell and Kester's perspective, the solution to the farm tenancy problem was cooperative farming, with the federal government facilitating home ownership and the sharing of farm equipment, gins, and barns. As a number of historians have shown, however, these cooperatives failed to provide enough relief for the massive number of landless. Small family farms were declining dramatically all over the nation. Small Delta farms, even with the aid of the FSA, could not compete with the large-scale corporate plantations. Nevertheless, some of the black families who became landowners under the FSA program established enough economic independence to become some of the early leaders of the post–World War II civil rights movement.[88]

The STFU's campaign to ensure that sharecroppers and tenants received their fair share of federal relief programs, and its reports of peonage cases, heightened black people's awareness of their citizenship rights. H. B. Brown illustrated this increased awareness when he wrote to Secretary of Agriculture Henry Wallace reporting that his landlord in Luxora, in Mississippi County, had taken his subsidy and applied it to his commissary account. Knowing that such action violated the AAA regulations, Brown demanded, "I want to be treated as thou I was a man and a Citizan."

Because of STFU legal assistance, croppers were able to file complaints with lawyers, exercising a most basic right of citizenship for which families in Elaine had died. In one instance, Powell Willis wrote on behalf of tenants who had been sent to the county farm north of Earle for their union activities. Although the people had been released, Willis wrote that "we is not satisfied for we was not gealty [*sic*] but they worked us 22 day we want to call a lawyer and have a law suit For you no it is not legal to miss treat people when they have not vylatied [*sic*] the law." Many of the people had been at home when they were arrested and were not on another's private property. "We want pay for the time they maked us work," he insisted. Other black people, emboldened by the union, sought to vote. In the all-black community of Edmundson, several men and women who had paid their poll taxes went to vote in a special election held in 1937 for U.S. senator. When they arrived, they were told to leave and that officers were on their way to arrest them. On the way home, officers stopped the eighteen people, searched them, and said "they [the white men] were running the election."[89] Without the STFU, these people may not have dared to exercise these rights of citizenship—acts of courage that marked an important chapter in the African American freedom struggle in the American Congo.

The STFU reached its peak in 1937, claiming thirty to thirty-five thousand members in several states. By the end of 1939, there were forty, down from a peak of approximately two hundred locals the previous year, and its membership was largely limited to Woodruff and St. Francis counties.[90] But the union did not fade away completely. It resurfaced after World War II began, when black workers once again faced opportunities outside of the region. The STFU addressed the concerns of those left behind to work on the plantations, pressing planters to pay fair wages and combating the terror that never seemed to end.

It may be useful to distinguish between the largely white union leadership and the predominantly black majority membership in terms of the legacy of the organization. For the black locals drew from a tradition of challenging the plantation system in all of its manifestations, including segregation and disfranchisement—a tradition that white people simply did not share. Seen in this light, the STFU was not a culminating point in the history of the plantation South, nor was it necessarily a bridge to the later civil rights struggle of the 1960s. The union was simply another stage in the ongoing struggle that black people had been waging against the alluvial empire since its inception, and in some cases, since slavery. The struggle in the 1930s differed in the degree of outside help that arrived from the Socialist and Communist parties and with the intrusion of a more elaborate liberal state than existed during World War I. New Deal policies, while harmful in some ways, combined with the Depression itself to open a space, however small, for yet another organized challenge to the horrors of the American Congo.

In the immediate scheme of things, the STFU lost its campaign to forge a permanent labor union for agricultural workers in the Delta. In the long run, however, black people continued their struggle for freedom, justice, and citizenship, a journey that was hastened by a second world war and yet another call for black people to offer their lives and labor in service to a Jim Crow nation. But experiences in the 1930s strengthened black people for this final stage of their journey toward citizenship. As they entered the next war, they had with them the support of a national labor movement whose increasing power could only bolster the drive for equality. And they could look to the increasing successes of the NAACP in fighting Jim Crow in the courts.

6 | A War within a War

World War II changed the face of the world. The Western colonial powers saw their empires collapse under the weight of revolution and the demands of their former subjects for freedom and independence. Thus, the anticolonial struggles unleashed by World War I achieved their goals with World War II, but only with a great deal of bloodshed. For twenty years after the war, the peoples of Asia, Africa, and the Americas fought wars of liberation against their former imperial masters and the native bureaucrats who managed their empires. A subsequent Cold War divided the world into Manichean halves: capitalism and communism, democracy and totalitarianism, Western Christianity and Soviet Atheism. Liberation movements, like it or not, had to choose sides.

The experience of the alluvial empire was no different from that of other colonies. World War II, which followed massive changes created by the Great Depression and New Deal, expanded the political consciousness of African Americans in the American Congo. Southern black people—men and women—fought all over the globe in a war to make the world safe for democracy. Having battled side by side with white American troops, as well as "coloured" soldiers from the various colonies, they returned to the Delta with a renewed determination to fight Jim Crow and to secure equality and freedom. The war had also raised the expectations of those who had remained behind to work in the fields and factories. During the war, a growing civil rights movement had pressed the federal government to end segregation and discrimination in industrial jobs, on public transportation, and in the armed forces. A. Phillip Randolph's threatened March on Washington in 1941 forced President Roosevelt to create a federal agency, the Fair Employment Practices Committee, to investigate discrimination in war industries.

Civil rights organizations also grew during the war years. While the

NAACP continued its legal efforts against Jim Crow, new organizations joined the fight. In the North, the Congress of Racial Equality (CORE) was founded in 1942, and in the South in 1938, the Southern Conference for Human Welfare was formed by southern and northern liberals, socialists, communists, and labor activists, including Eleanor Roosevelt. The NAACP won its first major victory in its legal battle against segregation in 1938, when the U.S. Supreme Court ordered Missouri's all-white law school to admit Lloyd Gaines. Soon after, in 1944, the court ended the white primary in the South, opening the way for black people to vote. The institutional mechanisms for fighting inequality, both within and outside the South, had grown and were mobilized for a protracted struggle for civil rights.[1]

The wartime freedom struggle in the Delta, then, did not occur within a national or global vacuum. It drew strength from organized labor, especially the CIO and the STFU, which continued to organize farm workers during the war. It was connected through the NAACP and other organizations to the emerging civil rights movement in the North and the anticolonial movements in the falling imperial world. And it produced indigenous organizations in the Delta as veterans returned from the war. But the freedom struggle in the Delta, like other liberation movements, was also encouraged in the postwar years by the founding in 1945 of the United Nations, with its stated commitment to human freedom and justice. The UN's creation of the Human Rights Charter in 1948 further signaled to the world and to the Delta that human rights had become a global issue endorsed by the Western democracies. The United States, and especially planters in the alluvial empire, could no longer profit from, even as they denied, the oppressive and undemocratic nature of their society.

None of these events escaped the attention of Delta black people—or white planters. The planters had also sent their sons to fight around the globe. Like their black counterparts, white southerners encountered other peoples and other worlds—some fought alongside African American, as well as colonial, troops. For most, the war had strengthened their commitment to white supremacy. Yet experiences abroad had also led some white southerners to question their own world of segregation and disfranchisement. During and after the war, the white supremacist South faced newer challenges from within its ranks. The rulers of the alluvial empire watched carefully as other empires, in the face of revolution, teetered on the brink of collapse. And they observed with trepidation the growing militancy of

African Americans around them. For all of the power they exercised on both regional and national levels, Delta planters did not know which fate would be theirs.

World War II ended the Great Depression by shifting the country to a full employment economy. Once again, thousands of black and white southerners left the depressed countryside for jobs in cities or to serve in the military. The Yazoo Delta's rural population fell 19 percent during the 1940s; 10 percent of its black residents left.[2] As they had in World War I, planters sought to retain a surplus of cheap workers. Similarly, black people who remained at home once again refused to work on these terms. Planters and workers again struggled over wages and working conditions. Unlike during World War I, however, workers in the American Congo had help from a reorganized STFU that represented their claims for justice.

During the war years, planters scrambled for sharecroppers and wage workers. Despite the AAA-induced labor displacement in the previous decade, the Yazoo Delta still operated 90 percent of its farms with tenants. Sharecropping had declined by only 9.4 percent during the 1930s.[3] The Depression-era surplus labor force was replaced by fewer workers demanding higher wages and sharecroppers demanding fair crop settlements. In addition, the mechanization of cotton, begun in the 1930s, slowed during the war with the military's need for steel. Since the 1930s, planters had hoped to decrease their operating expenses by reducing labor costs. During the war they found themselves once again trying to secure sharecroppers and wage laborers. The full mechanization of cotton would not come until the early 1960s.

By 1943, workers had declined the customary one dollar per hundred pounds (laboring six-day weeks, and ten- to twelve-hour days) and were receiving $2.50 or more. They also used their newfound economic bargaining power to determine how much money they needed to make each week, and once they had achieved their goal, refused to return to the fields. High wages allowed some workers greater control over their time, and some worked only two days a week.

Some families moved into nearby towns where the women found work as maids, cooks, and as laundresses, and the men hired out as day laborers on their own time and not that of the landowners. According to one Mississippi planter, "Some good substantial tenants have moved off . . . and built little shacks in town out of these Government grain bins that they had to offer for sale, and there have been probably a hundred of them erected in Cleveland, where this farm labor has moved with the expectation of drawing four or five dollars a hundred for cotton picking."[4]

Women and children received military allotment checks from their husbands, sons, or brothers, and, as they had during World War I, used them to break their dependence on the planters. Many moved into nearby towns and villages. Black women's independent income blatantly challenged planter authority, and their refusal to work on the plantations proved a crucial loss. A 1945 article in the leading newspaper of the Mississippi planters, the *Delta Farm Press,* revealed the planters' frustration when it claimed that at least fifty thousand people, mostly women, had refused to work in the fields. Chiding the women for working only two days a week and living off of dependent checks for the remaining time, the editor challenged the women's sense of responsibility and patriotism: "The Government has been very liberal with its people. Your husband goes off to war and Uncle Sam sends you a check. If you quit work and live on that check you are not helping the government which is helping you." Such actions, he warned, merely aided Hitler, for if "your husband or son is in the army and he comes home with one leg or arm broken, it may have been your fault. Just because you have enough to live on," the article righteously concluded, "does not give you the right to loaf."[5]

Planters explained black people's efforts to control their labor in terms of racism or bad character. According to W. M. Garrard, Jr., the "Delta negro is so constituted that they will not pick but so much cotton, and the higher the price per hundred, the less he will pick." Another planter complained that he had a black woman laborer who had always quit after she had made twenty dollars. "The psychology of the negro is this," he explained. "They have a task. When they get that task they know what that will mean in money." A fellow landowner, L. L. Green, agreed with this view, observing that the "average town negro has a certain amount he wants to make each day and if he can pick it by dinner, he sits down until that truck comes along. If it takes him half way into the evening, he will go to that point," he complained, "but they have a certain amount that they are going to make each day regardless of the price. As the prices goes up, when he gets two or three dollars, whatever he has in mind to make, he quits." And on top of all of this, planters saw workers using their gasoline and tire rations to ride all over the Delta, not in search of work, but to find the best fishing places.[6] As these landowners' complaints revealed, black people used their newfound higher wages to gain control over their own time.

High picking and chopping wages during the war turned the tables on the planters and undermined the sharecropping system that planters needed to maintain. Oscar Johnston of the Delta and Pine Land Company complained of croppers planting their fields and then abandoning them during the lay-by season of mid-July or early August, when they moved into nearby towns and villages and hired out as day laborers at higher wages during harvest season. Yet he saw this as a calculated move on their part, for in August they could tell if they would break even after the harvest. Croppers knew, he argued, that if they stayed, on September 1 they would owe their landlords furnishings for five or six months; one-half the cost of fertilizer, insecticides, and cost of application; a fee for picking sacks; costs for transporting the cotton to the gin; and one-half the cost of ginning the cotton itself. Under such circumstances, Johnston said that it was normal for the landlords to allow people to stay in homes free of charge, and with free fuel, until they could pick cotton for wages. He saw this as a crisis measure designed to keep enough labor on the plantations for harvest time and hopefully to keep them over into the next year to avoid the expense of recruiting and hiring new families.[7]

Croppers were thus able to squeeze the planters for their own ends during the war. H. G. Lowry complained that on his Indianola plantation there were "some darkies now borrowing money to carry them over to cotton picking, and those same darkies worked two or three days a week last month and the month before. I don't know whether it is because they are afraid they will die before they use it [money] up or not," he said, "but they will not work until it is gone."[8]

Planters hated paying higher wages and fairer crop settlements, and as they had always done in the American Congo, they continued to use coercion and theft in dealing with their workers. For example, when in 1945 Sally B. Love had made eighteen bales of cotton without acquiring any debts on the Sweet Brothers plantation in Widener, Arkansas, she expected to receive a full settlement. Instead, the planter refused to pay for the final bale until the field was scrapped and every pound of cotton picked. Lee Dora Bryson faced in 1943 a similar problem when she and her husband harvested four bales and went to settle with the landlord, who refused until all of the crop had been harvested, insisting that since the family owned a truck they might leave once they had received their money. The Brysons, who belonged to the STFU and the NAACP, claimed that the landlord had settled with every other family on the plantation.[9]

Planters continued to steal their tenants' parity checks, violate wage and crop agreements, overcharge commissary accounts, and cheat them on cotton weights. Letters from sharecroppers who belonged to the existing STFU locals revealed that many of these problems were still inherent in the plantation system, and demonstrated how little New Deal measures had done to protect and improve the lives of plantation workers. For example, H. N. Williams of Gould, Arkansas, claimed that planters in his area had hired labor at certain wages and paid much lower ones after the harvest. "It aint no law to make a man hire me," he wrote, "but it art to make him pay what he promas to pay . . . a man cant get what he work far how can he live."[10]

While some sharecroppers abandoned their crops in order to work for higher wages as pickers, others complained instead of being forced to leave their crops after the cotton had been planted and chopped, as they had during World War I. Planters did this in order to deny the workers their share of parity checks and to save on additional furnish bills. For example, in Arkansas James Graham had made a sharecrop with landowner G. R. Vardaman in 1942, and on June 24 Vardaman pulled a gun on the cropper and threatened to kill him. Graham argued that the planter did this to scare him off the plantation in order to secure control of the crop due to abandonment. This tactic allowed the planter to own all of the crop without having to settle with tenants after the harvest, freeing him to hire wage labor for the fall picking.[11]

Landowners continued to cheat their tenants on their gin receipts. Planters either owned their own gins or ordered their croppers to use certain ones and required the operators of those gins to turn all gin and compress receipts directly over to them. According to O. C. Morgan in Rockdale, Mississippi, planters told their croppers where to gin their cotton, made them pay 35 cents per hundred pounds for ginning, $3.00 for bagging and ties, and $1.25 for hauling. Few tenants ever saw their receipts and had to accept the planter's version of how much their cotton weighed, its grade, and the price received for it.[12]

Other complaints centered on the continued charging of high interest rates on cash advances and on furnish bills at the commissaries. Although Arkansas had a usury law establishing legal interest rates at 10 percent, many planters charged rates as high as 40 percent. Nor were workers allowed to see their accounts. Art Landers of Rockdale, Mississippi, complained that planters refused to give the croppers itemized statements, instead paying them money for their cotton and seed and then lumping all of the other expenses into one sum. Lewis Thompson of Widener, Arkansas, wrote in 1943 that "we doesnt get our bills at all. We don't know wheather we pay celling prices or owner celling prices." He requested that the Office of Price Administration post the government-imposed ceiling prices in public places and in newspapers.[13]

Finally, planters continued to abuse the AAA program. Parity checks were still delivered directly to planters, who either did not pay their workers any of their share of the payments, or gave them less than their due. The STFU forwarded one hundred such cases to the USDA in 1942 alone.[14] The Lee Wilson Company found creative ways of keeping the parity money that lawfully belonged to some of their tenants: plantation-riding bosses were listed as renters, who dutifully signed over their parity checks to the company.[15] And as usual, violence often surrounded the parity payments. In Pickens, Mississippi, Willie Joe Waites and his brother-in-law severely beat their former tenant, Ollie Hoover, who had refused to turn over his parity check.[16]

Both the STFU and UCAPAWA continued to organize separately in the Delta. The STFU continued to press the workers' demands to the federal government. UCAPAWA also had locals on plantations. For example, in 1941, an FSA supervisor evicted several families from the Missco Resettlement Community near Wilson, Arkansas, for belonging to the local UPACAWA chapter. The supervisor claimed that he had been acting on the advice of the planter-dominated Mississippi County Advisory Board for the FSA. The CIO representative in Memphis, Harry Koger, successfully pressed the national agency to keep the workers in their community.[17]

UCAPAWA also had a local on the giant Lee Wilson plantation. The union demanded that the company pay its workers in cash rather than in "brozene"; it supported the organization of buying clubs to allow sharecroppers and wage workers to bypass the commissary; and it encouraged the formation of cooperatives on government-purchased lands. Koger had also discovered that the Wilson company had displaced hundreds of sharecroppers and replaced them with tractors. Despite the increased mechanization, however, the Wilson company still needed large gangs of wage workers to chop and pick the cotton.[18]

Koger was also actively organizing black mill workers in the Chicago Mill and Lumber company mills in Helena, Arkansas, and Greenville, Mississippi. He secured an FBI investigation into the mob action of fifty white American Federation of Labor workers in Helena, who had beaten him and another organizer and tarred and feathered them before running them out of town.[19] And in Greenville, black members of the Carpenters and Joiners Union walked off the job at the Chicago Mill and Lumber plant when a black man was fired for fighting with a white worker. They protested the retainment of the white worker and the dismissal of the black laborer.[20] Thus, the CIO actively organized in Memphis and throughout the Delta during the war, but the STFU was to have the greatest influence in helping farm workers present their demands for justice to the wartime governmental agencies.

H. L. Mitchell and the STFU played a crucial role in presenting to federal officials cases of planter abuses during the war. He went beyond mere appeals, however, by initiating a program with the Farm Security Administration and the War Manpower Commission (WMC) to recruit southern plantation laborers during the off-season to work in other parts of the country. Since the average plantation worker had only 125 days of full-time employment in a year, such a program made sense from the perspective of an efficient use of wartime manpower. During November and December of 1942, the STFU-FSA program transported more than two thousand black and white laborers to the Southwest, where picking wages were four dollars per hundred pounds for long-staple and two dollars for short-staple cotton; and in January and February, they sent five hundred to the Florida citrus groves. Later, others went to New Jersey to work in the canneries. Overall, during World War II, the program sent approximately thirteen thousand southern rural workers to jobs outside of the South.[21]

Delta planters were outraged over the STFU-FSA program, even though 90 percent of the workers returned to their homes to harvest cotton. By linking his union with a federal jobs program, Mitchell had demonstrated the power that his organization could exert. The union's potential was not lost to the landowners. Many resorted to direct coercion to prevent workers from leaving by invoking vagrancy laws, the draft, and taking away gasoline and tire rations. Planters also directed their energies toward driving the STFU from the Delta. Angered over the labor program and over the union's continued efforts to organize in plantation country, Delta planters moved to protect themselves and their labor force from what they perceived as radical influences.

Mississippi planters came to reflect the bunker mentality that their counterparts in Arkansas had demonstrated in the 1930s in response to the STFU. By the early war years, however, planters in the alluvial empire saw themselves threatened from larger forces at work in the nation. While they had welcomed the AAA in the 1930s, they did not support the social welfare legislation that followed after 1935. Landowners did not support the passage of legislation that provided for Social Security, the recognition of labor unions, or the payment of a minimum wage and the enforcement of maximum hours. They came to view the Democratic Party as being dominated by the CIO, communists, Jews, and civil rights organizations. Their growing alienation with the Democratic Party, and their hostility to the social changes that the Depression had accelerated, shaped planter responses to the renewed STFU activity in the Delta.[22]

Mississippi planters used their trade organization, the Delta Council, to counter the STFU. The organization's executive secretary, Mrs. Dorothy Lee Black, was certain that "subversive movements are here in the Delta and they are hard at work. Individual vigilance alone cannot nullify their influence." She concluded, "It takes organized representation."[23] Black called for strong action against the union because the "increasing agitation and activity among the negroes of the Delta seriously threatens the unity as well as the economy of this area. The council has always sought to further the relationship between the races in this area," she argued, "and it is my personal opinion that now, as never before, we should make some effort to combat the dissension and unrest which are being fomented through outside interest, literature, and people."[24]

The Delta Council and Black made eradication of the STFU a primary goal. Black had actually attended an STFU meeting in Memphis, where she was "left with no doubt" that the organization favored not only social and political equality but also intermarriage. After receiving numerous reports from Mississippi landowners about union organizing, she asked a local black minister and leader of the Delta and Pine Land Company's Pastors' Conference, H. H. Humes, to spy on union activities in the region. Humes, the editor of the planter-funded black newspaper, the *Delta Leader*, contacted postmasters for a list of those sharecroppers receiving union literature and reported the information back to the planters.[25]

Black noted that in order to counter union activities, planters in Washington County, Mississippi, had used Farm Bureau dues paid by tenants to dispense health, sanitation, farming, and "general social education" information among their workers. "Maybe we should work with the Farm Bureau Federation to develop a program of work among the negroes setting them straight as to the manner in which they are being used by the selfish interest behind their present dissension." She wrote to Walter Sillers, Jr., that "we need to tell our negroes of the true facts and prevent their being exploited by selfish interests."[26] Sillers went further in his wishes, hoping that "when the war is over the army might take control and kick these devils [labor organizers] out."[27]

Planters in both Arkansas and Mississippi launched a massive membership drive on their plantations for the American Farm Bureau Federation. According to Walter Sillers, Jr., the Farm Bureau represented the best organized way for meeting the threat posed by labor unions. He argued that planters must have a national organization to represent both themselves and their workers, for "free enterprise in agriculture and the free action of agricultural labor is greatly and dangerously threatened." Nor could planters afford any divisions within their ranks, argued Sillers, for this must be a fight of "all for one and one for all."[28] Thus, in the early 1940s, landowners signed their farm workers into the Farm Bureau and deducted the dues from their settlements, or if they were wage workers, before they received their wages. In Mississippi, planters led croppers to believe that the Farm Bureau was responsible for their parity checks. Indeed, the bureau had actually posted a sign at the local AAA offices that read, "Pay your Farm Bureau Dues Here: The Farm Bureau is responsible for getting your AAA payments." In many instances, planters forced croppers to pay their dues when cashing their parity checks. In a sense the bureau had been responsible for the AAA checks due to their lobbying efforts in Congress. Given the planters' coercive actions, however, such subtleties were lost in the translation.[29]

During the war years, bureau membership drives were successful. Of the 28,901 members in Mississippi in 1941, 19,000 were in six Delta counties, and 13,000 of these were black sharecroppers and day laborers. Most workers never knew they were members until settlement time, when they received their wages, or when they received the *Farm Bureau News*. And once they belonged, they were not allowed to participate in the organization. Moss Matthews, for example, worked on the Terrell plantation in Bolivar County and had been a member of the bureau for three years. He was told to join in order to receive his portion of the parity payments. He had never attended a meeting, known when or where they were held, or participated in any organizational elections. When day laborer Judge Mitchell protested over having dues deducted from his wages, he was told that joining the bureau would keep cotton prices higher, leading to an increase in his wages. Even when workers refused to join the union, planters deducted the dues.[30]

Arkansas planters did much the same as their counterparts across the river, though they tended to simply deduct the $2.50 dues without reference to parity checks. Since Arkansas had more STFU members, croppers tended to protest more frequently and were threatened and often evicted. In 1940 alone, H. L. Mitchell collected forty affidavits regarding Farm Bureau abuses.[31]

Planter efforts to combat the STFU and to retain cheap workers transcended local concerns, but wartime needs superceded planter interests. Throughout the war planters battled with government officials—whose aim was to win the war—over price controls, wages, and the labor supply, and with their workers who sought better economic opportunity, either in wartime industries or on the land. Officials in Washington were split over whether to support the planters or the laborers, thus leading them to pursue policies that often appeared contradictory.

During World War II, Delta planters sought to protect their cotton prices from the wartime controls of the Office of Price Administration, while simultaneously ensuring that farm wages did not rise. These goals brought them into direct conflict with Secretary of Agriculture Claude R. Wickard and War Manpower Commissioner Paul McNutt, as well as with other leaders of wartime agencies. Landowners specifically sought to destroy the authority of the War Manpower Commission (WMC) over labor distribution. In 1942–1943, the WMC, through the U.S. Employment Service (USES), designated certain regions as having either a shortage or surplus of labor. The USES then worked with the Farm Security Administration to house and transport workers from one area to another. Planters were especially angry when the WMC tagged Memphis, Tennessee, and the Delta and hill sections surrounding it as surplus areas. As a result of this decision, the STFU was allowed to organize its own program of sending farm workers to other regions.[32]

The FSA and the USES also controlled the importation of Hispanic migrant labor. In 1942, the United States and Mexico arranged for the importation of Mexican labor, provided that workers received thirty cents an hour, unemployment compensation, housing, medical care, and transportation. Growers needed USES certification that local workers were not available before they requested Hispanic migrant labor. The FSA then transported the workers, monitored contracts, and insured grievance procedures. Delta growers and their western counterparts opposed both the welfare measures required of them as well as FSA intervention in their labor relations.[33]

Large-scale producers also clashed with Secretary of Agriculture Wickard's efforts to provide decent wages for farm workers. Wickard argued that cotton workers deserved a fairer income if they were to compete with rising wages paid in wartime industries. When the Office of Price Administration was created in 1942 to control inflation by establishing price ceilings and wage controls, Wickard argued against them for agricultural workers whose average hourly wage was thirty cents (compared to eighty cents in industry). Consequently, Wickard withheld government regulation until farm wages reached $2,400 annually. This policy promised opportunity for thousands of underpaid plantation workers who seldom averaged $500 a year.[34]

The Farm Bureau and the National Cotton Council combined forces with the Delta Council and the Agricultural Council of Arkansas to fight what they viewed as a policy of low farm prices and high wages. From their perspective, American industries were making great profits from war contracts while the industrial working class had higher wages to pay for more expensive foodstuffs. Planters did not think that they should carry the burden of Roosevelt's anti-inflation plan, arguing that the price of cotton, not government laws, determined wages. According to P. F. Williams, chairman of the Coahoma County Mississippi Farm Labor Committee, "Cotton farmers in this area have always figured that they could pay a wage scale on a per hour basis equivalent to the price of cotton. In other words," he continued, "if cotton is worth twenty cents per pound (approximate value at the present time) the farmer can afford to pay an average of twenty cents per hour for labor." If farmers were to pay thirty to forty cents, Williams argued, then the government must raise the price of cotton.[35]

Delta planters adamantly opposed Wickard's attempt to equalize farm and industrial wages, and they fought with the government over the issue of labor supply. Wartime industries and the draft, they insisted, had depleted their workforce, leaving them mainly with women and children who picked whenever they had a notion to and at exorbitant wages. Planters had a relative definition of surplus and scarcity, however, since they had always relied on additional labor from the hill sections, where crops matured earlier, and from nearby villages and towns. This "surplus" labor force had served to keep down wages. Wartime opportunities reduced this outside labor pool, raising the bargaining power of those workers who remained on the land. Planters and workers struggled over the definitions of surplus and shortage, and both presented their views to the federal government.

Delta planters lobbied hard in Washington to control federal policies relating to labor recruitment. In 1942, Congress passed the Tydings Amendment, deferring farm workers from military service and rescinding the deferment should a worker leave the farm for industry without official approval. While this bill satisfied some of the planters' concerns for an adequate labor supply, they still complained over what they perceived as a scarcity of labor. Consequently, they aimed to remove the responsibility for farm labor from the WMC and its affiliates, placing it in the USDA. They succeeded in April of 1943, with the passage of Public Law 45. This law created the Emergency Farm Labor Supply program and achieved all of the planters' and Farm Bureau's goals. Not only was the farm labor program placed in the USDA, but also an autonomous agency, the War Food Administration (WFA), was created within the department to administer the nation's food program and to recruit both foreign and interstate labor. The measure regarding the recruitment of foreign labor excluded Wickard's earlier policy of requiring that such labor receive a minimum of thirty cents an hour and a guarantee of at least four days a week of work. Roosevelt further weakened Wickard's power by appointing Chester Davis, a friend of southern planters and the Farm Bureau, as head of the WFA.[36]

Planters scored another success by having attached to Public Law 45 the Pace Amendment, which prevented the government from spending any funds to establish minimum wages and maximum hours, to regulate housing, or to recognize collective bargaining for farm workers. The amendment further required a county agent's signature before federal funds were used to send local farm workers to other regions to work, a measure that clearly targeted the STFU-FSA labor program. As extensions of planter power, county agents kept workers under their thumbs.[37]

Critics on the local and national levels saw the legislative measures for what they were: the triumph of large-scale growers over their workers' efforts to secure decent wages and working conditions. As a writer in the *Memphis Commercial Appeal* noted, farm workers were the only segment in the economy denied the chance to improve their conditions during the war. No other group, he said, was asked to make this sacrifice. Some questioned why cotton deserved a special place in the war production program. Oscar Johnston and the National Cotton Council insisted that the staple was essential to the war effort, not only because it provided material for uniforms and other military necessities, but also because it created cotton seed oil, a food. Skeptics countered that it took more acreage and labor to produce cotton oil than it did soybeans and other oil-producing crops. The National Cotton Council, in response to its critics, warned Midwestern producers of the consequences should the 11 million people involved in southern cotton production divert their efforts to raising soybeans and grains. Still others questioned increased cotton production when the country already had a two-year surplus. Radical journalist I. F. Stone noted that capitalist agriculture had never been a more profitable business, with the Office of Price Administration having shown that from 1939 to 1942, farm prices increased two and one-half times more than wage costs per unit output and four times the costs of total output per unit. Furthermore, 1942 was one of the best years in agricultural production, with total increases of 14 percent over 1941, a rise in per capita income of 116 percent over 1939 (in real dollars), and a 72 percent increase in purchasing power. The rate of return on investments for farmers went from 4.2 percent in 1939 to 13.4 percent in 1942, while the producers' share of consumer dollars rose 27 percent. In addition to all of these gains, the government paid out $697 million in agricultural subsidies, an increase of one-fifth over the payments in 1941.[38] Planters in the alluvial empire thus achieved exorbitant profits, with the help of the federal government and at the expense of farm workers.

Southern farm workers, through the STFU and organized labor, challenged planter claims of a shortage and their argument that plantation workers must remain in the region year round. Mitchell and others noted that planters controlled all of the relevant agencies that determined whether or not workers moved or were drafted, and they questioned the denial of farm labor mobility for better wages. As black union organizer and vice president of the STFU F. R. Betton explained to a Congressional committee, "Some of the younger farm workers fearing that they will be frozen for the duration in the county they now live in, have refused to accept deferment and have gone into the army." These men chose to serve the country by joining the Army rather than working one-third of the time. They also made fifty dollars a month in the military, far more than on the plantation.[39]

Bretton's predictions were soon realized as county agents, with the help of the local AAA committees, determined if a labor surplus existed and whether or not workers could leave the area. Exaggerating their need for labor, growers prevented any croppers or day laborers from leaving their counties after 1942. Further, the Tydings Amendment empowered planters to defer farm workers from the draft, and they used this authority, and their influence with local draft boards, to defer or draft workers depending on whether they would labor on the planters' terms. Deferment of men was especially significant because it meant keeping the entire family on the farm. If a husband, son, or brother left, he would send dependent checks back to their families, who might then leave the farms for towns to work as they chose. The STFU received numerous letters and reports of county agents refusing to sign releases and of threats to draft those who did try to leave. In Arkansas, for example, planters forced their sharecroppers to sign five-year contracts or face being drafted. Some planters presented their sharecroppers with contracts, claiming they came from the AAA—although they refused to let the workers read the agreement. Others secured Selective Service forms and took them to their tenants, promising to keep them out of the military if they worked for five years. H. L. Mitchell reported that a large number of union members had been confronted with these demands and that when they refused, were kicked off the land and drafted.[40]

County agents lived up to the STFU's expectations by refusing to sign releases for those workers who wanted to go elsewhere for employment and, with local law enforcement, threatening those who tried to leave. H. L. Mitchell received letters from 156 families regarding the FSA program, and of those, county agents denied 131 of the applicants' requests to leave. When a planter in Drew, Mississippi, overheard R. Booker, the president of the Ruleville, Mississippi, local, talking with people about working in Florida after the crops had been gathered, he sent a deputy to warn Booker against labor enticement. "Booker," he said, "you don't know anything about this Mississippi delta, do you? Why you would be killed in a little while if this was known. Every planter in Sunflower County would help do so because that Union is against the planters and their way of life." The deputy, with the help of three others, took the union dues that Booker had collected, telling him, "This damn thing was going to cause one of the greatest controversies that had ever been in Miss. . . . and before this will be put through they will suffer death and you had better keep out of the way as that is the best thing for you." In Booker's view, planters in Sunflower County were "very criminal to colored people."[41]

By 1943, the Arkansas State Farm Labor Committee ordered extension agents not to sign labor releases for industrial work and told them to check dependency cases for individuals who received state relief during cotton picking time. Thus, when 150 workers arrived at the train station in Brinkley, Arkansas, for transportation to jobs outside of the state, the director of the State Employment Service refused to certify their request after planters expressed fears the workers would not return. The experience of these prospective travelers probably represented the norm, for according to H. L. Mitchell, as of November 15, 1943, county agents had denied the applications of 2,200 workers who had applied for work based on the passage of Public Law 45.[42]

Despite their success in preventing workers from leaving, landowners still searched for additional sources of labor and used every means at their disposal to acquire them. When Colonel Long, head of the Mississippi Selective Service, met with the Delta Council about the draft, he argued that the main issue for planters centered on how to "reach the idle and make them work." A planter himself, Long wanted the government to understand the true nature of the plantation worker, who was "a man relatively easy-going, not particularly ambitious and raised in an atmosphere of lethargy." Many agreed with Walter Sillers, Jr., that "negroes don't make good soldiers. They can make a better contribution to the war effort in the fields producing food, feed, and fiber."[43]

Many petitioned the state penitentiary for the return of former workers. For example, one Bolivar County planter petitioned the Parchman State Prison pardon board to release two black men who had been sentenced in 1939 to ten years of incarceration for stealing a cow from another black couple. He argued that these men had been punished enough, and were "sorely needed by their respective families in the conduct of cotton farming operations in this time of labor scarcity." Another landowner requested a pardon for one of his workers serving a three-year sentence for shooting with intent to kill. He claimed that the laborer, who had been a "strawboss," or manager, was a "good white man's negro" whom he was "much attached to."[44]

Oscar Johnston requested the release of Willie Hobbs, who had killed a black woman and had served two years of a life sentence. "His family has been on this place for over twenty-five years," wrote Johnston. "His father died about a year ago and his mother needs him to help make the crops." Nor did Johnston stop at the state level. When Willie Hill, the son of one of his sharecroppers, was indicted for manslaughter in Chicago, Johnston hired a lawyer to obtain a three-year probation for him with the understanding that Hill be placed in his custody. Johnston thanked the lawyer for the "pains you have taken to help our 'nigger' who is paying probably a well deserved penalty for leaving his 'kith and kin' and going off to live up there among a lot of 'yankees.'"[45]

These letters not only indicated the extremes to which planters went to obtain workers, but revealed even more the nature of the relationship between landlords and sharecroppers and the role local authorities played in maintaining labor control. Delta planters had commonly shaped whether their workers were arrested and tried for crimes, especially if they involved black people harming other black people. Indeed, the U.S. Employment Service had initially operated through county sheriffs, who helped them to "comb" the countryside and villages for pickers. Planters had the power to have their people arrested for various crimes, but they could also excuse such infractions of the law when it suited their purposes. The harshness and arbitrary nature of Mississippi law was evident as well, for two men could receive ten years for stealing a cow while another man got only three years for manslaughter. As with the draft, the county extension agency, and relief programs, planters controlled fully the croppers' access to land, labor, and civil rights. In spite of their complaints, planters had their way in most cases regarding labor control. They invoked anti-enticement and vagrancy laws, they persuaded the local U.S. Employment Service boards not to advertise jobs in industry or construction until after the harvest, and the government eventually provided them with prisoners of war, Japanese internees, and after 1942, Hispanic migrant labor.[46]

Delta planters initially opposed the use of Japanese internee labor, insisting, as one prominent banker observed, that they might remain in the region after the war and, "instead of having one racial problem we will have two." He argued also that they would eventually own a large part of the land if allowed to remain. He may have known of California growers' concerns of Japanese landownership.[47]

Prisoners of war, Mexicans, and Texas-Mexicans provided the major alternative sources of labor during the war. But planters complained that none could pick cotton as cleanly as black workers; the new workers tended to pull rather than pick the cotton, thus lowering the grade. Nevertheless, Arkansas employed 8,000 prisoners of war in the fall of 1944 while Mississippi used 3,000. By the war's end, Mississippi had also used from 8,000 to 10,000 Mexican workers.[48]

While planters justified their use of outside labor in terms of a labor shortage, the STFU protested that planters aimed to use the additional men to depress wages for workers. Both employers and employees had responded to the increasing demand for more soldiers and defense jobs as the war intensified in 1944 and 1945, depleting further the labor supply in the towns and on the plantations. Mississippi claimed to have lost 43 percent of its farm population from 1940 to 1944, with a 24 percent shortage occurring in 1944. Arkansas fared no better, producing its 1944 crop with fifty thousand fewer workers than when the war began. Yet statistics tell only part of the story, for those left behind were mainly children, women, and the elderly. Women were not only picking and chopping—they had always done that—but now they plowed and operated tractors, repaired fences, and painted buildings. Black schools held classes only half-days during peak seasons, for planters argued that ten- and eleven-year-old boys had to pick 150 pounds after lunch. Landowners also complained of losing their skilled workers such as mechanics and tractor drivers. This loss, they argued, was compounded by the shortage in farm machinery, spare parts, ploughs, hay balers, and hoes.[49]

Despite these shifts in population, the STFU and plantation workers continued to insist that an adequate labor supply existed and that the issue confronting both planters and laborers was not one of scarcity, but of decent wages. In their view, the use of migrant and prisoner-of-war labor represented the planters' direct response to the demands of farm workers for decent wages. The STFU had held wage conferences since 1940 establishing the rates that workers expected, such as thirty cents an hour for a ten-hour day, or the equivalent in piece work (number of pounds picked, ditches dug, and so on) as well as guaranteed employment for 75 percent of their work days during the year, at a rate of three dollars a day.[50]

By 1943, the union was demanding a cotton-picking wage of three dollars per hundred pounds, and distributed leaflets throughout the Delta. An average worker, in one day, picked from 150 to 200 pounds of cotton. Union efforts proved especially effective in Memphis, where ten thousand seasonal day workers formed the labor force for many of the plantations across the river in Arkansas and in northern Mississippi. When the Tri-State Farm Labor Committee set the wage at $1.25, only two thousand workers went to pick cotton. Landowners urged black churches to close on Sundays and to send parishioners to the fields, but none answered the call. Since most of the Memphis farm workers were women and children who received dependent checks, they did not have to go out and work for what they considered inadequate wages.[51] The persistent refusal to work for low wages drove the cotton-picking wages to as high as $2.50 that year, and by the next, in 1944, the wage had reached $3.00.

In 1945, the STFU continued raising its wage demand, up to $3.50, and they expected to obtain it since one-third of the 1944 crop remained in the fields in some places. Mitchell now insisted that workers deserved an annual income of $625 that could only be earned by receiving $5.00 per ten-hour day during the 125 days of full employment available to them on the plantations. The $3.50 wage represented that amount.[52] By this time, planters were fed up with the union and its demand for high wages. Delta planters met in the summer of 1945 and agreed to ask the secretary of agriculture to appoint a state wage board that would arrange for each county to hold public hearings and an election to establish a wage ceiling. They argued that high wages had stolen profits from the tenants, who had to hire outside pickers at outrageous wages.[53]

By asking for a ceiling, planters in reality sought to retain their sharecroppers on the usual terms of low wages. Sharecroppers did in World War II as they had in the previous war. As picking wages rose, they left their crops and picked cotton. If their tenants left and picked elsewhere for wages, then planters lost control over the amount of cash their workers had access to. As we have seen earlier, with the sharecropping system, enough deductions could be made at settlement time to ensure that croppers got the amount of cash planters wanted them to have. Thus, landowners forced tenants to pay not only for the labor, but for production costs as well, a strategy that planters had followed since the founding of the alluvial empire. Nor did landowners want to pay an hourly wage, for they then lost control over the harvest. If workers picked on an hourly basis, they did not have to work as hard as when they picked on a piece rate; with a piece rate, workers had to pick long, hard hours to collect enough cotton to bring in an adequate income. Workers knew this, and since planters refused an hourly rate, they sought to keep the picking wage high enough to prevent having to work ten-hour days.

A wage ceiling also aimed at destroying the STFU. When the Delta Council met to discuss the ceiling, Mitchell was certainly on the members' minds. Oscar Johnston saw a federal ceiling as the only way to prevent organized labor from demanding five dollars per hundred and then striking if it was not forthcoming. Yet Hugh L. Gary was skeptical of governmental action, noting that a "good many people in our area . . . fear organized labor on our plantations the most. People are afraid if we use the Federal Government they will insist on having labor represented."[54]

Despite the private discussions of their fears of organized labor, when the Arkansas and Mississippi planters officially requested a ceiling, they gave as their reason the tremendous war-induced shortage of labor. In reality they no longer controlled the amount they paid their workers, for wages had risen from $1.00 per hundred pounds in 1940 to as high as $4.50 in some areas in 1944. As the administrative officer of the Mississippi AAA and chair of the ceiling hearings observed, "It is well known for many years here in the Delta you have held meetings here in the fall to agree upon a fair price for picking." Under a wage ceiling, however, "you have the federal government to help you."[55]

Wage hearings were held in the Delta in August. The landowners constituted the majority of those testifying, with a few selected sharecroppers and tenant farmers also heard. The hearings revealed the various ways the planters and workers understood the changes occurring in their region, and described the response of both to worker efforts to improve their conditions. At the Belzoni hearings, one planter complained that "all you hear out here now among the labor is that they are going to get five dollars a hundred or else. They just got their minds set on four or five dollars." W. M. Garrard, Jr., in Sunflower County testified that he had one sharecropper who wanted to turn his crop back over to him to harvest and pick for wages. Still another planter in Arkansas blamed the croppers and small renters for raising wages, for those with large families picked their own crop first. On the last day of their harvest, many of these farmers either raised the picking wage on their own crop, or sent a neighbor into town to bid up the wages. Then the entire family went into town and hired out as pickers for the higher wages that they had in part been responsible for raising. And in Greenwood, a landowner claimed that younger people picked their crops first and then hired out to pick their father's crop at five dollars per hundred. "The young darkies will get it all picking the cotton," he said.[56]

Despite wartime shortages, many insisted that workers were around, provided the price was right. "Clarksdale is full of pickers," claimed one planter. "Every house is packed and jammed, and a great proportion of them were tenants and very few worked in industry. They have moved here because they know that they can get just as much or more money picking cotton than they can living out on the plantations and fighting the whole year."[57]

Picking and chopping wages also affected other aspects of the local economy, especially the cotton oil mills and compresses and the unskilled labor market in Delta towns. For example, one planter said that the high wages in 1944 had shut down the laundries in Vicksburg, while most towns complained of having no cooks or maids during harvest and chopping season. Domestic workers made from ten to twelve dollars a week, but at prevailing farm wages, they made more than that in a few days picking and chopping cotton. The oil and compress industry especially concerned planters, for if workers left these jobs, cotton could not be ginned or the seed crushed. In 1944, the federal ceiling on oil and compress wages was fifty cents per hour for a ten-hour day, or $4.20 per day at a time when pickers brought home daily six to seven dollars.[58]

Other planter testimony revealed the methods that planters urged in dealing with reluctant workers. One Leland, Mississippi, planter, who had forty-six families that "come and go" on his plantation, devised incentives to retain them. "I am going to put electricity in the houses, I am going to see that they get radios, and get it first hand, instead of the cooked up stuff by the labor people. Let's let them know the facts. I don't blame the Negro," he concluded, "he just can't make the grade. And I am not making it." He had "borrowed money on everything but my wife this year to keep going."[59]

Others were less willing to concede anything to their workers. Many agreed with Russell Kearney that "if you force them they will pick for $1.75." If planters stick to a ceiling, he was certain pickers would not "sit down" the way they had in 1944 in the Delta counties surrounding Memphis. A. L. Lelouis agreed: "They are not going to strike. They might pretend to strike, but they will pick cotton if the police put them out of town, or get them for vagrancy. If a man doesn't show some means of livelihood, he should be made to work."[60]

In spite of the planter-dominated hearings, some workers and union members testified. G. E. Ray, a cotton picker in Greenville, told how high rents and grocery prices called for better wages. He asked that the ceiling reflect the increasing food prices, noting that a sack of flour had increased from seventy-five cents to two dollars. "I will thank you for as much as the OPA can stand," he said. "The fellow picking the cotton has the house rent to pay and has to eat, and his clothes on top of that." Ray requested a ceiling of three dollars, while his wife requested four.[61]

Union representatives testified and challenged the entire premises of the hearings. Harry Koger, of UCAPAWA, said that farm workers suffered more during the war because of inflation. The government protected growers' markets, yet did little to shield workers from the ravages of high prices and low wages. Koger especially criticized landowners' attempts to pit farm workers against each other: "We deplore the attempts of some persons who try to show that the interests of sharecroppers and other farm labor are not the same." David Burgess, of the Board of Home Missions of the Congregational Church of Christ, worked with farm workers and agreed with Koger that sharecroppers also picked cotton, and were thus not in conflict with day laborers. He also observed that mechanization would eventually drive these people off the land, and wondered why, in the meantime, planters sought to hold them down.

Burgess's concerns fell on deaf ears. The state wage boards held elections in September in which planters and sharecroppers were to vote on a wage ceiling. Mississippi got a ceiling of $2.10 and Arkansas one of $2.05 per hundred pounds.[62] The STFU immediately challenged the legality of the entire proceedings, arguing that farm workers had not been adequately notified of the hearings and elections. Indeed, planters coerced many of those who voted. Nor did farm workers have representation on the wage stabilization committees headed by the Extension Service. The AAA committees enforced the ceilings in each county, and most elections occurred in the commissaries, where workers voted in front of the planters. For these reasons, the STFU sought unsuccessfully to prevent the elections, and afterward sought an injunction to stop the ceiling's implementation. In the Arkansas Delta, 9,356 had voted for and 2,757 against the ceiling, while in the Yazoo Delta, the vote was 21,713 for and 315 against. Most workers did not vote.[63]

Mitchell failed in his efforts to secure an injunction, but he did launch a campaign among sharecroppers and day workers to secure an annual wage of not less than $625, or a daily wage of five dollars for the 125 days of work during the season. The union did not succeed in securing a minimum wage, nor in protecting plantation laborers from the reduced income resulting from the ceiling. It did withhold labor from the fields, however, prompting planters and their local newspapers to complain in December and January that from 33 to 40 percent of the cotton had remained in the fields.[64] Despite this loss of labor, planters reaped the largest income in their history, exceeded only by the previous year. Pleased with their efforts to control wages, landowners sought unsuccessfully to impose a ceiling on cotton chopping wages in the spring of 1946. The following fall, Mississippi alone secured a ceiling of $2.60 per hundred pounds. The STFU protested to no avail.[65]

While the STFU failed in its attempts to defeat a wage ceiling, it had succeeded during the war years in helping farm workers to obtain higher wages. Despite planter shenanigans, workers made more money during the war than they had in the Great Depression. Surely the continued presence of the union and its persistent actions on behalf of the croppers and wage workers contributed to the growing political consciousness among black people in the American Congo. For in challenging their employers, black workers also tested planter dominance of their social and political world.

African Americans in the Delta, like other people throughout the colonial world, increasingly challenged the system of white supremacy and those who enforced it. They manifested their changing political consciousness on many different levels. As in World War I, Delta black people demanded better education, housing, and jobs; a fair judiciary; and an end to police violence and terror. But this time, they insisted on the vote, and they challenged more directly Jim Crow, both in public facilities and on the military bases that dotted the region. In all of these ways, black people asserted their demands for freedom and justice during and after the war.

One of the earliest signs of an increasing black political consciousness centered on the ways that black people addressed each other and themselves. Planters observed this new development in 1941 with great concern, and complained, like their counterparts in the various western empires, of a "growing race consciousness" in their alluvial empire. "We have noted," said one planter, "that when they speak of themselves they speak as 'negroes' and not as 'colored people.' They do not choose as their officers the most talented, whitest, most attractive of their group, but invariably select the blackest among them."[66] Another landowner and superintendent of schools in Coahoma County noted that whenever he went into the black community on his plantation seeking the whereabouts of a tenant, each worker would address the other with the title of Mr. or Mrs.[67]

When sociologist Arthur Raper conducted a survey of Coahoma County in 1941, he found a widespread recognition of the changes that had occurred among black people. "While in the county, we heard from ever so many sources, Negro and White," he wrote, "that the Negroes were becoming more aware of their second-rate citizenship status." An agent of the Farm Security Administration told Raper that "even the poorer Negroes are becoming convinced that they are mistreated here."[68]

Further evidence of black people's determination to secure citizenship occurred in Clarksdale in 1941 at the annual agricultural fair for black people, one of the major cultural events in the African American community. Several prominent white people had asked for a meeting with black leaders during the fair to discuss the reasons for migration. Black people agreed, but demanded that the meeting occur in the newly built city auditorium, the finest public space in Clarksdale, and that they be allowed to parade, two thousand strong, through the streets on the way to the meeting. The white leaders agreed, hoping to give some greater evidence of their interests in retaining black people in the county and in keeping them satisfied. The county agent and president of the state Farm Bureau also attended.[69]

At the meeting, black leaders submitted a sheet listing the various reasons for the migration, including poor education and housing, police brutality, and poor collection of garbage in black communities. But the most provocative discussion occurred around the issue of voting. The editor of a local newspaper and former lieutenant governor, E. D. Schneider, defended the white primary that allowed only white people to vote in the Democratic primary, and the poll tax that restricted black people's voting. Schneider stated that black people in Mississippi would never vote. Black people booed him. An editor of a black newspaper in Little Rock rose and spoke after Schneider. He affirmed without question that black people in Mississippi would soon vote. If necessary, he continued, bloodshed would occur in Mississippi as well as on foreign soil to secure democracy at home. Black people at the meeting insisted that their problems could be resolved by providing their people with better education and political rights.

Schneider's newspaper had featured a page entitled the "Colored Page Messenger," which covered black community affairs, and even used titles when referring to African Americans. After his speech, however, numerous people canceled their subscriptions. Schneider sought unsuccessfully to woo them back by insisting that he was their friend and had only been realistic in his comments. Later, Schneider approached Miss Lucille Rodgers Johnson, an African American supervisor for the northern-sponsored Jeanes Fund schools in the county, explaining to her that he was the black people's best friend. Miss Johnson replied, "Were you worrying about social equality and the like? Now, let's not get things mixed up here. We do want to have our rights, but we don't want to associate with you any more than you want to associate with us."[70]

Young people were also exposed to the increasing demand for equality. School Promotion Day, a major annual event in the Clarksdale black community, brought children to the Agricultural High School from all over the county to celebrate their promotion to the next grade. In 1941, they presented a pageant entitled *Cavalcade of Freedom* that described the African American struggle for freedom in American history. The play was based on materials distributed by the liberal Commission on Interracial

Cooperation in Atlanta. While we cannot know exactly how this play affected the students, one might imagine that exposure to African American history influenced some of them, who in turn may have shared these ideas when they returned to their rural homes and communities. In fact, the presence of the commission's materials in the school indicated that at least one teacher, and probably more, sought to instill more awareness in the students of black history and the black political struggle.[71]

In 1944, another investigator found in that same county that "ideas about 'rights' are being introduced in a few instances to Negro sharecroppers through Negro preachers and their educated white and Negro friends." He also noted that the STFU had used preachers in its organizing campaigns and thus had received some of the blame for increasing this awareness. This observation illustrated further the importance of the STFU during the war years in raising rural people's consciousness.[72]

Unlike during the previous world war, then, there were increasing demands in the Delta during World War II for black citizenship that included the right to vote. The differences between the black demands in the two wars centered on the changes that had occurred following World War I, not the least of which was the emergence of the NAACP's legal battles against disfranchisement and Jim Crow, and for civil rights. Its support for the men accused of murder in the Elaine Massacre signaled a determination to fight Jim Crow justice. And the NAACP's success in dismantling the southern white Democratic primary in 1944, in *Smith v. Allwright,* provided the legal justification for black people to register and vote. Unlike during World War I, black people now looked to the U.S. Supreme Court for support in their emerging civil rights movement. And they also drew strength from the network of civil rights organizations, including the STFU and the CIO, that had emerged in the late 1930s and early 1940s and whose goals partly centered on reinstating the vote for African Americans. In short, the national and international context had shifted, and black people in the Delta moved with the changing political terrain. Further, returning veterans, as they had in the first war, came home with a renewed determination to secure their rights.

The struggle for the vote in the Delta involved the traditional linkages of organizations in the towns to those in the countryside. As we have seen throughout the first half of the twentieth century, through fraternal and religious organizations and through family networks rural peoples were connected to the towns, and vice versa. And the membership of these organizations often cut across class lines. Thus, members of fraternal and religious organizations, as well as the NAACP, were not solely from the middle and professional classes. These connections shaped the voting rights struggles. And, as during World War I, returning veterans returned to their towns and plantations, and linked up with their families and these organizations to once again fight for their rights.

In 1940, W. H. Flowers, a young lawyer in Pine Bluff, formed one of the most important organizations, the Committee on Negro Organizations (CNO). Flowers claimed that a "blackout of democracy" existed in Arkansas. He proposed the creation of an independent mass political organization that aimed to "revolutionize the thinking of people of Arkansas." Its purpose was to provide an organization to serve the "social, civic, political and economic needs of the people." The CNO demanded that black people secure their rights in government in order to fight "un-American activities . . . enslaving the Negro people," and to devise a "system of protest" to end these actions.

The platform called for equalization of school facilities, teachers' salaries, and graduate education; for the appointment of black people to state and local policymaking boards; for better housing, jobs, and health services; for equal opportunities in wartime industries and the armed services; for a fair allocation of farm benefits to include sharecroppers and tenant farmers; for equal facilities for black people; and for the vote. The cornerstone of the CNO sought to "secure widespread, organized political participation."[73]

The CNO's platform included goals for both town and rural people, and Flowers took his platform on the road, speaking to black community organizations all over the state. In 1940, he held his first statewide "Meeting on Negro Organization" in a black landowning FSA community located in Lakeview, Arkansas. Phillips County officials sought to prevent the meeting (Lakeview was only a few miles from Elaine), but Flowers prevailed. By the end of the year, he had held sixteen mass meetings with four thousand people attending.

His organization filed claims against relief agencies for discrimination, secured the appointment of a black census enumerator in St. Francis County, and launched a massive political education campaign that encouraged black people to pay their poll taxes. Flowers's organization helped lay the groundwork, preparing black people for the lengthy struggle for the vote. By 1948, he had built the Pine Bluff NAACP into an organization with 4,382 members, an indication that the war had produced a long-term commitment to winning equality and justice.[74]

Returning black veterans also formed organizations to win the vote.[75] In Little Rock, veteran Charles Bussey organized the Veterans Good Government Association, and Jeff Hawkins, also a veteran, formed the East End Civic League. These organizations, combined with the NAACP, linked up with rural churches and organized voting rights groups. Mrs. Annie Mae Bankhead, who lived on a plantation outside of Little Rock, illustrated how these organizations affected political life on the plantations. Until the war years, she recalled, black people on plantations could buy their poll taxes, but they were not permitted to vote.[76] This changed during World War II, however, when "somebody had this dream that things was gonna change. And they began—you could begin to hear it in the churches around in the little meetings where blacks met, that this organization called the NAACP was working on the government in the demand that the Negro in the South be allowed to vote." Many people on the plantations now believed that achieving the vote was a possibility and began to organize their neighbors into buying their poll taxes.[77] Bankhead said that veterans organized the campaign: "You see a lot of those black men came back home with no privilege. And they were organizing themselves." Veterans combed the countryside, according to Bankhead, speaking in churches and urging people to buy their poll taxes and prepare to vote.

After hearing the veterans speak during the war years, Bankhead became an organizer. She got the poll tax books and sold the receipts to people on her plantation. She also took her cause to the local ministers in her plantation village, seeking to convince them of the need to discuss politics from their pulpits. Politics was "nothing but good government," she insisted, and "good government started from the church, Jesus started it." She persuaded one preacher to talk about the poll tax, voting, and citizenship, and then he convinced the other two preachers in the area to do the same.[78]

In 1940, J. R. Robinson of the Arkansas Negro Democratic Association unsuccessfully petitioned the state Democratic Party to open the white primary to black voters.[79] Several black people challenged the white primary again in the 1942 elections in Pine Bluff, Little Rock, and Conway.[80] In 1944, once the U.S. Supreme Court had declared the white primary illegal, black people increasingly went to the polls. In Pine Bluff, five hundred black people voted in the 1947 Democratic primary, out of a total vote of 2,767. Many came to the polls with an NAACP-endorsed list of candidates attached to their poll receipts. All but one of the candidates whom black people supported won.[81]

Black people in Mississippi also organized a Progressive Voters League to urge people to vote. Many tried to vote in the 1942 election, but were turned away. The state election officials also forbade the counting of absentee ballots cast by the state's black soldiers, even though Congress had passed a measure legalizing the soldier's vote. The most violent confrontation came when black people sought to test the Supreme Court decision in the *Allwright* case by voting in the 1946 election. As in Arkansas, returning veterans led the campaign urging black people to the polls. The most widely known attempt to vote was when Medgar Evers led returning veterans down the streets of his hometown of Decatur to vote in the 1946 primary against Mississippi's renowned racist senator Theodore Bilbo. Turned away from the polls by a mob, the men returned with their guns, yet they were still refused the vote. Similar incidents occurred all over the state during the election as black people, sometimes violently, were refused the vote. People were whipped and beaten; one man was even killed.[82]

Many black voters blamed the incendiary speeches of Senator Theodore Bilbo for the violence surrounding the 1946 elections. Bilbo had insisted that white people should resort to any means necessary to prevent black people from voting. "You and I know what's the best way to keep the nigger from voting. You do it the night before the election."[83] Planter Walter Sillers, Jr., Speaker of the State House of Representatives, said that in his home county of Bolivar, white people had been posted at every poll to challenge black voters.[84] In response to the violent election, fifty Mississippians, including some white people, filed a complaint with the U.S. Senate Committee to Investigate Campaign Expenditures, claiming that Bilbo had subjected black people to a reign of terror. The NAACP and the Progressive Voters League, with chapters in several towns and cities, including some in the Delta, led in the effort to secure an investigation. A committee that included other southern senators held hearings in Jackson. At least two hundred black people from all over the state, including members of the middle class, farm workers, and laborers, came to tell their stories of intimidation. The committee ruled in favor of Bilbo, arguing that he had neither incited the violence nor prohibited black people from voting. Yet black people's participation in the election of 1946 in Mississippi, as well as in the earlier ones in Arkansas, signaled that black people intended to vote, and unlike during the previous war, they would engage in the struggle until their right was acknowledged.[85]

Delta black people also directly challenged Jim Crow during and after the war. They filed legal suits, staged boycotts, and openly defied the customs of segregation. In Warren, Arkansas, black people launched a boy-cott in 1941 against the Pastime theater to protest police brutality. Officer Jess Crawford had kicked Mrs. O. Z. Jackson, a well-known member of the Mount Carmel Baptist Church, when she refused to wait in an alley until all of the white patrons had bought their tickets. Mrs. Jackson's husband, a member of the NAACP, contacted Flowers and the CNO to orga-nize the boycott. Flowers announced, "These ruthless and heathen of-ficers should not be tolerated."[86]

Public transportation became a site for challenging segregation. For those who had sent their family members to serve in the fight against fas-cism, and for the veterans themselves, the humiliation of sitting in Jim Crow seats on the trains and buses no longer seemed tolerable. A mail car-rier in Pine Bluff, Mr. Potts, received a beating and a fine of twenty-five dollars for riding in the white section of a bus on his way to work.[87] In Winona, Mississippi, twenty-six-year-old Turner E. Brown was whipped for refusing to say "yes sir" to a bus driver on the Tri-State bus line.[88] Trav-elers from outside the South also challenged the Jim Crow practices in transportation. Two white men, one a soldier and another an Arkansas cit-izen, refused to sit in the white section of a train as it entered Arkansas.[89] Like black people all over the South, African Americans in the Delta in-creasingly refused to submit to the practice of white supremacy.

Black people challenged these affronts to human dignity with legal ac-tion. In Mississippi, Mrs. Eva Williams Turner filed a civil liberties suit against the Tri-State Bus Company for being thrown off a bus when she refused to sit in the Jim Crow section. Reverend Harry Bartie filed a simi-lar suit for $10,000 against the bus company after a ticket agent had beaten him up when he asked for information regarding a bus schedule. Another minister, W. H. Blackman, sought $11,000 in damages in a case against the Pure Oil Company and its manager of a gas station in Mount Olive, Mississippi. The minister had stopped at the station to buy milk for his one-year-old child and the manager had struck him with a wrench. While the result of these cases is unknown, their significance lies in black people taking legal action against Jim Crow.[90]

Black people also sued law officers who mistreated them. In Crittenden County, notorious for its violence during the 1930s against members of the STFU, seventy-year-old L. A. Millsaps filed a civil liberties suit against the town marshal of West Memphis, a state highway patrolman, the county jailer, and an attorney. The lawyer, Cecil B. Nance, had been as-signed to Millsaps when Millsaps was accused of murdering his stepson.

Nance forced him to admit to a murder he did not commit, threatening him with the electric chair. Millsaps was promised a twenty-one-year suspended sentence if he would leave Arkansas and give Nance the deed to his 160-acre farm.[91] In another case, two black men sued a patrolman in West Memphis for beating them.[92] These cases and others illustrated black people's willingness to use the courts in their fight for civil rights.

White southerners who had long beaten and murdered black people without punishment now were more likely to be held accountable for their actions. In Jonesboro, Arkansas, a manager of the Jonesboro Transfer Company, along with his brother and sister, were charged with the shooting of Ralph Donaldson, a black man. In another case, the Circuit Court in Jonesboro awarded $500 in actual and $625 in punitive damages to John Bennett against two white men from Marianna who had beaten him on a highway. And in Mississippi, a white soldier received a three-year sentence for stabbing a black man who had refused to give him fifty cents.[93]

Delta black people also sought to break down the barriers in employment and in government jobs. In St. Francis County, a black woman, Miss Ivory G. Black, had applied to become a census enumerator in the black town of Edmundson. When the state census office denied her application, W. H. Flowers launched a successful campaign to hire Miss Black, as well as other enumerators. Black people, he argued, should take the census in the rural areas where the majority of people were African American.[94] Beauticians in Pine Bluff, too, demanded that the State Board of Cosmetics hire black inspectors for their beauty shops. Several cities and towns, including Pine Bluff, organized chapters of the state Colored Beautician Association.[95]

W. B. Harper in Greenville, Mississippi questioned the advertising of jobs in the local newspaper. Writing in 1947 to the prominent editor, Hodding Carter, Jr., regarding the way the *Delta Democratic Times* referenced every job ad with the precaution "whites only," he noted, "We negroes realize our position and none of us would open ourselves to embarrassment by applying for a job unless it is emphasized that a colored person is wanted. Why keep reminding him," he continued, "that the color of his skin, regardless of those qualifying traits which he might possess, makes all the difference in the world." Harper signed his letter with "yours for a real Democracy."[96]

While black people challenged Jim Crow and white supremacy at home, black soldiers tested their oppression in the military, both during and after their return from service. They actively wrote letters protesting outra-

A War within a War | 221

geous racist statements, particularly those of Mississippi senator Theodore Bilbo claiming that black men made poor soldiers, that they raped white European women, and that they would rape southern women when they returned. Private Reuben C. Smith sent a map to the senator entitled "In the Line of Duty," showing where black soldiers had played a role in the Far East. "Frankly speaking," he wrote, "we soldiers are tired of your lies referring to the 13,000,000 Negroes in the United States. Every time one reads the hometown newspaper there is always some of your dirty remarks stating: 'The negro will not work, he cannot soldier. All he's good for is making trouble.'" If black soldiers were not working, he insisted, "tell me just who in the *Hell* were responsible for the opening of the Old Burma Road and the building of Ledo road. Sixty-five percent of the soldiers were Negroes, and there's a *grave* for every mile."[97]

Another letter entitled "The Voice of the Colored Workers of the Navy Department" told Bilbo that "With glee and irony of mind and heart we write these few lines, to a fanatic person, who ultimately, undoubtedly will become insane. Why are you sitting there worrying your mind as to the progress of the Negro of America . . . is hopelessly beyond our comprehension, knowing within yourself that our race has started on the wheels of progress, nothing but god can stop us." The soldiers admonished Bilbo, "It took the white race 1,944 years to accomplish what you have . . . it only took the negro race in spite of segregation only 85 years to become an outstanding race giving your people more and more competition in every field of labor, industry, commerce, and entertainment. When our boys return it will be time enough for them to whip hell out of the average southerner who remains as backward and ignorant as you appear to be. You are very dense. *May God help you, he is the only one that can.*"[98]

Private A. Burns wrote from a military base in Mississippi, challenging Bilbo's determination to "hold to the color line." In his view, this would have excluded many white men a long time ago. "We negroes are satisfied to stay with our own race and all that we want is to be a citizen of the U.S.A." Burns then defined what he meant by citizenship: "To have the privilege to work as any other citizen to support our families. And who ever are to run this government under which we must live. We should have a right to help select the ones for that purpose." He continued: "We men of color who are giving our all for democracy (not white supremacy) are trying to make this world a better place in which to live. When Hitler and the Axis are defeated and we return to our homes, we pray that our white brothers will at least treat us fair."[99]

Black soldiers who served on military bases in the South protested the police brutality and the segregated practices there. In 1941, at Camp Van Doren, Mississippi, black soldiers "rioted" when the military police killed a black private in Centreville.[100] Others, like soldiers in Camp Shelby, Mississippi, tested the military's segregated policies. In 1945, black soldiers refused to move out of a small block of seats that had been reserved for white personnel in a theater that had been built entirely for black troops. When the military police ordered them to vacate the seats, they refused, forcing the closing of the establishment.[101]

Delta planters worried about the presence of black troops in their region, and about the growing demands for citizenship they heard from black people on their plantations and in their towns. J. W. Bradford, a lawyer and planter who was president of the Yazoo-Mississippi Delta Levee Commission, noted that black people wanted integration, fair treatment in retail stores, and uniform wage scales, all of which required federal laws. In 1943, following an integrated meeting in Greenville, Bradford warned, "We are sitting right under the mouth of a gun. I think we face the worst situation now we have faced since just prior to Reconstruction days." The potential outcome of the growing assertiveness was not in doubt. "We are going in the future," wrote another member, "to get quite close to the time when the darkey will be protected by Federal law in his vote in the South, and we all know what that will mean in Mississippi."[102]

Greenville lawyer Charles W. Wade told Bilbo in 1943 that the "Negro situation in Mississippi is becoming so serious that unless some steps are taken by the government to quiet them, there will be real, and terrible, trouble." He reported that a litany of "disgusting acts," including the incident at Centerville when black soldiers "openly state that they were going to clean out Mississippi," the alleged rape of a white woman by six black soldiers near Camp McCain in Grenada, and "the Federal Government's lack of concern over such conduct together with the recent attempt to convict several persons in a Federal Court in Southern Mississippi because of the lynching of a negro, is causing grave concern among the white population here."

Wade had served two years in the Phillippines, an experience that led him to see the racial problem back home in a broader perspective. "I know that from personal observation," he wrote, "that regardless of what administration controlled newspapers say about how loyal the Filipino is, he hates our white skin, and so does every other yellow and black man, and no amount of kindness and coddling will make them like us." Wade insisted that the "jap side of this war is strictly a race matter, and if you public officials think that it has not had its weight with the black and yellow people in this country, you are just as far behind as you were before Pearl harbor." Wade then observed presciently that "this negro question in the South is not as local as the government wishes to believe. It's going to be a world-wide race movement, and you people who call the turns had better get your ears to the ground if you wish to continue to enjoy the advantages of white supremacy."[103]

While Wade was right about the global nature of the "race" issue, other white southerners drew a different lesson from the global consequences of the war. A prominent citizen of Greenville, Mrs. Betty Carter, wrote to her journalist husband, Hodding, that "the time has come when—while people like those in the Middle East are far down on the social scale from us—we have to decide what we want to do—compete with Egypt and her fellah labor or cooperate? There is no other choice: do we want constantly to be *fighting to keep down* so-called backward races and backward countries or do we want to recognize the inevitable and help them and so at least have their good will and a chance for our own economic betterment in a better world?" Carter insisted, "This applies as much to the Negro problem as to the world problem. The Nazis thought they would petrify things on a slave-master basis. Well, that idea's dead, or ought to be. It's too late for that sort of thing."[104] Both Carters would become outspoken critics of their native South after the war.

Although Carter and Wade came from different sides of the political fence in Greenville, they both saw the increasing link between the emerging freedom struggle at home and the one abroad. Events nearer the Delta also drove home that southern racial practices were now under an international microscope. When François Georges, the Haitian minister of agriculture, was invited to attend a National Agricultural Commission meeting in Biloxi, Mississippi, the local hotels refused him a room once it became apparent that he was not white. The Haitian government launched an official protest.[105]

Black people in the Delta also saw the global dimensions of their struggle for civil rights. Writing from Drew County, Arkansas, in 1942, Reverend A. Reed told the NAACP, "Since all of the darker races of the world are asking what freedom shall they enjoy after the war, and while we the Negro American citizens are still being denied our franchise and since we are taxed without representation, and knowing as we do the heroic struggle you have and are still making," it "has dawned upon my mind that now is the psychological time to organize chapters all up and down this country." The minister and farm worker saw these chapters as important in sending "prepared men to sit around the peace table to fight for the Negro's full franchise after the war is over." Later, in 1950, after the creation of the United Nations and the writing of the Human Rights Charter, Reed wrote to his Congressman, urging him to support civil rights legislation and informing him that "human rights precede all other rights, and there can never be any freedom as long as a majority group directs the individual life of the minority group." Why, he explained, "can't you see that we too are citizens and entitled to all of the rights and privileges of any other citizens of this country?" In addition, as the Cold War heated up in 1950, and the United States became—in the rhetoric of the time—the champion of democracy around the world, Reed wrote to his senator, John McClellan, that "DEMOCRACY in reality must be practiced HERE, before we can SELL the idea to others."[106]

While Reed was the president of his local NAACP chapter, he was also a farm hand and minister. His invocation of the language of human rights and the rhetoric of the Cold War indicated his own awareness, and perhaps the awareness of those who surrounded him on the plantations, that the local freedom struggle that he and others in the Delta were engaged in drew strength from larger forces operating around the world. People like Reed were giving planters a warning: the world had changed and black people aimed to use those changes to secure democracy and citizenship. Planters recognized as much. Walter Sillers, Jr., in a letter to Senator James Eastland in 1950, observed that black people were "well ahead of us" in organizing. "They hold meetings nearly every week throughout the whole Delta counties, and are well organized," he wrote, "and should an emergency arise they know exactly where to go and what to do, while our people are disorganized and would scatter like a covey of flushed quail." Sillers feared that "you can't arouse our folks to the dangers of the situation."[107]

Sillers and his fellow planters also faced challenges from within their ranks. Sargent Willie Jones, a white Mississippian, wrote in a letter to *Yank* magazine, "Until I came into the Army I hated Negroes. It wasn't anything they did to me; I just didn't like them. Since I have been in the ETO [European Theater] I have fought from D-Day to VE-Day with Negro soldiers. I was wounded twice in one foxhole and a Negro saved my life" under heavy fire. "Many Negro soldiers have died on the front for American soldiers who thought Jim Crow was right. So if Germans can have freedom after they have caused so much suffering and destruction, why not let the negro race have what they fought for? I feel that they should, and a lot of southern GIs feel the same way."[108]

Needless to say, Delta planters disagreed with Jones's assessment of black soldiers. But conditions had changed dramatically during and after the war, challenging planter definitions of citizenship. Gone were the days when any American could define citizenship in the racist and discriminatory terms that Oscar Johnston did in 1943. "I subscribe to the theory that full rights of citizenship," he wrote, "including the right to hold public office in the USA, should be limited to white gentiles. I should oppose any move to discriminate against any 'minority group,' but I do not class as discrimination laws and regulations preventing intermarriage between the races or preventing interracial associations which might and usually do lead to breaches of the peace."[109]

Black people in the Delta rejected this white supremacist conception of citizenship. Returning from yet another war, fought with a Jim Crow army to make the world safe for democracy, African Americans had leverage this time around. An emerging Cold War, which led the United States to woo Africa, made the loyalty of African Americans at home all the more important. Escalating mechanization of the rural South signaled the limited future of sharecroppers, even as planters remained dependent on their labor until the 1960s. Meanwhile, a growing grassroots freedom struggle in the South was linked ever more strongly with a national civil rights movement and its organizations, which included the CIO. The coalition of civil rights and labor groups was forcing changes in court decisions, in military policy, in the Democratic Party platform, and finally, in legislation. No Elaine Massacre followed in the wake of World War II, for national and international events had made atrocities of this scale inconceivable immediately after the war. The world of 1945 was vastly different from that of 1919, and the ferocity of African American protest reflected this change.

World War II was the death knell for the American Congo, as it was for western colonial empires. The alluvial empire that had existed in the Arkansas and Mississippi Delta confronted challenges from inside and out over the next two decades. Thousands of rural southerners, black and white, did not return to its debilitating economy. The war had opened up new possibilities in West Coast shipyards, the aerospace industry, and in northern factories. Although many others chose to remain on Delta land, life was not the same as before the war.

With the war over, factories were free to produce tractors. Simultaneously, the search for a mechanical cotton picker that could harvest a high grade of cotton, and for new herbicides to kill the weeds, continued until each was perfected in the late 1950s. In the immediate postwar years, mechanization occurred slowly, ensuring continued need for black labor. But during the 1950s, sharecropping fell precipitously. For example, in Phillips County, Arkansas, the number of tenants fell from 2,994 to 1,060 over the decade. Black people began to work more often as seasonal pickers and choppers, or as tractor drivers. The Mississippi Delta in 1958 harvested 27 percent of its crops with machinery: by 1964 this amount had reached 81 percent.[110] By the 1960s, thousands of Delta black people were living off of federal food relief programs and other forms of welfare, working only in the fall and spring for whatever wages the planters paid.

In the midst of these technological changes, black people, just as during other trying times, continued their battle for justice. They knew that their labor was needed even as the mechanization process evolved, and they continued to fight for justice within the changing plantation economy. Veterans returned home, war weary and world wise, and joined forces with their families who had themselves developed a new political awareness. They used the educational benefits provided for them in the GI Bill to attend college or trade school. Neither they nor their families intended to return to the horrors and injustices of their past labors. Like their counterparts in the postwar liberation struggles occurring throughout Africa and Asia, black southerners launched a movement for their equality that would eventually force the nation, including white southerners, to legislate for their basic civil rights and grant black people the protection of the law. When the Student Non-Violent Coordinating Committee (SNCC) arrived in the Arkansas and Mississippi Delta in the early 1960s, its organizers found that black people continued to confront landowners over questions of wages and access to federal relief, such as the food commodity program, welfare benefits, and agricultural subsidies—as well as over the continued theft of black people's property and police brutality. Both SNCC and CORE workers found that black people carried guns and were not afraid of using them. And they encountered strong women leaders on the plantations and in the nearby towns who provided essential leadership in the civil rights struggle of the 1960s.

Many freedom fighters of the 1960s drew from a long tradition of political struggle that had characterized the alluvial empire from its inception. It was a struggle marked by assertions of human dignity and demands for economic justice. Some, like Mrs. Carrie Dilworth of Gould, Arkansas, had organized during the 1930s and 1940s for the STFU, and lived to participate in the struggle of the 1960s. Others, like Mrs. Fannie Lou Hamer of Sunflower County, Mississippi, drew strength from her mother, who carried a gun to the fields in her lunch bucket to protect herself and her family from planter violence. Still others, like landowning families in Holmes County, Mississippi, used their independence as property owners to support the SNCC workers as they entered their region.[111]

These three life stories are just a few examples of the Delta freedom struggle. Two world wars, the Great Depression, combined with the work of grassroots labor and civil rights organizations and embattled but useful federal programs, had politically strengthened the core of rural black people. This constellation of national and local forces emboldened African Americans to shift from individual efforts to an organized collective struggle, giving birth to the post–World War II civil rights movement. It also linked the liberation of black people to that of former colonial peoples throughout the world. As the nation moved past mid-century, a new era of political struggle and commitment was emerging, one that would fulfill on a national and international scale the kind of citizenship that African Americans at the turn of the century had only glimpsed in the American Congo.

Notes

Introduction

1. William Pickens, "American Congo: Burning of Henry Lowry," *Nation*, March 23, 1921. The Congo has recently been the subject of two excellent books: Adam Hochschild, *King Leopold's Ghost: A Story of Greed, Terror, and Heroism in Colonial Africa* (New York: Houghton Mifflin, 1998), and Sven Lindquist, *Exterminate All the Brutes: One Man's Odyssey into the Heart of Darkness and the Origins of European Genocide* (New York: New Press, 1996).

2. The literature on peasant and worker resistance to colonialism and capitalism is enormous. Any discussion of the subject must begin with Eric Hobsbawm, *Primitive Rebels: Studies in Archaic Forms of Social Movements in the Nineteenth and Twentieth Centuries* (New York: W. W. Norton, 1959), and Eric Wolf, *Peasant Wars in the Twentieth Century* (New York: Harper and Row, 1970). See also the multivolume works of the Freedmen and Southern Society Project at the University of Maryland, beginning with Ira Berlin, Thavolia Glymph, Steven F. Miller, Joseph P. Reidy, Leslie Rowland, and Julie Saville, eds., *Wartime Genesis of Free Labor* (Cambridge: Cambridge University Press, 1990). For works on regions outside of the United States, see Walter Rodney, *The Making of the Guyanese Working People, 1881–1905* (Baltimore: Johns Hopkins University Press, 1981); Frederick Cooper, Thomas C. Holt, and Rebecca J. Scott, *Beyond Slavery: Explorations of Race, Labor, and Citizenship in Postemancipation Societies* (Chapel Hill: University of North Carolina Press, 2000); Ann Laura Stoler, *Capitalism and Confrontation in Sumatra's Plantation Belt, 1870–1979* (New Haven: Yale University Press, 1985); Allen Isaacman, *Cotton Is the Mother of Poverty: Peasants, Work, and Rural Struggle in Colonial Mozambique* (Portsmouth, N.H.: Heinemann, 1996).

3. For an overview of the imperialist era, see Eric Hobsbawm, *The Age of Empire, 1875–1914* (New York: Pantheon, 1987). On the expansion of corporate agriculture into the colonies, see George L. Beckford, *Persistent Poverty:*

Underdevelopment in Plantation Economies in the Third World (New York: Oxford University Press, 1972).

4. Harold D. Woodman, "Postbellum Social Change and Its Effects on Marketing the South's Cotton Crop," *Agricultural History* 56 (January 1982): 215–230. See also Robert F. Brandfon, *Cotton Kingdom of the New South: A History of the Yazoo Mississippi Delta from Reconstruction to the Twentieth Century* (Cambridge, Mass.: Harvard University Press, 1967).

5. For a discussion of this region, see Brandfon, *Cotton Kingdom of the New South;* James C. Cobb, *The Most Southern Place on Earth: The Mississippi Delta and the Roots of Southern Identity* (New York: Oxford University Press, 1992); Jeannie M. Whayne, *A New Plantation South: Land, Labor, and Federal Favor in Twentieth Century Arkansas* (Charlottesville: University of Virginia Press, 1996); John C. Willis, *Forgotten Time: The Yazoo-Mississippi Delta after the Civil War* (Charlottesville: University of Virginia Press, 2000); Harold D. Woodman, "The Reconstruction of the Cotton Plantation in the New South," in Thavolia Glymph and John J. Kushma, eds., *Essays on the Postbellum Southern Economy* (College Station: Texas A&M University Press, 1985); and Woodman, *New South, New Law: The Legal Foundations of Credit and Labor Relations in the Postbellum Agricultural South* (Baton Rouge: Louisiana State University Press, 1995). See also Neil McMillen, *Dark Journey: Black Mississippians in the Age of Jim Crow* (Urbana: University of Illinois Press, 1989), and Leon Litwack, *Trouble in Mind: Black Southerners in the Age of Jim Crow* (New York: Random House, 1998).

6. For a discussion of peonage, see Pete Daniel, *The Shadow of Slavery: Peonage in the South, 1901–1969* (Urbana: University of Illinois Press, 1969). See also Alex Lichtenstein, *Twice the Work of Free Labor: The Political Economy of Convict Labor in the New South* (London: Verso, 1996), and Karen Shapiro, *The Battle against Convict Labor in the Tennessee Coalfields, 1871–1896* (Chapel Hill: University of North Carolina Press, 1998).

7. Harold D. Woodman, "Post–Civil War Southern Agriculture and the Law," *Agricultural History* 53 (January 1979): 319–335.

8. I am drawing on the distinction made by Antonio Gramsci between state (or political) and civil society. According to Gramsci, civil society is composed of the educational, religious, and associational institutions, while the state, or political society, consists of the courts, legislatures, and elections. In bourgeois democracies, the latter are theoretically separate from the former. Gramsci argued that the elaborate structure of liberal democracy–elections, legislatures, courts–created a facade of popular control and participation and served as the means through which the bourgeoisie obtained the consent to govern. In the plantation South, however, planters removed African Americans from political society. Moreover, they collapsed state and civil society, for the same people controlled both. See Joseph V. Femia, *Gramsci's Political Thought: Hegemony, Consciousness, and the Revolutionary Process* (London: Oxford University Press, 1987), pp. 26–29, and Antonio Gramsci, *Selections*

from Prison Notebooks, ed. and trans. Quintin Hoare and Geoffrey Nowell Smith (New York: Monthly Review Press, 1971), pp. 206–278. See also Jean L. Cohen and Andrew Arato, *Civil Society and Political Theory* (Cambridge, Mass.: MIT Press, 1994). The finest application of Gramsci's work to explaining a society's specific historical development remains Eugene Genovese's masterful *Roll, Jordan, Roll: The World the Slaves Made* (New York: Pantheon, 1972).

9. On lynching in the South, see Fitzhugh Brundage, *Lynching in the New South: Georgia and Virginia, 1880–1930* (Urbana: University of Illinois Press, 1993); for the postcards of lynchings, see James Allen, *Without Sanctuary: Lynching Photography in America* (Santa Fe: Twin Palms, 2000). For the development of segregation and disfranchisement, see C. Vann Woodward, *Origins of the New South, 1877–1914* (Baton Rouge: Louisiana State University Press, 1951); and John W. Cell, *The Highest Stage of White Supremacy: The Origins of Segregation in South Africa and the American South* (Cambridge: Cambridge University Press, 1982). On planter hegemony, see Genovese, *Roll, Jordan, Roll* and *The World the Slaveholders Made: Two Essays in Interpretation* (New York: Pantheon, 1969). For a discussion of planter hegemony in the New South, see Stanley B. Greenberg's excellent *Race and State in Capitalist Development: Comparative Perspectives* (New Haven: Yale University Press, 1980).

10. Charles M. Payne, *I've Got the Light of Freedom: The Organizing Tradition and the Mississippi Freedom Struggle* (Berkeley: University of California Press, 1995), p. 405.

11. Cooper et al., *Beyond Slavery;* Barbara J. Fields, *Slavery and Freedom on the Middle Ground: Maryland during the Nineteenth Century* (New Haven: Yale University Press, 1985); Lawrence N. Powell, *New Masters: Northern Planters during the Civil War and Reconstruction* (New Haven: Yale University Press, 1980); Joseph P. Reidy, *From Slavery to Agrarian Capitalism in the Cotton Plantation South, Central Georgia, 1800–1880* (Chapel Hill: University of North Carolina Press, 1992); Julie Saville, *The Work of Reconstruction: From Slave to Wage Laborer in South Carolina, 1860–1870* (Cambridge: Cambridge University Press, 1994).

12. For a discussion of black women's participation in political struggles and in defining citizenship, see Elsa Barkley Brown, "Negotiating and Transforming the Public Sphere: African American Political Life in the Transition from Slavery to Freedom," *Public Culture* 7 (Fall 1994): 107–146; Rebecca Scott, "Fault Lines, Color Lines, and Party Lines," in Cooper et al., *Beyond Slavery;* Leslie A. Scwhalm, *A Hard Fight for We: Women's Transition from Slavery to Freedom in South Carolina* (Urbana: University of Illinois Press, 1997); and the forthcoming work of Thavolia Glymph on slave and free women.

13. Resistance literature has become a field unto itself. The concept of resistance, however, weakens the actual nature of black peoples' struggles. African Americans, at least in the Delta, were actively engaged in fighting for their

rights and challenging their oppression, often violently. For an example of this literature, see James C. Scott, *Domination and the Arts of Resistance* (New Haven: Yale University Press, 1990).

14. Eric Foner, *Nothing but Freedom: Emancipation and Its Legacy* (Baton Rouge: Louisiana State University Press, 1983).

15. John Dittmer, *Local People: The Struggle for Civil Rights in Mississippi* (Urbana: University of Illinois Press, 1994), Chana Kai Lee, *For Freedom's Sake: The Life of Fannie Lou Hamer* (Urbana: University of Illinois Press, 1999); Payne, *I've Got the Light of Freedom;* Youth of the Rural Organizing and Cultural Center, *Minds Stayed on Freedom: The Civil Rights Struggle in the Rural South* (Boulder, Colo.: Westview Press, 1991). See also Aldon Morris, *The Origins of the Civil Rights Movement: Black Communities Organizing for Change* (New York: Free Press, 1984); and Greta deJong, *A Different Day: African American Struggles for Justice in Rural Louisiana, 1900–1970* (Chapel Hill: University of North Carolina Press, 2002).

1. The Forging of the Alluvial Empire

1. Eric Hobsbawm, *The Age of Capital, 1848–1875* (New York: Pantheon, 1975); Immanuel Wallerstein, *The Modern World-System II: Mercantilism and the Consolidation of the European World-Economy, 1600–1750* (London: Academic Press, 1980); Robert L. Brandfon, *Cotton Kingdom of the New South: A History of the Yazoo Mississippi Delta from Reconstruction to the Twentieth Century* (Cambridge, Mass.: Harvard University Press, 1967); George L. Beckford, *Persistent Poverty: Underdevelopment in Plantation Economies of the Third World* (New York: Oxford University Press, 1972).

2. For a discussion of the New South economy, see C. Vann Woodward, *Origins of the New South, 1877–1914* (Baton Rouge: Louisiana State University Press, 1951); Gavin Wright, *Old South, New South: Revolutions in the Southern Economy since the Civil War* (New York: Basic Books, 1986). On the coal fields in Alabama and Tennessee, see Daniel L. Letwin, *Interracial Unionism: Alabama Coal Miners, 1878–1921* (Chapel Hill: University of North Carolina Press, 1998), and Karen A. Shapiro, *A New South Rebellion: The Battle against Convict Labor in the Tennessee Coalfields, 1871–1896* (Chapel Hill: University of North Carolina Press, 1998); on the growth of the textile industry, see David Carleton, *Mill and Town in South Carolina, 1880–1920* (Baton Rouge: Louisiana State University Press, 1982).

3. The counties lying wholly within the Yazoo Delta are Bolivar, Coahoma, Humphreys, Issaquena, Leflore, Quitman, Sharkey, Sunflower, Tunica, and Washington. Other counties situated partially in the Yazoo Delta include Carroll, Holmes, Panola, Tallahatchie, Warren, and Yazoo. The Arkansas counties defined as the Delta plantation region include Chicot, Crittenden, Desha, Lee, Phillips, and Mississippi, and portions of Arkansas, Ashley, Craighead, Cross, Drew, Jefferson, Lincoln, Lonoke, Monroe, Poinsett,

Pulaski, St. Francis, and Woodruff. See E. L. Langsford and B. H. Thibodeaux, *Plantation Organization and Operation in the Yazoo-Mississippi Delta Area*, Bureau of Agricultural Economics, Technical Bulletin no. 682 (Washington, D.C.: U.S. Department of Agriculture, 1939), and E. G. Nourse, "A Preliminary Survey of Land Tenure in Arkansas," *University of Arkansas Bulletin* 13 (August 1919). Lumber companies and plantations also grew along the Louisiana side of the river.

4. Brandfon, *Cotton Kingdom of the New South;* Jeannie M. Whayne, *A New Plantation South: Land, Labor, and Federal Favor in Twentieth Century Arkansas* (Charlottesville: University of Virginia Press, 1996); John Willis, "On the New South Frontier: Life in the Yazoo-Mississippi Delta, 1865–1920," Ph.D. diss., University of Virginia, 1991, pp. 121–126.

5. *Southern Lumberman,* December 12, 1906, p. 13, and July 12, 1912, pp. 43–46 (hereafter cited as *SL*).

6. *SL,* November 1, 1901, pp. 10–11, and December 25, 1904, p. 54.

7. Deanna Snowden, ed., *Mississippi County, Arkansas: Appreciating the Past and Anticipating the Future* (Little Rock, Ark.: August House, 1986), pp. 47, 50; "Robert E. Lee Wilson," *Delta Historical Review* (Spring 1998): 1–4.

8. Snowden, *Mississippi County,* p. 47.

9. Ibid.

10. Ibid., p. 46.

11. Ibid., pp. 50, 68.

12. Dan A. Rudd and Theo. Bond, *From Slavery to Wealth: The Life of Scott Bond: the Rewards of Honesty, Industry, Economy, and Perseverance* (Madison, Ark.: Journal Publishing, 1917), pp. 32–49, 52–60.

13. Ibid., pp. 126–139.

14. Steven Reich, "The Making of a Southern Sawmill World: Race, Class, and Rural Transformation in the Piney Woods of East Texas, 1830–1930," Ph.D. diss., Northwestern University, December 1998. Many thanks to the author for providing me with a copy of his dissertation. See also John C. Willis, *Forgotten Time: The Yazoo-Mississippi Delta after the Civil War* (Charlottesville: University of Virginia Press, 2000).

15. Corliss Curry, "Early Timber Operations in Southeastern Arkansas," *Arkansas Historical Quarterly* 19 (Summer 1960): 111–118; *SL,* February 1, 1902, p. 5; September 20, 1913, p. 36; and May 15, 1902, p. 8.

16. *SL,* October 12, 1911, p. 34, and October 26, 1912, p. 28; Whayne, *New Plantation South,* pp. 86–112; Nourse, "Preliminary Survey," p. 17.

17. *SL,* December 25, 1905, p. 46; "The Choctaw Lumber Company: An Illustrated History," *SL,* May 2, 1908, pp. 1, 32–34.

18. Reich, "Making of a Southern Sawmill World"; Whayne, *New Plantation South.*

19. *SL,* February 22, 1908, p. 39.

20. Ibid., August 30, 1913, p. 36.

21. Ibid., November 9, 1907, pp. 31–32.

22. Ibid., March 25, 1905, p. 19; May 14, 1912, p. 29; and August 31, 1919, p. 32.

23. J. A. Fox, *Garden Spot of the Mississippi Valley* (St. Louis: Barnes-Crosby Company, 1902), p. 29.

24. *SL,* December 23, 1916, p. 31.

25. Ibid., July 7, 1917, p. 23.

26. Quoted in James C. Cobb, *The Most Southern Place on Earth: The Mississippi Delta and the Roots of Southern Identity* (New York: Oxford University Press, 1992), p. 98.

27. The Southern Alluvial Land Association, *The Call of the Alluvial Empire: Containing Authentic Information about the Alluvial Region of the Lower Mississippi Valley, Particularly the States of Arkansas, Tennessee, Mississippi, and Louisiana* (Memphis: Hood, 1919), p. 5. See earlier versions; for example, *The Call of the Alluvial Empire: Facts about the Alluvial Region of Arkansas, Mississippi, and Louisiana* (Memphis: Hood, 1917).

28. Ibid., pp. 5, 7, and 15.

29. Ibid., p. 17.

30. Ibid., p. 9.

31. Ibid., p. 29.

32. Ibid., p. 31.

33. Woodward, *Origins of the New South;* Paul M. Gaston, *The New South Creed: A Study in Southern Mythmaking* (New York: Random House, 1970); Barbara Jeanne Fields, "The Advent of Capitalist Relations: The New South in a Bourgeois World," in Thavolia Glymph and John J. Kushma, eds., *Essays on the Postbellum Southern Economy* (College Station: Texas A&M University Press, 1985), pp. 73–94; Harold D. Woodman, "The Reconstruction of the Cotton Plantation in the New South," in Glymph and Kushma, *Essays,* pp. 95–119; Woodman, *New South—New Law: The Legal Foundations of Credit and Labor Relations in the Postbellum Agricultural South* (Baton Rouge: Louisiana State University Press, 1995); and James C. Cobb, "Beyond Planters and Industrialists: A New Perspective on the New South," *Journal of Southern History* (February 1988): 45–68. For a discussion of yet another selling of the South, see James C. Cobb, *The Selling of the South: The Southern Crusade for Industrial Development, 1936–1980* (Baton Rouge: Louisiana State University Press, 1982); and Wright, *Old South, New South.* One of the finest discussions of southern progressivism remains Jack Temple Kirby, *Darkness at the Dawning: Race and Reform in the Progressive South* (Philadelphia: Temple University Press, 1972).

34. Willis, *Forgotten Time,* pp. 50–54.

35. Ibid., p. 188.

36. Ibid., pp. 128–129.

37. Ibid., pp. 129–144.

38. Ibid., pp. 1–4, 114–173. Steven Reich has made a similar argument for the

decline of black landownership in the Piney Woods of East Texas. In 1910, Reich found that blacks owned 40 percent of the land in 1910, with rates as high as 55 percent in some counties in 1900 and to around 80 percent in 1910. See Reich, "Making of a Southern Sawmill World," pp. 73–74.

39. M. A. Crosby, "The Present Status of Farm Management Work in Alabama and Mississippi," January 9, 1915, and Crosby, "Report on Delta Farms," January 13, 1914, RG 83, Bureau of Agricultural Economics (BAE), entry 133, National Archives, Washington, D.C. in James B. Grossman, ed., *Black Workers in the Era of the Great Migration* (Frederick, Md.: University Publications of America, 1985), microfilm, reel 22.

40. Barton W. Currie, "Sky High Cotton as Raised on a Huge Plantation," *Country Gentleman,* February 10, 1917, pp. 10–11.

41. Ibid.

42. Ibid.

43. Howard A. Turner, "The Bledsoe Plantation," November 10, 1913, RG 83, BAE, entry 133, in Grossman, *Black Workers in the Era of the Great Migration,* reel 22.

44. Gene Day, "A 40,000-Acre Cotton Farm," *Country Gentleman,* August 1, 1914, p. 1322.

45. Ibid.

46. Howard A. Turner, "Mississippi Delta Planting Company," November 14, 1913.

47. Ibid.; Harold D. Woodman, "Post–Civil War Southern Agriculture and the Law," *Agricultural History* 53 (January 1979): 319–335.

48. Turner, "Mississippi Delta Planting Company."

49. Currie, "Sky High Cotton," p. 243.

50. Ibid.

51. Turner, "Mississippi Delta Planting Company"; Howard A. Turner, "An Account of Runnymede Plantation, Leflore County, Mississippi, January 11, 1916," RG 83, BAE, entry 133, in Grossman, *Black Workers in the Era of the Great Migration,* reel 22.

52. Turner, "Mississippi Delta Planting Company."

53. Ibid.

54. Crosby, "The Present Status of Farm Management Work in Alabama and Mississippi," and Crosby, "Report on Delta Farms."

55. Turner, "Account of Runnymede Plantation."

56. Howard A. Turner, "Dunleith Plantation," January 17, 1916, RG 83, BAE, entry 133, in Grossman, *Black Workers in the Era of the Great Migration,* reel 22, and ibid.

57. Turner, "Account of Runnymede Plantation."

58. "Labor Management on Some Plantations in the Yazoo-Mississippi Delta," January 17, 1916, in Grossman, *Black Workers in the Era of the Great Migration,* reel 22; Turner, "Dunleith Plantation."

59. Thirteenth U.S. Census (1910).

60. E. A. Boeger and E. A. Goldenweiser, *A Study of the Tenant System of Farming in the Yazoo-Mississippi Delta* (Washington, D.C.: U.S. Department of Agriculture, bulletin 337, January 13, 1916), pp. 1, 8, 10.

61. The new plantation region of the early twentieth century included some former slaveholding counties such as Arkansas, Chicot, Desha, Jefferson, LaFayette, and Union. Because of the vast drainage programs, however, the largest plantation section entailing also the highest percentages of tenancy and African Americans encompassed those counties that lay along the banks and bottoms of the Arkansas, Mississippi, and White rivers in northeastern and southeastern Arkansas.

62. Nourse, "Preliminary Survey," p. 47.

63. Thirteenth and Fourteenth U.S. Censuses (1910, 1920).

64. Ibid.

65. Nourse, "Premliminary Survey," p. 47.

66. Ibid., p. 59.

67. Ibid., p. 61.

68. Barton W. Currie, "The Backbone of America: Farming in the Drainage District of Arkansas," *Country Gentleman*, February 6, 1915, pp. 218–219.

69. Alfred Holt Stone, "A Plantation Experiment," in *Studies in the American Race Problem* (New York: Double Day and Page, 1908).

70. E. Richardson, "Tentative History of Mississippi Delta," p. 20, RG83, BAE, Land Tenure section, project files, box 18, National Archives, Washington, D.C.; and Willard B. Gatewood, "Sunnyside: The Evolution of an Arkansas Plantation, 1840–1945," *Arkansas Historical Quarterly* 50 (Spring 1991): 22. See also Pete Daniel, *The Shadow of Slavery: Peonage in the South, 1901–1969* (Urbana: University of Illinois Press, 1969); and Alex Lichtenstein, *Twice the Work of Free Labor: The Political Economy of Convict Labor in the New South* (London: Verso, 1996).

71. A. C. Hervey to Attorney General, February 14, 1911, US Department of Justice, Mail and Files division (hereafter cited as Justice Dept. Mail), file 155735, in *The Peonage Files of the U.S. Department of Justice,* Pete Daniel, ed. (Frederick, Md.: University Publications of America, 1989), microfilm, reel 13.

72. Petition Signed by Fourteen Families in Marked Tree, Arkansas, in William G. Whipple to Attorney General, May 23, 1912, Justice Dept. Mail, file 161148, reel 13.

73. Arthur Stahl to George W. Wickersham, May 10, 1912, file 162055; William H. Martin to Attorney General, March 13, 1914, file 170912; and A. G. Woodson to George W. Wickersham, October 10, 1911, file 158823, all in Justice Dept. Mail, reel 13.

74. W. H. Dunblazier to Attorney General, May 13, 1915, Justice Dept. Mail, file 176183, reel 13.

75. J. Bernstorff to Philander C. Knox, April 3, 1909, Justice Dept. Mail, file 1485-44-2, reel 13.

76. "The Meaning of Peonage," *Colliers,* July 24, 1909, Justice Dept. Mail, file 9787-03-5, reel 13.

77. William G. Whipple to William Wallace, Jr., January 13, 1914, Justice Dept. Mail, file 111884-9, reel 13.

78. J. H. Miller to Justice Department, March 13, 1909, Justice Dept. Mail, file 9787-03-2, reel 13.

79. Pete Daniel, "Commentary," *Arkansas Historical Quarterly* 50 (Spring 1991): 90–92.

2. Tensions of Empire

1. Frederick Cooper, *Decolonization and African Society: The Labor Question in French and British Africa* (Cambridge: Cambridge University Press, 1996), p. 29. For a discussion of African American intellectuals and the larger black Atlantic world, see Winston James, *Holding Aloft the Banner of Ethiopia: Caribbean Radicalism in Early Twentieth Century America* (New York: Verso Press, 1998), and Robin D. G. Kelly, "'But a Local Phase of a World Problem': Black History's Global Vision, 1883–1950," *Journal of American History* 86(December 1999): 1045–1077.

2. Quoted in the *Dallas Express,* August 11, 1917, in *The Tuskegee Institute News Clipping Files,* John W. Kitchens, ed. (Ann Arbor, Mich.: University Microfilm Incorporated, 1976), 6:0532 (hereafter cited as TCF).

3. James C. Cobb, *The Most Southern Place on Earth: The Mississippi Delta and the Roots of Southern Identity* (New York: Oxford University Press, 1992), p. 115.

4. Peter Gottlieb, *Making Their Own Way: Southern Blacks' Migration to Pittsburgh, 1916–1930* (Urbana: University of Illinois Press, 1987); James Grossman, *Land of Hope: Chicago, Black Southerners, and the Great Migration* (Chicago: University of Chicago Press, 1989); Joe William Trotter, *Black Milwaukee: The Making of an Industrial Proletariat, 1915–45* (Urbana: University of Illinois Press, 1985); Neil McMillen, *Dark Journey: Black Mississippians in the Age of Jim Crow* (Urbana: University of Illinois Press, 1989). See also U.S. Department of Labor, Division of Negro Economics, *Negro Migration in 1916–1917* (Washington, D.C.: U.S. Department of Labor, 1919); Emmett J. Scott, "Letters of Negro Migrants, 1916–1918," *Journal of Negro History* 4 (July 1919): 290–340; Scott, "Additional Letters of Negro Migrants, 1916–1918," *Journal of Negro History* 4 (October 1919): 412–475.

5. Charles S. Johnson, "Migration Study: Mississippi Summary," 1917, National Urban League Papers, ser. 6, box 86, Manuscripts Division, Library of Congress, Washington, D.C.

6. For a discussion of the evolution of sharecropping laws and contracts, see Harold D. Woodman, *New South, New Law: The Legal Foundations of Credit and Labor Relations in the Postbellum Agricultural South* (Baton Rouge: Louisiana State University Press, 1995).

7. Johnson, "Mississippi Summary."

8. *Sunflower (Miss.) Tocsin,* November 9, 1916.

9. *Baltimore Afro American,* January 26, 1918, TCF, 6:0594.

10. Johnson, "Mississippi Summary."

11. Ibid.

12. Gilbert Fite, *Cotton Fields No More: Southern Agriculture, 1865–1980* (Lexington: University of Kentucky Press, 1984), pp. 94–95.

13. Johnson, "Mississippi Summary."

14. G. B. Ewing to Arkansas State Council of Defense, October 23, 1918, Arkansas Council of Defense Papers, located in the Arkansas History Commission, Little Rock, Ark., hereafter cited as ACD.

15. Minutes of the Arkansas State Council of Defense, January 21, 1918, ACD.

16. G. B. Ewing to Arkansas Council of Defense, October 23, 1918, ACD.

17. Henry Snowden Stabler, "Draining the South of Labor," *Country Gentleman,* September 8, 1917, p. 1372.

18. Johnson, "Mississippi Summary."

19. Minutes of the Arkansas State Council of Defense, January 21, 1918, RG 62, U.S. Council of National Defense Papers, State Councils, General Correspondence, box 692, Washington National Records Center, Suitland, Md.; Johnson, "Mississippi Summary"; *Leland (Miss.) Enterprise,* June 15, 1919. For another discussion of changing consumptive patterns among Delta black people, see Ted Ownby, *American Dreams in Mississippi: Consumers, Poverty, and Culture* (Chapel Hill: University of North Carolina Press, 1999).

20. "Arkansas Cotton Belt's Prosperity Brings Autos to Negro Tenants," *St. Louis (Mo.) Star,* November 16, 1917, TCF, 4:1015.

21. For the creation of wartime agencies, see David M. Kennedy, *Over Here: The First World War and American Society* (New York: Oxford University Press, 1980). For a discussion of the liberal state during this time, see Alan Dawley, *Struggles for Justice: Social Responsibility and the Liberal State* (Cambridge, Mass.: Harvard University Press, 1991).

22. Arthur H. Fleming to Several Southern State Councils of Defense, "Organization of Negroes," July 24, 1918, RG 62, Council of National Defense Papers, Field Division, Winterbotham Correspondence, 15-QA, box 859.

23. W. H. Smith to W. E. Gifford, June 27, 1917, RG 62, Council of National Defense Papers, State Councils, box 665.

24. States Relations Service memorandum to County Agents, August 2, 1918, RG 16, U.S. Secretary of Agriculture Papers, Accession 234, drawer 267, National Archives, Washington, D.C.

25. Captain N. M. Cartmell, who was in charge of recruiting for the district of Arkansas, said that the draft quota for Arkansas between April 1, 1917, and June 30, 1917, was 3,000, but only 719 had reported for registration. Arkansas State Council of Defense Memorandum, n.d., RG 62, Council of National Defense Papers, State Councils, box 692. See also E. H. Crowder to

Charles H. Brough, November 6, 1917, RG 163, U.S. Selective Service System, 1917–1919, State Files, Arkansas, box 86, Washington National Records Center, Suitland, Md. (hereafter cited as SSS).

26. C. H. Brough to E. H. Crowder, November 2, 1917, RG 163, SSS, 1917–1919, State Files, Arkansas, box 88.

27. J. W. Johnson to E. H. Crowder, November 8, 1918, RG 163, SSS, State Files, Arkansas, box 89.

28. *Memphis (Tenn.) Commercial Appeal,* June 6, 1917.

29. J. P. Burks to Lloyd England, July 28 and August 23, 1918, RG 163, SSS, State Files, Arkansas, box 86.

30. T. S. Frazier, "Report of Inspection Made of State Headquarters, Little Rock, Arkansas, September 28, 1918, RG 163, SSS, State Files, Arkansas, box 86; *Helena (Ark.) World,* October 3, 1917. Gerald Schenk found that Georgia planters actually denied draft information to their tenants, allowing the planters to then collect the bounty. I did not find evidence of this in the Delta, but that does not mean that it did not happen. See Gerald Schenk, "Race, Manhood, and Manpower: Mobilizing Rural Georgia for World War I," *Georgia Historical Quarterly* 81, no. 3 (Fall 1997): 632–633.

31. My discussion of the southern draft is drawn from the fine essay by Jeanette Keith, "The Politics of Southern Draft Resistance, 1917–1918: Class, Race, and Conscription in the Rural South," *Journal of American History* 87 (March 2001): 1335–1361.

32. Ibid., p. 1346.

33. Quoted in ibid., p. 1350.

34. The 1910 census had listed the number of men of twenty years of age as 28 percent in Arkansas and 55 percent in Mississippi. *(Little Rock) Arkansas Gazette,* August 18, 1917.

35. LeRoy Percy to B. B. Humphreys, May 26, 1917, Percy Family Papers, box 9, Mississippi Department of Archives and History, Jackson, Miss.

36. E. H. Crowder to Charles H. Brough, September 9, 1917, RG 163, SSS, State Files, Arkansas, box 89.

37. E. H. Crowder to Lloyd England, December 29, 1917, and England to Crowder, January 5, 1918, RG 163, SSS, State Files, Arkansas, box 89.

38. E. H. Crowder to Lloyd England, September 14, 1917, RG 163, SSS, State Files, Arkansas, box 88; E. H. Crowder to Lloyd England, December 29, 1917, and England to Crowder, January 5, 1918, RG 163, SSS, State Files, Arkansas, box 89.

39. James W. Maynard, "Alleged Irregularities in the District Exemption Board for South Mississippi," June 3, 1918, RG 163, SSS, State Files, Mississippi, box 176.

40. Senator Thaddeus H. Caraway to President Woodrow Wilson, September 28, 1917, and Dr. O. Howton to War Department, September 28, 1917; both in RG 163, SSS, State Files, Arkansas, boxes 88 and 86, respectively.

For numerous instances of planters attempting to secure exemptions for family members, see James W. Maynard, "Alleged Irregularities in the District Exemption Board for Southern Mississippi," June 2, 1918, ibid.

41. L. G. Dean, et al. to E. H. Crowder, February 18, 1918, RG 163, SSS, State Files, Arkansas, box 177.

42. John Sharp Williams to Woodrow Wilson, October 28, 1918, and E. D. Cavett to Williams, October 19, 1918, RG 163, SSS, Mississippi, box 178. The review board saw it differently, finding that Graham had been duly advised by "reputable whites" to register and had willfully defied the law. Brigadier General Eric Scales to U.S. Adjutant General, November 7, 1918, RG 163, SSS, Mississippi, box 178.

43. Quoted in Keith, "Politics of Southern Draft Resistance," p. 1351.

44. G. B. Ewing to Arkansas State Council of Defense, October 3, 1918, ACD. For concerns about allotments in Mississippi, see A. M. Pepper to E. H. Crowder, August 15, 1918, RG 163, SSS, State Files, Mississippi, box 178; for Arkansas, see J. E. Stevenson to E. H. Crowder, August 15, 1917, SSS, State Files, Arkansas, box 88. See also Fon Louise Gordon, *Caste and Class: The Black Experience in Arkansas, 1880–1920* (Athens: University of Georgia Press, 1995), pp. 121–138; Randy Finley, "Black Arkansans and World War One," *Arkansas Historical Quarterly* 49 (Autumn 1990): 249–277; and Emmett J. Scott, "Letters of Negro Migrants of 1916–1918," *Journal of Negro History* 4 (October 1919): 412–475.

45. For a discussion of the black middle class and bourgeois uplift, see Kevin Gaines, *Uplifting the Race: Black Leadership, Politics, and Culture in the Twentieth Century* (Chapel Hill: University of North Carolina Press, 1996). On Du Bois and his closed ranks article in the *Crisis,* see Mark Ellis, "'Closing Ranks' and 'Seeking Honors': W. E. B. Du Bois in World War I," *Journal of American History* 79 (June 1992): 96–124. For a discussion on India, see Hugh Tinker, "India in the First World War and After," *Journal of Contemporary History* 3(1968): 89–107.

46. P. L. Dorman to Reverend A. J. Rooks, September 2, 1918, ACD.

47. Charles E. Sullenger to Wallace Townsend, October 2, 1918, ACD; R. B. Keating to Wallace Townsend, June 6, 1918, ACD; Arkansas State Council of Defense Minutes, September 2, 1918, RG 62, Council of National Defense Papers, Field Division, box 857.

48. *Sunflower (Miss.) Tocsin,* January 29, 1919.

49. Ibid., April 8, 1918.

50. *Leland (Miss.) Enterprise,* May 4, 1918.

51. Ibid., May 25, 1918.

52. Ibid., May 25 and November 2, 1918.

53. *Sunflower (Miss.) Tocsin,* November 1, 1917.

54. Ibid., October 25, 1917.

55. Edwin Bevens to Lloyd England, October 11, 1918, ACD.

56. *Helena (Ark.) World,* August 30, 1917. Another large organization, the

Royal Circle of Friends, also endorsed the war. *Arkansas Gazette*, September 4, 1917.

57. *Sunflower (Miss.) Tocsin*, November 22, 1917.

58. *Arkansas Gazette*, August 4, 1917.

59. John Roland, "Cotton Hands That Stay: How Some Mississippi Plantation Owners Hold Their Renters and Croppers," *Country Gentleman*, December 22, 1917, pp. 4–5.

60. Ibid., pp. 21–22.

61. Ibid.

62. *Memphis Commercial Appeal*, August 22, 1917, the *Hampton University Peabody Newspaper Clipping File* (Alexandria, Va.: Chadwyck-Healy, 1987), item 229.

63. Johnson, "Mississippi Summary"; *Sunflower (Miss.) Tocsin*, January 24, 1918.

64. *Sunflower (Miss.) Tocsin*, May 2, 1918.

65. Jack Wilson to John R. Shillady, April 11, 1919, NAACP Papers, group 1, box C2. The NAACP Papers are located in the Library of Congress Manuscripts Division, Washington, D.C.

66. *Pittsburgh Courier*, March 22, 1919, NAACP Papers, group 1, box C373.

67. A. N. Meeks to Wallace Townsend, July 31, 1918, ADC.

68. John R. Shillady to Woodrow Wilson, September 25, 1918, RG 174, U.S. Department of Labor Papers, Chief Clerk's Files, box 18, file 8\102-E, National Archives, Washington, D.C.

69. W. R. Smith to Lloyd England, March 26, 1918, ACD.

70. A. B. Fairfield to Arkansas State Council of Defense, June 8, 1918; K. G. Morley to Wallace Townsend, October 31 and November 4, 1918, folders 57, 240, ACD.

71. H. O. Pate to Arthur H. Fleming, September 19, 1918; Fleming to Pate, September 24, 1918, RG 62, Council of National Defense Papers, State Councils, Arkansas, box 721.

72. *St. Louis (Mo.) Post* to Secretary of Labor W. B. Wilson, October 4, 1918, RG 174, U.S. Department of Labor Papers, box 139, file 129\14B; *Sunflower (Miss.) Tocsin*, May 9, 1918.

73. *Sunflower (Miss.) Tocsin*, July 11, 1918.

74. *SL*, July 27, 1918, p. 27.

75. L. L. Cantrell to Wallace Townsend, October 8, 1918, ACD.

76. Lloyd England to Chairmen, County Councils of Defense, August 13, 1918, ACD.

77. Minutes, Arkansas State Council of Defense, January 2, 1918, ACD.

78. *Helena (Ark.) World*, August 30, 1917.

79. Arkansas State Council of Defense Circular Letter no. 23, February 16, 1918, ACD; C. T. Carpenter to Lloyd England, July 25, 1917, ACD.

80. *Leland (Miss.) Enterprise*, June 29, 1918.

81. *New Orleans (La.) Times-Picayune*, n.d., TCF, 5:4540.

82. Lloyd England to County Councils of Defense, n.d., ACD.

83. J. B. Densmore to W. B. Wilson, May 29, 1918, RG 174, U.S. Department of Labor Papers, 1907–1942, box 139.

84. U.S. Employment Service Bulletin, May 17, 1918, ibid.

85. R. A. Nelson to State Council of Defense, October 9, 1918; Theo Rectin to U.S. Commissioner of Agriculture, October 21, 1918; A. B. Fairfield to Wallace Townsend, December 13, 1918, all in ACD.

86. *Helena (Ark.) World,* June 5, 1918.

87. Ibid., October 16, 1917.

88. Major W. H. Loving to the Chief, Military Morale Section, September 27, 1918, RG 165, Secretary of War Papers, Office of Chief of Staff, Military Intelligence Division, in Theodore Kornweibel, ed., *Federal Surveillance of Afro-Americans, 1916–1925* (Bethesda, Md.: University Publications of America, 1986), reel 22.

89. Colored Boy of the 409th Reserve Labor Battalion to Arkansas State Council of Defense, January 7, 1919, folder 1, ADC.

90. McMillen, *Dark Journey,* pp. 314–315.

91. See applications for charters in NAACP Papers, group 1, ser. G, Branch Files, 1913–1939, boxes 11–12. For inquiries, see Scott Bond to John R. Shillady, June 4, 1919, box G12; R. D. Mitchell to NAACP, August 3, 1921, box G11; and Robert E. Jones to Dr. E. C. Morris, 1915, group 1, ser. C, Administrative Files, 1906–1940, box 1.

92. For a discussion of Du Bois's positions on the war and for his criticism of the treatment of returning soldiers, see Elliot Rudwick, "W. E. B. Du Bois: Protagonist of the Afro-American Protest," in John Hope Franklin and August Meier, eds., *Black Leaders of the Twentieth Century* (Urbana: University of Illinois Press, 1982).

93. W. E. B. Du Bois, "We Should Worry," *Crisis* (June 1917); "The Black Man in the Great War," *Crisis* (June 1919).

94. D. Whipple to A. M. Briggs, July 5, 1917, RG 65, Department of Justice Papers, Bureau of Investigations, in Kornweibel, *Federal Surveillance of Afro-Americans,* reel 19.

95. P. L. Dorman to State Council of Defense, December 31, 1918, ACD.

96. *Leland (Miss.) Enterprise,* September 6, 1919.

97. Captain F. Sullens, Memo to Major Brown, November 30, 1918, RG 65, Department of Justice, Bureau of Investigation, in Kornweibel, *Federal Surveillance of Afro-Americans,* reel 22. Military regulations made it illegal to prevent any honorably discharged soldier from wearing his uniform for up to three months after discharge. *War Department Bulletin* no. 16, June 22, 1916, p. 83. I am grateful to John Slonaker, Chief Reference Historian, U.S. Army Military History Institute, Carlisle, Pa., for finding this reference for me.

98. Quoted in McMillen, *Dark Journey,* p. 306.

99. *Mobile (Ala.) Register,* May 28, 1919, TCF, 10:0381; *New Orleans (La.) Times-Picayune,* June 18, 1919, TCF, 10:0381.

100. *SL*, August 5, August 23, and October 18, 1919.

101. *Memphis Commercial Appeal*, August 24, 1919, TCF, 9:0898.

102. *Jackson Daily News*, August 30, 1919, and unidentified clipping, TCF, 9:0921.

103. Ibid.

104. *Chicago Defender*, September 27, 1919, TCF, 9:0895.

105. *Birmingham (Ala.) Reporter*, September 20, 1919, TCF, 9:0900.

106. *New York Age*, June 14, 1919, TCF, 9:0936.

107. A White Son of Mississippi to the *Crisis*, March 18, 1919, NAACP, group 1, Box C2.

108. *Chicago Whip*, September 13, 1919; "Asks Governor if He Approves of Murder," NAACP Press Release, NAACP, group 1, box C350.

109. For the numerous lynchings in both Arkansas and Mississippi, see NAACP Papers, group 1, boxes C349, C350, C360, and C389. See also McMillen, *Dark Journey* and Todd E. Lewis, "Mob Justice in the 'American Congo': Judge Lynch in Arkansas during the Decade after World War I," *Arkansas Historical Quarterly* 52 (Summer 1993): 156–184.

110. *New Orleans (La.) Times-Picayune*, June 18, 1919, TCF, 10: 0382.

3. The Killing Fields

1. For a discussion of the postwar years, see Eric Hobsbawm, *Age of Extremes: A History of the World, 1914–1991* (New York: Pantheon, 1994); Charles S. Maier, *Recasting Bourgeois Europe: Stabilization in France, Germany, and Italy in the Decade after World War I* (Princeton, N.J.: Princeton University Press, 1975); and Barrington Moore, Jr., *Injustice: The Social Bases of Obedience and Revolt* (White Plains, N.Y.: M. E. Sharpe, 1978). For a discussion of 1919 in the Atlantic world, see Neil Evans, "Red Summers," *History Today* 51 (February 2001): 28–33; Evans, "Across the Universe: Racial Conflict and the Post-War Crisis in Imperial Britain, 1919–1925," *Immigrant and Minorities* 9 (July 1994); and Philippa Levine, "'Battle Colors': Race, Sex, and Colonial Soldiery in World War I," *Journal of Women's History* 9 (Winter 1998).

2. For a discussion of Red Summer, see William M. Tuttle, Jr., *Race Riot: Chicago in the Red Summer of 1919* (New York: Atheneum, 1970); Steven A. Reich, "Soldiers of Democracy: Black Texans and the Fight for Citizenship, 1917–1921," *Journal of American History* 83 (March 1996): 1478–1504.

3. Kieran Taylor, "'We Have Only Just Begun': Black Organizing and White Response in the Arkansas Delta, 1919," *Arkansas Historical Quarterly* 58 (Autumn 1919): 270.

4. Lawrence N. Powell, *New Masters: Northern Planters during the Civil War and Reconstruction* (New Haven: Yale University Press, 1980).

5. The Helena Businessmen's League, "What the Business Men's League Means to Helena, Arkansas," (1913), reprinted in the *Phillips County Historical Quarterly* 28 (Spring 1990): 19. (Hereafter cited as *PCHQ*.)

6. Gerard B. Lambert, *All Out of Step: A Personal Chronicle* (New York: Doubleday, 1956), pp. 73–74.

7. John Thomas Moore, "Collections as Told to Me and How I Saw It," *PCHQ* 35 (Spring 1997): 5–24. See also E. M. Allen, "The Story of Elaine, Arkansas," pp. 30–32; Mary L. Demoret Jones, "Elaine, Arkansas," pp. 33–37; and Willie Mae Countiss Kyte, "Elaine, Arkansas," pp. 38–51, all in *PCHQ* 34 (Fall 1996).

8. Lambert, *All Out of Step*, pp. 67–68.

9. Ibid.

10. Ibid., pp. 72–79; Jones, "Elaine, Arkansas," p. 34.

11. Lambert, *All Out of Step*, pp. 71–72.

12. Manuscript Census for Searcy and Mooney Townships, Fourteenth U.S. Census (1920).

13. *Helena World,* May 20, May 30, August 10, August 17, and November 16, 1917.

14. *SL,* April 27, 1918, p. 22.

15. *Helena World,* July 11 and November 16, 1917.

16. "Memoranda on Tenancy in the Southwestern States," Extracts from the Final Report of the United States Commission on Industrial Relations," quoted in Arthur I. Waskow, *From Race Riot to Sit-In: A Study in the Connections between Conflict and Violence* (New York: Doubleday, 1966), p. 122.

17. Ida B. Wells-Barnett, *The Arkansas Race Riot* (Chicago: Hume Job, 1920), pp. 13–18. I am grateful to Tom Dillard for providing me with a copy of this important source.

18. Harold D. Woodman, *New South, New Law: The Legal Foundations of Credit and Labor Relations in the Postbellum Agricultural South* (Baton Rouge: Louisiana State University Press, 1995), pp. 65–66.

19. Gilbert Fite, *Cotton Fields No More: Southern Agriculture, 1865–1980* (Lexington: University of Kentucky Press, 1984), p. 95. Fite notes that while cotton had reached a high of forty-three cents per pound in the summer of 1919, it had declined to an average of thirty-five cents at harvest time. Local prices varied, however, and the only methods for determining the prices offered in Phillips County are those cited in the contemporary sources.

20. Wells-Barnett, *Arkansas Race Riot,* p. 13. See also U. S. Bratton to David Y. Thomas, September 5, 1921, David Y. Thomas Papers, 1:2, University of Arkansas, Fayetteville, Special Collections.

21. U. S. Bratton to Frank Burke, November 6, 1919, Arthur I. Waskow Papers, State Historical Society of Wisconsin, Madison.

22. This account is based on a court case in Arkansas in 1921. See Woodman, *New South, New Law,* p. 85.

23. George B. Sanger, ed., *The Statutes at Large: Treaties and Proclamations of the United States of America from December 1863 to December 1865,* vol. 13 (Boston, 1866), pp. 535–536.

24. Wells-Barnett, *Arkansas Race Riot,* p. 49.

25. Ibid., pp. 48–49.

26. Most studies of black fraternal associations have focused on their bourgeois nature. See William A. Muraskin, *Middle-Class Blacks in a White Society: Prince Hall Freemasonry in America* (Berkeley: University of California Press, 1975), and Loretta J. Williams, *Black Freemasonry and Middle-Class Realities* (Columbia: University of Missouri Press, 1980). John Michael Giggie discusses the role of lodges in the rural Delta, but his evidence is limited. See Giggie, "God's Long Journey: African Americans, Religion, and History in the Mississippi Delta, 1875–1915," Ph.D. diss., Princeton University, 1997, pp. 54–90. Information regarding black societies in rural areas is extremely difficult to find.

27. This entire account is taken from O. S. Bratton to U. S. Bratton, November 5, 1919, Waskow Papers.

28. Ibid.

29. Ibid.

30. Grif Stockley, *Blood in Their Eyes: The Elaine Race Massacre of 1919* (Fayetteville: University of Arkansas Press, 2001), pp. xxiii; *Helena World,* October 2, 1919, in J. W. Butts Collection, Helena Public Library, Helena, Arkansas; Jeannie Whayne, "Low Villains and Wickedness in High Places: Race and Class in the Elaine Riots," *Arkansas Historical Quarterly* 58 (Autumn 1999): 285–313.

31. On Moore and the cutting of the phone lines, see article, n.d., in TCF, 10:0857. On the Elaine Massacre, see Waskow, *From Race Riot to Sit-In; J. W. Butts and Dorothy James, "The Underlying Causes of the Elaine Race Riot of 1919," *Arkansas Historical Quarterly* 20 (Spring 1961): 95–104; O. A. Rodgers, "The Elaine Riots of 1919," *Arkansas Historical Quarterly* 20 (Spring 1961): 142–150; B. Boren McCool, *Union, Reaction, and Riot: A Biography of a Race Riot* (Memphis: Memphis State University Bureau of Social Research, June 1970); M. Langley Biegert, "Legacy of Resistance: Uncovering the History of Collective Action by Black Agricultural Workers in Central East Arkansas from the 1860s to the 1930s," *Journal of Social History* (Fall 1993): 73–99; Jeannie Whayne, "Low Villains and Wickedness in High Places"; Kieran Taylor, "We Have Just Begun," *Arkansas Historical Quarterly* 58 (Autumn 1999): 265–284. The best accounts of the legal struggles and their implications are Richard C. Cortner, *A Mob Intent on Death: The NAACP and the Arkansas Riot Cases* (Middletown, Conn.: Wesleyan University Press, 1988), and Stockley, *Blood in Their Eyes.* A trusty is a prisoner who has won the trust of officers with his good behavior and is allowed to work outside of the cell in various privileged jobs.

32. Stockley, *Blood in Their Eyes,* pp. 15–16; *Helena World,* October 2, 1919, copy in Butts Collection.

33. L. S. (Sharpe) Dunaway, *What a Preacher Saw through a Key-Hole in Arkansas* (Little Rock, Ark.: Parke-Harper, 1925), pp. 103–104.

34. Clipping, *Memphis Press,* October 4, 1919, Waskow Papers.

35. Bessie Ferguson, "The Elaine Race Riot," master's thesis, George Peabody College for Teachers, August 1927, pp. 83–84. I am grateful to Tom Dillard for providing me with a copy of this important source.

36. Dunaway, *What a Preacher Saw*, pp. 108–109. Unfortunately, Dunaway did not provide a source for his figures of the death toll. But I agree with lawyer Grif Stockley that Dunaway had no reason to lie, especially since he accepted the planters' and the Army's interpretation that black people had staged an insurrection. See Stockley, *Blood in Their Eyes*, pp. 36–37.

37. Lambert, *All Out of Step*, p. 76.

38. Ibid., p. 77.

39. Ibid., p. 75.

40. Ibid., p. 78.

41. Mr. Glass's niece, Mrs. Ruth Jackson, kindly related this account and also provided me with a photograph of her uncle. She could not recall how Glass's daughter got home from Elaine. Interview with Mrs. Ruth Jackson, October 23, 1998, Snow Lake, Arkansas.

42. *Helena World*, October 3, 1919, typescript in Butts Collection.

43. Ibid. In a handwritten note on the transcript, Butts wrote that D. A. Keeshaw, an undertaker, had said that bullets from James Meyer's gun had actually killed Lilly.

44. Reverend A. H. Miller, *How I Succeeded in My Business* (n.d., n.p.). Dr. Robert Miller, mayor of Helena, Arkansas, kindly provided me with a copy of his grandfather's memoir.

45. Cortner, *Mob Intent on Death*, p. 86.

46. Grif Stockley provides the best account of these trials. See Stockley, *Blood in Their Eyes*, pp. 106–137, and *Helena World*, November 5–6, 1919, in Butts Collection.

47. Waskow, *From Race Riot to Sit-In*, pp. 135–136; Stockley, *Blood in Their Eyes*, pp. 62–63.

48. Stockley, *Blood in Their Eyes*, pp. 64–65.

49. *Helena World*, October 2 and October 5, 1919, transcript in Butts Collection.

50. Stockley, *Blood in Their Eyes*, p. 65.

51. Grif Stockley argues that Brough "rolled over" to support the Committee of Seven in its efforts to publicize its narrative of events. He supposedly secured from these men a pledge that no black people would be lynched. Stockley, *Blood in Their Eyes*, pp. 77–78.

52. This entire account is taken from the *Helena World*, October 6–7, 1919.

53. Ibid.

54. It is entirely possible that the sharecroppers knew of Lane's program, for the Southern Alluvial Land Association supported and publicized the program all over the Delta. Engineers in charge of land reclamation had claimed that 7,000 acres of cut-over land existed in the Arkansas and Mississippi Delta and insisted these lands be used for the veteran land program. See *SL*, November

16, 1918, p. 23; November 23, 1918, p. 26; and December 21, 1918, p. 24. See also Anne Wintermute Lane and Louise Herrick Wall, eds., *The Letters of Franklin K. Lane: Personal and Political* (Boston: Houghton Mifflin, 1922), pp. 285–290.

55. This view was also reflected in the press and in the government reports that were written. For quotes, see *Helena World,* October 2–7, 1919.

56. *Arkansas Gazette,* October 8, 1919, TCF, 10:0653.

57. Harry Anderson to Charles H. Brough, October 7, 1919, box 4:55, Brough Papers, University of Arkansas, Fayetteville.

58. Walter White, "Massacring Blacks in Arkansas," *Nation,* December 6, 1919, pp. 715–716; White, "The Race Conflict in Arkansas," *Survey* 43 (1919): 233–234, and "The Real Causes of Two Race Riots," *Crisis* 19 (December 1919): 56–62. See also Monroe N. Work to John R. Shillady, April 19, 1920, NAACP mss., Waskow Papers.

59. E. M. Allen to David Y. Thomas, January 4, 1920, Thomas Papers, 1:2.

60. For a discussion of the Cotton Association's meeting, see Fite, *Cotton Fields No More,* p. 95. Some of those attending recommended that farmers place their cotton gradually on the market to prevent lowering high wartime cotton prices. Despite this advice, farmers planted a large crop in 1920, beginning a decade of overproduction and low prices. The authors of the union's literature may have confused the drive for controlled cotton production with their own efforts to market their crops at decent prices, though their use of this conference may never be known. The union members probably also discussed Secretary Lane's proposal to aid returning soldiers in securing cheap farmland and houses.

61. Wells-Barnett, *Arkansas Race Riot,* pp. 8, 9, 11. Actually, cotton sold for forty-three cents in June 1919, and had declined to thirty-five cents by harvest time, though local prices fluctuated. See Fite, *Cotton Fields No More,* p. 95.

62. Wells-Barnett, *Arkansas Race Riot,* pp. 13–14.

63. Ibid., p. 14.

64. Ibid., pp. 15–16.

65. Ibid., pp. 16–18.

66. Ibid., pp. 20–21.

67. Stockley, *Blood in Their Eyes,* and especially Cortner, *Mob Intent on Death,* pp. 84–200. Evidence suggests that many Arkansas officials and leading citizens wanted the cases dismissed. Most telling was the action of Arkansas Attorney General J. S. Utley, who simply filed a demurrer when Frank Moore's lawyers, Scipio A. Jones and E. L. McHaney, filed a writ of habeus corpus with the Arkansas federal courts—thereby effectively accepting the new evidence of Jones and Smiddy and their account of events at Elaine (p. 131).

68. *Moore v. Dempsey* U.S. 595 (1923), pp. 87–88.

69. Ibid., pp. 88–89.

70. Ibid., pp. 92–95.

71. Ibid., pp. 95–99.

72. "The Real Causes of Two Race Riots," p. 61; U. S. Bratton to Walter White, January 11, 1923, Waskow Papers; Storey cited in *Pittsburgh Courier,* June 30, 1923, TCF, 19:0727.

73. Mrs. Ruth Jackson, interview with the author, October 23, 1998, Snow Lake, Arkansas; I visited John Morrow in a nursing home in Helena in October of 1998. Unfortunately he was dying of cancer, though he still tried to talk to me. Thus, I could only gather secondhand accounts from friends with whom he had spoken, such as Reverend C. B. Bingham and Freddie Lee Hollywood. I interviewed Dr. Robert Miller on several occasions in Helena in 1998 and 1999. He became the first African American mayor of Helena, Arkansas, in 1998.

74. Mrs. Gladys Hammond, interview with the author, October 31, 1998, Elaine, Arkansas. I am grateful to Nashid Madyun for arranging this interview. Stella Seals, interview with the author, Wilson, Arkansas, October 1998.

75. Capt. Guy G. Bratton to U. S. Bratton, November 16, 1919, Waskow Papers, and "Oblige to Uncle Sam," November 14, 1919, RG 60, General Records of the Department of Justice, Straight Numerical Files, 1904–37, box 1284, National Archives, College Park, Md. I am grateful to Greta deJong for finding and providing me with this letter.

76. Wells-Barnett, *Arkansas Race Riot,* pp. 19–20.

77. Ibid., p. 20.

78. Cortner, *Mob Intent on Death,* pp. 197–199.

79. Ibid., pp. 107–109.

80. *Helena World,* October 3, 1919, transcript in Butts Collection.

81. Ibid., October 6, 1919. For a discussion of Fannie Lou Hamer, see Chana Kai Lee, *For Freedom's Sake: The Life of Fannie Lou Hamer* (Urbana: University of Illinois Press, 1999), p. 11. Black revolutionary Robert F. Williams always credited his grandmother, who carried a gun, for shaping his political views, especially those regarding armed self-defense. See Timothy B. Tyson, *Radio Free Dixie: Robert F. Williams and the Roots of Black Power* (Chapel Hill: University of North Carolina Press, 1999), p. 164. See also Greta deJong, *A Different Day: The African American Freedom Struggle and the Transformation of Rural Louisiana, 1900–1970* (Chapel Hill: University of North Carolina Press, 2002). For the role of black women in struggles on the plantations, see Rebecca J. Scott, "Fault Lines, Color Lines, and Party Lines: Race, Labor, and Collective Action in Louisiana and Cuba, 1862–1912," in Frederick Cooper, Thomas C. Holt, and Rebecca J. Scott, *Beyond Slavery: Explorations of Race, Labor, and Citizenship in Postemancipation Societies* (Chapel Hill: University of North Carolina Press, 2000), pp. 61–106. For black women's role in struggles during the era of emancipation, see Leslie Schwalm, *A Hard Fight for We: Women's Transition from Slavery to Freedom in South Carolina* (Urbana: University of Illinois Press, 1997), and the forthcoming work of Thavolia Glymph on slave and free women.

82. *New York City Call*, January 26, 1920, for union account; also *New York Globe*, January 23, 1920; *Montgomery (Ala.) Advertiser*, January 22, 1920; *Boston Herald*, January 22, 1920, all in TCF, 12:04559. For the military report, see Major Robert Q. Poag to Director of Military Intelligence, January 22, 1920, RG 60, Department of Justice Papers, Glasser Files, Kornweibel, *Federal Surveillance of Afro-Americans*, reel 16.

83. Cortner, *Mob Intent on Death*, p. 15.

84. Neil McMillen, *Dark Journey: Black Mississippians in the Age of Jim Crow* (Urbana: University of Illinois Press, 1989), p. 174.

85. *Atlanta Constitution*, February 22, 1920; *Chicago Defender*, April 14, 1920, TCF 12:0406. An account of the Vick murder also appeared in the *St. Louis Daily Journal*, February 6, 1920, TCF 12:0406.

86. For an example of a leading lodge member who belonged to the NAACP and had attended the association's antilynching convention, see W. L. Purifoy to John R. Shillday, May 21, 1919, NAACP Papers, group 1, box C3. For the role that churches and fraternal orders played in the Great Migration, see James Grossman, *Land of Hope: Chicago, Black Southerners, and the Great Migration* (Chicago: University of Chicago Press, 1989), p. 92.

87. F. W. Lynch, "Negro Activities throughout the South—Arkansas," December 31, 1920, RG 165, Department of War, General and Special Staffs, Military Intelligence Division, in Kornweibel, *Surveillance of Afro-Americans*, reel 19.

88. C. T. Schade to Department of Justice, October 4, 1919, RG 60, Department of Justice Papers, in Kornweibel, *Surveillance of Afro-Americans*, reel 12.

89. Fred S. Dunn, "Report Made at Little Rock, for Period June 3–10, 1921," RG 60, Department of Justice Papers, General Intelligence Division, 158260-1-27, as cited in Waskow Papers.

4. The Black People's Burden

1. Lucy Oliver, interview with the author, June 26–27, 1998, Wilson, Arkansas. I am indebted to Stella Seals for introducing me to Mrs. Oliver, who was born in 1902. Mrs. Oliver's parents had been slaves on the Craighead plantation, which Craig eventually purchased. Her grandfathers had both fought in the Civil War and had received land for their service. She spent her entire life as a sharecropper on Craig's plantation, watching the ownership change several times, though when I interviewed her, she had moved into an apartment with her grandchildren. Her brother married Lowry's daughter. Mrs. Oliver died a few months after the interview.

2. Ibid.

3. Ibid.; William Pickens, "The American Congo: Burning of Henry Lowry," *Nation*, March 23, 1921, in NAACP Papers, group 1, box C350.

4. Black people running for their lives commonly used turpentine to mask their scent from tracking dogs.

5. L. W. Washington to William Pickens, January 26, 1921, NAACP Papers, group 1, box C350.

6. Interview with Lucy Oliver; Pickens, "American Congo."

7. William Pickens's Arkansas Report, n.d., and W. A. Singfield to Pickens, February 2, 1921, NAACP Papers, group 1, box C350. For a discussion of peonage in the 1920s, see Pete Daniel, *The Shadow of Slavery: Peonage in the South, 1901–1969* (Urbana: University of Illinois Press, 1969).

8. Pickens, "American Congo."

9. Interview with Mrs. Lucy Oliver.

10. Ibid. The *Memphis Press* reported, "As the gasoline was poured over his chest and head the negro cried out some appeal of one of the many negro lodges of which he was a member." See January 27, 1921, in NAACP Papers, group 1, box C350. Based on the archival evidence, it seems that fraternal lodges played a major role in black political activity and consciousness in the Delta. But I have not found any further evidence of their local proceedings. The title of thirty-third-degree Mason was conferred on those individuals who were seen as having strong leadership qualities. "The peculiar duty of their mission is to teach and enlighten the brethren; to preserve charity, union, and fraternal love among them; to maintain regularity in the works of each degree, and to take care that it is preserved by others; to cause the dogmas, doctrines, institutes, constitutions, statutes, and regulations of the Order to be reverently regarded, and to preserve and defend them on every occasion; and, finally, everywhere to occupy themselves in works of peace and mercy." See Albert Gallatin Mackey, *An Encyclopedia of Freemasonry and Its Kindred Sciences* (Philadelphia: L. H. Everts, 1884), p. 702.

11. *Memphis Commercial Appeal,* January 28, 1921, and clipping from an unnamed Savannah, Georgia, newspaper, January 27, 1921, in NAACP Papers, group 1, box C350.

12. *Memphis Press,* January 27, 1921, in NAACP Papers, group 1, box C350.

13. Interview with Mrs. Lucy Oliver.

14. For changes in southern agriculture in the 1920s, see Gilbert Fite, *Cotton Fields No More: Southern Agriculture, 1865–1980* (Lexington: University of Kentucky Press, 1984), pp. 102, 120; Jack Temple Kirby, *Rural Worlds Lost: The American South, 1920–1960* (Baton Rouge: Louisiana State University Press, 1987); Pete Daniel, *Breaking the Land: The Transformation of Cotton, Tobacco, and Rice Cultures since 1880* (Urbana: University of Illinois Press, 1985); and Daniel, *Deep'n as It Come: The 1927 Mississippi River Flood* (New York: Oxford University Press, 1977).

15. Fourteenth and Fifteenth U.S. Censuses, 1920 and 1930.

16. See Robert A. Hill, *The Marcus Garvey and Universal Negro Improvement Association Papers* (Berkeley: University of California Press, 1987), vol. 7, pp. 986–987 and 990–991 for a list of the local chapters. For the earlier emigration movement, see Edwin S. Redkey, *Black Nationalist and Back-to-Africa Movements, 1890–1910* (New Haven: Yale University Press, 1969). Unfortunately, I have been unable to find further information on these chapters.

17. For a discussion of industrial workers and their methods of transmitting news to less educated laborers, see Herbert Gutman's classic essay, "Work, Culture, and Society in Industrializing America, 1815–1918," *American Historical Review* 78 (1973): 531–588. For the various ways that black people obtained and circulated information and news, see James Grossman, *Land of Hope: Chicago, Black Southerners, and the Great Migration* (Chicago: University of Chicago Press, 1989), pp. 92–97.

18. John C. Polk, M.D., J. A. Smith, Reverend J. H. Hammond, and Reverend W. B. Smith to NAACP, February 25, 1922, box C8; for information on antilynching, see Women's Club of Jackson, Tenn., to O. G. Villard, March 16, 1919, box C2, and William H. Harrison to Walter White, January 11, 1928, box G105; for copies of the *Crisis,* see H. G. Broadus to NAACP, October 15, 1928, box G12; for providing information on lynching, see J. W. Thompson to NAACP, February 2, 1927, box G12, Walter Eugene McDaniel to NAACP, September 9, 1921, box C8, A. T. Cunningham to NAACP, December 5, 1925, box G11, and Madison Price to NAACP, August 8, 1927, box G106; all in NAACP Papers, group 1.

19. Mrs. Roberta Johnson to NAACP, May 25, 1921; W. H. Wyatt to NAACP, August 14, 1921, both in NAACP Papers, group 1, box C8; J. F. Griffin to NAACP, October 15, 1922, NAACP Papers, group 1, box C10.

20. Reverend Thomas Jordan to NAACP, August 3, 1922, NAACP Papers, group 1, box C10.

21. Mrs. B. B. Johnson to J. W. Johnson, October 20, 1920, NAACP Papers, group 1, Box C6.

22. Miss Frankella Jackson to Robert Bagnall, 1929; Pickens to Jackson, March 29, 1929; Jackson to Bagnall, April 22, 1929; Jackson to Pickens, April 22, 1929; Jackson to J. W. Johnson, April 29, 1929; Charles Everett Martin to NAACP, June 10, 1931; Lizzie Pruitt to Walter White, June 14, 1931 and May 15, 1933; Reverend J. B. Keys to J. W. Johnson, December 8, 1926; May 24, 1927, all in NAACP Papers, group 1, box G12.

23. Scipio Jones to J. W. Johnson, October 29, 1927, NAACP Papers, group 1, box G12.

24. H. Y. Young to Robert Bagnall, March 23, 1922; W. B. Gloman to NAACP, June 1, 1924, NAACP Papers, group 1, box G13.

25. H. L. Henderson to Mary White Ovington, November 28, 1921, NAACP Papers, group 1, box G11.

26. Ibid.; Henderson to Joel Spingarn, August 26, 1922, NAACP Papers, group 1, box C386.

27. W. B. Coleman to NAACP, June 1, 1924, NAACP Papers, group 1, box G13; Josie Coleman, Letter included in NAACP Press Release, July 8, 1922; J. C. Coleman to NAACP, August 29, 1922; J. C. Coleman to NAACP, November 19, 1922, all in NAACP Papers, group 1, box C386.

28. Joe McHerring to NAACP, December 1, 1921, NAACP Papers, group 1, box G11.

29. Jim Coleman to NAACP, January 1, 1922, in ibid. The Coleman in this letter

and the following ones signed their names in various ways, sometimes as Colmon, others as Coleman.

30. Lucious Holiday to the NAACP, August 11, 1922, NAACP Papers, group 1, box C386.

31. James A. Churchill to Robert Bagnall, February 19, 1927; Miss Mary Williams to NAACP, January 26, 1928, both in ibid.; Affidavit of James Walker, December 9, 1926, Department of Justice, Peonage Files, 50–625, in Pete Daniel, ed., *The Peonage Files of the U.S. Department of Justice, 1901–1945* (Frederick, Md.: University Publications of America, 1989), reel 11.

32. Robert L. McLendon to General Stone, April 11, 1924, and McLendon to Department of Justice, May 4, 1925, in Department of Justice, Peonage Files, 50-632-1; 50-41-3, reel 11.

33. Letter from Arthur Jackson, December 17, 1924, Department of Justice, Peonage Files, 50-40-1, reel 11.

34. Manuel Tellez to Frank B. Kellog, December 4, 1925, Department of Justice, Peonage Files, 50-636, reel 10.

35. *Baltimore Afro-American,* November 27, 1926, TCF, 26:0094; *Chicago Whip,* November 6, 1926, NAACP Papers, group 1, box C387; Reverend B. J. Linden to James Weldon Johnson, April 18, 1921, NAACP Papers, group 1, box C386.

36. Jim Coleman to NAACP, February 2, 1921, and April 17, 1921; Reverend S.J. Bell to Joel Spingarn, April 16, 1921, both in NAACP Papers, group 1, box G11.

37. "In the Matter of Mims Wilson," August 8, 1921, Department of Justice Peonage Files, 50-550, reel 11.

38. J. W. G. Ratterree to U.S. District Attorney, March 19, 1928, Department of Justice, Peonage Files, 50-41-5, reel 11.

39. Robert Harris to James Weldon Johnson, April 11, 1922, NAACP Papers, group 1, box C386.

40. P. M. M. to Department of Justice, December 14, 1925, Department of Justice, Peonage Files, 50-92-1, reel 10.

41. Henry Evans to Department of Justice, April 8, 1921, Department of Justice, Peonage Files, 50-455, reel 10.

42. W. Rodgers to J. W. Johnson, April 2, 1921; Mississippi Peonage 1921, June 3–October 21, 1921, in NAACP Papers, group 1, box C386; *St Louis Independent,* April 8, 1920, TCF, 11:0210.

43. Pete Daniel, *The Shadow of Slavery: Peonage in the South, 1901–1969* (Urbana: University of Illinois Press, 1969), p. 148.

44. Affidavit of Sam Edwards, December 23, 1931, and Nugent Dodds to Secretary of the Treasury, March 15, 1932, Department of Justice, Peonage Files, 50-41-6, reel 11.

45. Calvin R. Ledbetter, Jr., "The Long Struggle to End Convict Leasing in Arkansas," *Arkansas Historical Quarterly* 52 (Spring 1993): 22–27; *Arkansas Gazette,* December 18, 1912; Acts of Arkansas (1913), act 69, sect. 9;

(1939), act 118, sec. 1. I am most grateful to Cary Cox of the Butler Center for Arkansas Studies for providing me with this state law.

46. Report Made by E. B. Hazlett, June 24, 1922, Department of Justice, Peonage Files, 50-611, Memphis file 273, reel 10.

47. Jim Coleman to NAACP, May 19, 1922, in NAACP Papers, group 1, box G11.

48. Reverend W. H. Booker to NAACP, February 2, 1922, NAACP Papers, group 1, box C386.

49. S. B. Argain to Joel Spingarn, June 1, 1921, NAACP Papers, group 1, box C386.

50. *Drew (Miss.) Leader,* September 5, 1924; *Leland (Miss.) Enterprise,* June 30, 1921; *Sunflower (Miss.) Tocsin,* February 23, 1928.

51. *Memphis Commercial Appeal,* September 4, 1925.

52. *Sunflower Tocsin,* March 16, April 6, and November 30, 1922; January 29, 1925; April 29, 1926; February 18, 1926.

53. *New York Call,* May 23, 1921, TCF, 13:0536.

54. Eric Hobsbawm, *The Age of Extremes: A History of the World, 1914–1991* (New York: Pantheon, 1994).

55. *New York Herald,* November 11, 1923, TCF, 18:0036.

56. Fourteenth and Fifteenth U.S. Censuses (1920 and 1930).

57. *Chicago Defender,* June 6, 1919, TCF, 11:0042; *St. Louis Argus,* December 17, 1926, TCF, 25:1020; *Montgomery (Ala.) Advertiser,* April 26, 1921; *Atlanta Constitution,* April 28, 1921, TCF, 14:0856. For a discussion of the Klan and whitecapping in northeastern Arkansas, see Jeannie Whayne, *A New Plantation South: Land, Labor, and Federal Favor in Twentieth Century Arkansas* (Charlottesville: University of Virginia Press, 1996), pp. 47–77.

58. *Cleveland Plain Dealer,* November 20, 1920, TCF, 11:0641; Anonymous to NAACP, January 4, 1921, NAACP Papers, group 1, box C7.

59. *Memphis Commercial Appeal,* November 21, 1921, and *Chicago Whip,* March 19, 1921, TCF, 14:0856; *Memphis Commercial Appeal,* December 28, 1921, TCF, 13:0480; *Norfolk Journal and Guide,* May 23, 1925, *Chicago Defender,* May 2, 1925, and *Baltimore Afro-American,* May 23, 1925, TCF, 23:0380; *Atlanta Constitution,* August 21, 1921, TCF, 13:0536.

60. *Dallas Express,* January 15, 1921, TCF, 13:0444.

61. *Cleveland Plain Dealer,* August 3, 1921, TCF, 13:0479; *St. Louis Argus,* September 2, 1921, *New York Telegram,* July 31, 1921, and *Atlanta Constitution,* June 11, 1921 in TCF, 13:0537; *Memphis Commercial Appeal,* May 23, 1923, TCF, 18:0841; *Memphis Commercial Appeal,* September 17, 1922, TCF, 18:0086; *Memphis Commercial Appeal,* July 30, 1926, TCF, 25:1009; *Chicago Defender,* July 8 and July 22, 1922, TCF, 16:0104.

62. *St. Louis Clarion,* September 28, 1923, TCF, 17:0398.

63. *Kansas City (Mo.) Sun,* July 28, 1923, TCF, 18:0141.

64. *St. Louis Clarion,* August 31, 1923; *Chicago Whip,* August 25, 1923; *Memphis Commercial Appeal,* August 28, 1923, all in TCF, 18:0350.

65. *Memphis Commercial Appeal,* July 10, 1922, TCF, 15:0797; *Memphis Commercial Appeal,* August 14, 1923, TCF, 18:0142.

66. Ibid., September 8, 1920.

67. Lewis, "American Congo," p. 175; Neil McMillen, *Dark Journey: Black Mississippians in the Age of Jim Crow* (Urbana: University of Illinois Press, 1989), pp. 225–253; *Memphis Commercial Appeal,* November 17, 1922, TCF, 15:0793.

68. *Leland (Miss.) Enterprise,* March 12, 1921; *Greenwood (Miss.) Democrat,* March 7, 1921, TCF, 13:0455; *Memphis Commercial Appeal,* August 15, 1925, *Memphis Commercial Appeal,* December 21, 22, 1925, and *Chicago Defender,* February 20, 1926, TCF, 25:0989.

69. *New York Tribune,* November 10, 1922, *Hot Springs Echo,* November 6, 1926, *Chicago Whip,* June 18, 1921, *New York Times,* August 2, 1922, *Brookhaven (Miss.) Leader,* May 25, 1927, and *New York Times,* December 21, 1926, all in NAACP Papers, group 1, boxes C349, 350, C360; *Montgomery (Ala.) Advertiser,* June 18, 1922, TCF, 15:0772; *Helena (Ark.) World,* April 5, 1921, and *Atlanta Constitution,* June 2, 1921, TCF, 13:0455; *Memphis Commercial Appeal,* June 6, 1922, TCF, 15:0765.

70. *New York Times,* December 21, 1926, NAACP Papers, group 1, box C359; *Memphis Commercial Appeal,* January 15, 1926, September 29, 1925, and June 6, 1922, TCF, 15:0765, 25:1008.

71. *Drew (Miss.) Leader,* December 21, 1923. Hamer's account uses the name Joe Pullian, but the newspaper accounts all used the name Pullen. See also Chana Kai Lee, *For Freedom's Sake: The Life of Fannie Lou Hamer* (Urbana: University of Illinois Press, 1999), pp. 16–17.

72. *Chicago Defender,* February 26, 1921, TCF, 13:0444; *Memphis Commercial Appeal,* March 1, 1923, TCF, 17:0339. Regarding the circus event, no newspaper title was listed for the May 22, 1925, clipping in TCF, 24:0583.

73. *New York Age,* June 25, 1927, TCF, 28:0638.

74. Charles S. Bouton to W. F. Callander, April 14, 1923, RG 83, BAE, Grossman, ed., *Afro Americans and the Great Migration,* reel 21; *Cleveland Advocate,* July 31, 1920, TCF, 11:0684.

75. Fourteenth and Fifteenth U.S. Censuses (1920 and 1930).

76. *Cleveland Advocate,* July 31, 1920, TCF, 11:0684.

77. *New Orleans Item,* May 1, 1923, TCF, 18:0730.

78. Fourteenth and Fifteenth U.S. Censuses (1920 and 1930).

79. *Memphis News Scimitar,* January 20, 1920, TCF, 11:0686.

80. *Birmingham (Ala.) Reporter,* June 24, 1920, TCF, 11:0686.

81. *Memphis Commercial Appeal,* December 3, 1922, and *Chicago Defender,* June 26, 1920, TCF, 11:0686.

82. T. J. Woofter, "The Negro on a Strike," *Journal of Social Forces* 2 (November 1923–September 1924): 84–88; *Atlanta Independent,* May 10, 1923, TCF, 18:0650.

83. *Atlanta Independent,* May 10, 1923.

84. *Memphis Commercial Appeal,* May 3, 1923.

85. Herschel Brickell, "Mississippi Is Changing Attitude toward Negroes," *New York Post,* May 22, 1920, TCF, 12:0601.

86. *Chicago Tribune,* September 11, 1923, TCF, 18:0804.

87. Ibid.

88. Director of Publicity to Editor of *Atlantic Monthly,* October 4, 1923, NAACP Papers, group 1, box C373; *St. Louis Argus,* October 26, 1923, TCF, 18:0769.

89. *Memphis Commercial Appeal,* May 6, 1923.

90. Mrs. Walter Sillers, Sr., n.d. (1920s), Walter Sillers, Sr. Papers, box 3, Sillers Family Papers, Roberts Memorial Library, Delta State University, Cleveland, Miss. (hereafter cited as Sillers Papers).

91. *Memphis Commercial Appeal,* September 11, 1923, and October 19, 1923.

92. Ibid.

93. Ibid., October 10, 1923.

94. *Sunflower (Ms.) Tocsin,* September 10, September 24, October 8, and December 10, 1925, and January 21, 1926.

95. *Memphis Commercial Appeal,* February 11, 1923.

96. Ibid., September 21, 1925.

97. Paper title illegible, February 15, 1926, TCF, 25:0599.

98. *Sunflower (Ms.) Tocsin,* July 20, 1922, and July 17, 1924, and *Memphis Commercial Appeal,* July 4, 1925, TCF, 22:0201.

99. *Memphis Commercial Appeal,* October 17, 1923.

100. *Sunflower (Ms.) Tocsin,* August 9, 1923.

101. Ibid., September 11, 1924, and September 17 and December 12, 1925.

102. *Cotton Farmer,* June 6, 1925, TCF, 22:0206.

103. *Manufacturer's Record,* October 25, 1923, pp. 103–106.

104. *Leland (Ms.) Enterprise,* September 24, and October 29, 1921.

105. *Mail and Evening Telegram,* November 12, 1926, TCF, 25:0055.

106. "Enticing Servants," 1926, in Oscar Johnston, General Correspondence, Delta and Pine Land Company Papers, Mitchell Memorial Library, Mississippi State University, Starkville.

107. Edgar Webster to LeRoy Percy, November 15, 1923, Percy Family Papers, box 11, Mississippi Department of Archives and History, Jackson.

108. Walter Sillers, Sr., to Robert Arnold, June 7, 1928, Sillers Papers, box 4.

109. Walter Sillers, Sr., to U.S. Department of Agriculture, April 9, 1926, and Sillers to Governor Frank O. Lowden, November 13, 1925, Sillers Papers, box 3.

110. Walter Sillers, Sr., to *Memphis Commercial Appeal,* n.d., 1920s, Sillers Papers, box 5.

111. John Sharp Williams to Florence W. Sillers, August 24, 1921, and Florence

Sillers Ogden to George McLaurin, May 26, 1923, Florence Sillers Ogden Papers, box 1, Sillers Papers.

5. Revolt against Mean Things

1. The literature on the rural South in the 1930s is vast. Two of the major works are Pete Daniel, *Breaking the Land: The Transformation of Cotton, Tobacco, and Rice Cultures since 1880* (Urbana: University of Illinois Press, 1985); and Jack Temple Kirby, *Rural Worlds Lost: The American South, 1920–1960* (Baton Rouge: Louisiana State University Press, 1987).

2. Daniel, *Breaking the Land,* p. 91; E. A. Boeger and E. A. Goldenweiser, *A Study of the Tenant Systems of Farming in the Yazoo-Mississippi Delta,* (Washington, D.C.: U.S. Department of Agriculture, Bulletin 337, January 13, 1916), p. 1; E. L. Langford and B. H. Thibodeaux, *Plantation and Organization in the Yazoo-Mississippi Delta,* Bureau of Agricultural Economics, Technical Bulletin no. 682 (Washington, D.C.: U.S. Department of Agriculture, 1939), pp. 42, 51; Paul E. Mertz, *New Deal Policy and Southern Rural Poverty* (Baton Rouge: Louisiana State University Press, 1978), p. 11.

3. Pete Daniel, *Deep'n as It Come: The 1927 Mississippi River Flood* (New York: Oxford University Press, 1977); and Nan Elizabeth Woodruff, *As Rare as Rain: Federal Relief in the Great Southern Drought, 1930–31* (Urbana: University of Illinois Press, 1985), p. 115.

4. Woodruff, *As Rare as Rain,* pp. 108, 111, 115, 123, 126.

5. Unsigned letter to NAACP, September 3, 1930; Booker to NAACP, October 11, 1930, NAACP Papers, group 1, box C387.

6. *Arkansas Gazette,* September 11, 1931; *Atlanta Constitution,* September 10, 1931; *Memphis Commercial Appeal,* September 13, 1931; *Montgomery (Ala.) Advertiser,* October 8, 1931; *Chicago Whip,* November 3, 1931; all in TCF, 38:0024. The newspaper reports did not identify the origin or the sponsor of the fliers.

7. Woodruff, *As Rare as Rain,* pp. 56–59, 116–117, 120.

8. *Pittsburgh Courier,* April 9, 1932; *Daily Worker,* April 13, 1932; both in TCF, 41:0273; *Chicago Defender,* February 2, 1931, TCF, 38:152.

9. Lement Harris, *My Tale of Two Worlds* (New York: International Publishers, 1986), pp. 120–128.

10. Harvard Sitkoff, *A New Deal for Blacks: The Emergence of Civil Rights as a National Issue; The Depression Decade* (New York: Oxford University Press, 1978), pp. 46–57.

11. *New York Age,* April 6, 1935, TCF, 49:0940; *Memphis Commercial Appeal,* March 14, 1934, TCF, 47:0052; M. S. Stuart to Roy Wilkins, August 8, 1933, NAACP Papers, group 1, box G106.

12. *Memphis Commercial Appeal,* March 14, 1934, TCF, 47:0052; *(Oklahoma City) Black Dispatch,* February 3, 1934, TCF, 47:0051. See also Roger D.

Tate, "Easing the Burden: The Era of Depression and New Deal in Mississippi," Ph.D. diss., University of Tennessee, 1978.

13. M. S. Stuart to John Ross, January 25, 1934, box G199; Nat Williams et al., WPA, Tunica, Miss., box C386; and Walter White to Harry Hopkins, September 9, 1936, box C386; all in NAACP Papers, group 1.

14. Numerous studies of the AAA exist, but one may begin with Daniel, *Breaking the Land,* pp. 91–109, and David Eugene Conrad, *Forgotten Farmers: The Story of Sharecroppers in the New Deal* (Urbana: University of Illinois Press, 1965).

15. Donald H. Grubbs, *Cry from the Cotton: The Southern Tenant Farmers' Union and the New Deal* (Chapel Hill: University of North Carolina Press, 1971), pp. 19–20.

16. H. L. Mitchell, *Mean Things Happening in This Land: The Life and Times of H. L. Mitchell, Cofounder of the Southern Tenant Farmers' Union* (Montclair, N.J.: Allanheld, Osmun, 1979), pp. 120–121.

17. Ibid., pp. 19–23. See also Conrad, *Forgotten Farmers,* pp. 24–25 for estimates of displacement, and Pete Daniel, *Breaking the Land,* pp. 91–109, 170–171 for planter profits.

18. J. Ross Bell to B. C. Barber, April 30, 1934, box 68; A. V. Dunbar to W. B. Camp, (n.d., 1936), RG145, General Correspondence, 1936–38, Dr. 429–430, Records of the Agricultural Stabilization and Conservation Service, Agricultural Adjustment Administration, National Archives, College Park, Md. (hereafter cited as AAA).

19. Daniel, *Breaking the Land,* pp. 178–179.

20. H. L. Mitchell, *Mean Things Happening,* pp. 35–36.

21. "1934 Leaflet Program," STFU Papers, box 1, located in the Southern Historical Collection, University of North Carolina, Chapel Hill (hereafter cited as STFU Papers); Grubbs, *Cry from the Cotton,* 42; Mitchell, *Mean Things Happening,* pp. 46–47.

22. Grubbs, *Cry from the Cotton,* p. 63.

23. For a discussion of these southern white radicals, see Anthony P. Dunbar, *Against the Grain: Southern Radicals and Prophets, 1929–1959* (Charlottesville: University of Virginia Press, 1981).

24. Grubbs, *Cry from The Cotton,* pp. 29–61.

25. Ibid., pp. 42–43.

26. Ibid., pp. 8, 29–61.

27. Mitchell, *Mean Things Happening,* pp. 82–84, 125, 136–137, 182.

28. Ibid., pp. 47–48.

29. Grubbs, *Cry from the Cotton,* pp. 67–68.

30. Fourteenth and Fifteenth U.S. Censuses (1920 and 1930).

31. Sue Thrasher and Leah Wise, "The Southern Tenant Farmers' Union," *Southern Exposure* 1 (Winter 1974): 7, 19.

32. Grubbs, *Cry from the Cotton,* p. 68.

33. Jeannie Whayne, *A New Plantation South: Land, Labor, and Federal Favor in Twentieth Century Arkansas* (Charlottesville: University of Virginia Press, 1996), pp. 184–218.

34. Thrasher and Wise, "Southern Tenant Farmers' Union," pp. 7, 19.

35. On African American religion see Eugene Genovese, *Roll, Jordan, Roll;* and on southern white religion, see Samuel S. Hill, *Religion and the Solid South* (Nashville: Abingdon Press, 1972). For earlier attempts at interracial unionism in the South, see Daniel L. Letwin, *Interracial Unionism: Alabama Coal Miners, 1878–1921* (Chapel Hill: University of North Carolina Press, 1998); and Eric Arnesen, *Waterfront Workers of New Orleans: Race, Class, and Politics, 1863–1923,* (New York: Oxford University Press, 1991).

36. On the Alabama Sharecroppers' Union, see Robin D. G. Kelly, *Hammer and Hoe: Alabama Communists during the Great Depression* (Chapel Hill: University of North Carolina Press, 1990). See also Thrasher and Wise, "Southern Tenant Farmers' Union," p. 20.

37. Howard Kester, "Ceremony of the Land," January 14, 1937, STFU Papers, box 7.

38. Ibid.

39. Grubbs, *Cry from the Cotton,* 63; Mark D. Naison, "Black Agrarian Radicalism in the Great Depression: The Threads of a Lost Tradition," *Journal of Ethnic Studies* 1 (1973): 47–65.

40. Thrasher and Wise, "Southern Tenant Farmers' Union," p. 29.

41. Ibid., p. 8.

42. Mitchell, *Mean Things Happening,* p. 81; Grubbs, *Cry from the Cotton,* pp. 84–85.

43. Thrasher and Wise, "Southern Tenant Farmers' Union," pp. 25–26.

44. Mitchell, *Mean Things Happening,* pp. 82–83; Grubbs, *Cry from the Cotton,* pp. 84–85.

45. Ibid.

46. Grubbs, *Cry from the Cotton,* pp. 86–87; Mitchell, *Mean Things Happening,* p. 87.

47. Grubbs, *Cry from the Cotton,* pp. 88–89.

48. Ibid., pp. 90–91, 100.

49. Ibid., pp. 91–92.

50. C. T. Atkinson et al., "Special Report on Strike Area in Eastern Arkansas," June 1936; A. G. Albright to J. M. Futrell, June 20, 1936, both in Futrell Papers, folder 431, located in the Arkansas History Commission, Little Rock, Ark. (hereafter cited as Futrell Papers). See also H. C. Malcom to McKinley, May 21, 1936, Futrell Papers, folder 434; *New York Times,* June 7, 1936, TCF, 52:0902.

51. Charles Flemming to J. M. Futrell, June 9, 1936, Futrell Papers, folder 432.

52. Grubbs, *Cry from the Cotton,* p. 102.

53. Ibid., pp. 102–104.
54. Mitchell, *Mean Things Happening,* pp. 87–92.
55. *New York Times,* November 26, 1936, TCF, 51:0791; *Memphis Commercial Appeal,* November 25, 1936, TCF, 51:0789.
56. *Memphis Commercial Appeal,* November 26, 1936, TCF, 51:0790; *New York Times,* November 26, 1936, TCF, 51:0791.
57. Testimony Taken in the Case of Negro Tenants and Sharecroppers Located in Tents in the Vicinity of Parkin, Arkansas, February 27, 1936, Futrell Papers, folder 431.
58. *Memphis Commercial Appeal,* February 29, 1936.
59. J. M. Futrell to Joseph P. Robinson, March 10, 1936, Futrell Papers, folder 434.
60. Joseph P. Robinson to J. M. Futrell, March 22, 1936, Futrell Papers, folder 434.
61. *Memphis Commercial Appeal,* March 12, 1935, TCF, 48:0958.
62. Ibid., May 26, 1935, TCF, 48:0958.
63. F. Raymond Daniell, "AAA Piles Misery on Sharecroppers," *New York Times,* April 15, 1935, TCF, 48:0965.
64. Union Members in Heth to H. L. Mitchell, February 20, 1936, STFU Papers, box 2; *Memphis Commercial Appeal,* March 7, 1935.
65. J. C. Brookfield to J. R. Butler, July 23, 1936; Roger Baldwin to J. M. Futrell, July 8, 1936, STFU Papers, box 4.
66. H. L. Mitchell to Norman Thomas, February 2 and February 15, 1936, box 2; Mary Lee Moore to H. L. Mitchell, May 23, 1936, box 3; Bob Miller to H. L. Mitchell, July 20, 1936, box 4; STFU Sample Cases, April 5, 1936, box 5, all in STFU Papers.
67. *Kansas City Call,* July 3, 1937, TCF, 54:0541.
68. News Release, May 28, 1937, STFU Papers, box 8.
69. William Tucker to J. R. Butler, October 26, 1937, STFU Papers, box 10; *Memphis Commercial Appeal,* May 28, 1937; Sam Barnes to H. L. Mitchell, August 28, 29, 1937; Barnes to Ray Wilson, October 15, 1937, STFU Papers, box 9.
70. *Memphis Commercial Appeal,* November 1, 1938, and October 9, 1938, TCF, 58:0511; Statement of Walter Biggs, October 13, 1937, and Statement of Jesse Rose, October 13, 1937, STFU Papers, reel 5.
71. STFU Press Release, October 2, 1937, STFU Papers, box 9; Brien McMahon to J .R. Butler, December 6, 1937, and Fred Isgrig to J. R. Butler, November 13, 1937, both in STFU Papers, reel 5.
72. Statement of Melvin Swinea, October 11, 1937, STFU Papers, reel 5.
73. Memo on Johnson Case, June 1939, and Louis Johnson to J. R. Butler, June 7, 1939, both in STFU Papers, reel 11.
74. Sample Cases, September 4–5, 1936, STFU Papers, box 5; J. F. Hynds to J. R. Butler, May 10 and May 13 1937, STFU Papers, reel 4.

75. Zero Mumford to J. R. Butler, April 27, 1940, STFU Papers, reel 14; STFU Organizers' Report, July 17, 1939, STFU Papers, reel 13.

76. Statement of Claude B. Cistrunk, April 4, 1940; Local 15 to J. R. Butler, March 26, 1940; Butler to Robert H. Jackson, March 28, 1940, all in STFU Papers, reel 14.

77. Oscar Johnston to FCSDA, April 6, 1936, in Oscar Johnston, General Correspondence, Delta and Pine Land Company Papers, Mitchell Memorial Library, Mississippi State University, Starkville.

78. Oscar Johnston to Clay East and H. L. Mitchell, February 20, 1934, in Oscar Johnston, General Correspondence.

79. Document dated May 4, 1937, in Oscar Johnston, General Correspondence.

80. F. R. Betton to J. R. Butler, November 17, 1939, STFU Papers, reel 13.

81. H. L. Mitchell to Steve Lucas, March 9, 1938, STFU Papers, reel 7.

82. A. J. Hicks to NAACP, April 1937, NAACP Papers, group 1, box G106.

83. Grubbs, *Cry from the Cotton*, pp. 168–169. See Grubbs for a fuller account of these divisions than presented here, especially his discussion of the Missouri Highway Demonstration and the fights it provoked between the two unions and their black members (pp. 180–184).

84. Thrasher and Wise, "Southern Tenant Farmers' Union," p. 28.

85. Grubbs, *Cry from the Cotton*, p. 184; Official Proceedings of the National Negro Congress, 1936, Chicago, in *The FBI file on the National Negro Congress* (Wilmington, Del.: Scholarly Resources, 1987), reel 1, box 1; Michael Honey, *Southern Labor and Black Civil Rights: Organizing Memphis Workers* (Urbana: University of Illinois Press, 1993).

86. Thrasher and Wise, "Southern Tenant Farmers' Union," p. 28.

87. Neil Foley, *The White Source: Mexicans, Blacks, and Poor Whites in Texas Cotton Culture* (Berkeley: University of California Press, 1997), p. 200.

88. Sidney Baldwin, *Poverty and Politics: The Rise and Fall of the Farm Security Administration* (Chapel Hill: University of North Carolina Press, 1968); Pete Daniel, *Breaking the Land*; Donald Holley, *Uncle Sam's Farmers: The New Deal Communities in the Lower Mississippi Valley* (Urbana: University of Illinois Press, 1975).

89. H. B. Brown to H. A. Wallace, September 4, 1938, RG145, AAA, entry 1, box 86; Powell Willis to H. L. Mitchell, June 10, 1936, STFU Papers, box 4. Those seeking to vote were W. M. Chapton, Will Rolly, Lendon Wafford, George Taylor, George Austin, Isham Rodgers, S. W. Austin, Joe Reeds, H. G. Guy, Mike Richons, Ed Freemon, W. C. Cummings, Mr. Davis, William Smith, Walter Hampson, Mary Baker, Will Pippin, and Willie Smith. See Affadavit, John Winson, October 25, 1937, STFU Papers, reel 5, and H. L. Mitchell to Walter White, July 18, 1941, STFU Papers, box 34. W. C. Cummings was listed on a complaint protesting the seizure of this land. See "Complaint," October 14, 1941, STFU Papers, box 36.

90. Mitchell, *Mean Things Happening*, p. 182, and Grubbs, *Cry from the Cotton*, p. 187.

6. A War within a War

1. Patricia Sullivan, *Days of Hope: Race and Democracy in the New Deal Era* (Chapel Hill: University of North Carolina Press, 1996); Michael Honey, *Southern Labor and Black Civil Rights: Organizing Memphis Workers* (Urbana: University of Illinois Press, 1993); John Egerton, *Speak Now against the Day: The Generation before the Civil Rights Movement in the South* (New York: Knopf, 1994).

2. James C. Cobb, *The Most Southern Place on Earth: The Mississippi Delta and the Roots of Southern Identity* (New York: Oxford University Press, 1992), p. 198.

3. Ibid., p. 197.

4. Fred Young to Walter Sillers, Jr., January 18, 1943, Sillers Papers, box 29; Greenville, Mississippi, Wage Hearings, August 22, 1945, p. 49, and Cleveland, Mississippi, Wage Hearings, August 23, 1946, p. 72, both in RG 224, Office of Labor, War Food Administration, Wage Stabilization Program, Cotton, Mississippi, National Archives, College Park, Md. (hereafter cited as Wage Hearings, with town of hearing).

5. *Delta Farm Press,* January 1, 1945.

6. Wage Hearings, Indianola, August 22, 1946, p. 26; Wage Hearings, Greenville, August 22, 1946, p. 37; Wage Hearings, Greenwood, August 22, 1945, p. 125; *Delta Farm Press,* April 6, 1944.

7. Oscar Johnston to Forrest Cooper, July 15, 1942, in Oscar Johnston, General Correspondence, Delta and Pine Land Company Papers, Mitchell Memorial Library, Mississippi State University, Starkville.

8. Wage Hearings, Indianola, August 22, 1946, p. 31.

9. Crop Settlement Complaints, Sally B. Love, 1945, STFU Papers, box 57; Lee Dora Bryson to H. L. Mitchell, December 1, 1943, STFU Papers, box 46.

10. H. N. Williams to H. L. Mitchell, June 14, 1943, STFU Papers, box 45; G. W. Mitcher to White House, May 18, 1943, RG 224, Office of Labor, General Correspondence, box 17, National Archives, College Park, Md. Both the STFU and the Office of Labor received numerous complaints of planter abuse in the Delta.

11. Case Report, STFU Legal Services Department, August 1942, STFU Papers, box 40. See also Charlie Vallance to Franklin D. Roosevelt, June 19, 1943, RG 224, Office of Labor, General Correspondence, box 16.

12. O. C. Morgan to H. L. Mitchell, December 19, 1942, box 41, and L. Williams to Mitchell, August 23, 1942, box 45, both in STFU Papers. See also Lula Jackson to NAACP, February 9, 1941; Secretary and officers of Panola, Mississippi, Branch of NAACP to NAACP, June 2, 1941; and F. Marshall to Tommie Knox, February 24, 1941, all in NAACP Papers, group 2, box A525.

13. Art Landers to J. R. Butler, February 9, 1941, box 32; Lewis Thompson to

H. L. Mitchell, July 30, 1943, box 45; Mitchell to Leon Henderson, May 19, 1942, box 39; Case Report, STFU, August 1942, box 40; *Jesse Carson v. W. E. Fallas,* 1945, box 52; STFU Press Release, January 20, 1945, box 53, all in STFU Papers.

14. Case Report, Legal Services Department, July and August 1942, box 40; see also J. E. Hynds to James P. Davis, April 25, 1942, box 39. All in STFU Papers.

15. *Birmingham Southern News Alamanac,* April 3, 1941, TCF, 71:0445.

16. *Atlanta Daily World,* April 23, 1942, TCF, 76:0973.

17. *Birmingham Southern News Advocate,* March 27 and April 3, 1941, TCF, 71:0045–46.

18. Ibid.

19. *Kansas City (Mo.) Call,* October 17, 1941; *Pittsburgh Courier,* October 18, 1941, both in TCF, 73:0595.

20. *Philadelphia Tribune,* May 8, 1943, TCF, 82:0966.

21. H. L. Mitchell to Lester B. Granger, June 21, 1943, box 45; Mitchell to Elmira Porter, November 6, 1942, box 41; Mitchell to Land Workers Bulletin, 1953, box 69, all in STFU Papers. See also Mitchell's conversation with Patterson, the Arkansas State Director of Employment Service, November 25, 1942, box 41, and the letters submitted by Mitchell describing the plight of these workers once they reached their destinations in Mitchell, "Statement Submitted to the Senate Committee on Agriculture," 1943, STFU Papers, box 44. For a discussion of the Farm Labor Program, see Nan Elizabeth Woodruff, "Pick or Fight: The Emergency Farm Labor Program in the Arkansas and Mississippi Deltas during World War II," *Agricultural History* 64 (1990): 74–85; Cindy Hahamovitch, *The Fruits of Their Labor: Atlantic Coast Farmworkers and the Making of Migrant Poverty, 1870–1945* (Chapel Hill: University of North Carolina Press, 1997).

22. A number of works exist on the reaction of southern politicians and planters to labor unions, civil rights organizations, and social legislation. See Egerton, *Speak Now against the Day;* Cobb, *Most Southern Place;* and Sitkoff, *A New Deal for Blacks: The Emergence of Civil Rights as a National Issue; The Depression Decade* (New York: Oxford University Press, 1978).

23. Radio Talk by Dorothy Lee Black, March 10, 1943, folder A-1, Delta Council Files of B. F. Smith, Delta Council Headquarters, Stoneville, Miss. Smith, the former executive secretary of the council, kindly allowed me to see his files, though I was not allowed to see the files of the council. The Delta Council was formed in 1935 as the Delta Chamber of Commerce to promote levee construction and economic development of the region. Reorganized in 1938 as the Delta Council, it added to its goals the reform of the plantation system to retain labor and to combat labor unions and civil rights advocates. For more on the council and its relationship to labor relations and the plantation in the 1940s, see Nan Elizabeth Woodruff, "Mississippi Delta Planters

and Debates over Mechanization, Labor, and Civil Rights in the 1940s," *Journal of Southern History* 60, no.2 (May 1994): 263–284.

24. Dorothy Lee Black to Walter Sillers, Jr., January 1, 1943, Sillers Papers, box 29.

25. Dorothy Lee Black to Walter Sillers, Jr., November 12, 1942; Black to Sillers, February 9, 1943; Sillers to Black, February 10, 1943, all in Sillers Papers, box 29.

26. Dorothy Lee Black to Walter Sillers, Jr., January 1 and March 13, 1943, Sillers Papers, box 29.

27. Walter Sillers, Jr., to Archie Toler, February 15, 1943, Sillers Papers, box 29.

28. Walter Sillers, Jr., to H. R. Adams, July 31, 1942, Sillers Papers, box 15.

29. H. L. Mitchell to Will Alexander, April 1, 1942, STFU Papers, box 39.

30. Ibid.; *McGehee (Ark.) Times,* April 29, 1943. The six Mississippi Delta counties were Bolivar, Coahoma, Quitman, Sunflower, Tunica, and Washington; see H. L. Mitchell, "The Farm Bureau in the South," April 17, 1942, STFU Papers, box 39.

31. Mitchell, "Farm Bureau in the South"; see also Affidavit of John Alford, March 3, 1942, STFU Papers, box 39.

32. *Memphis Commercial Appeal,* April 6, 1943; for the FSA role in the farm labor program, see Otey M. Scruggs, "The Bracero Program under the Farm Security Administration, 1942–1943," *Labor History* 3 (Spring 1962): 149–168. See also Arthur J. Holmaas, *Agricultural Wage Stabilization during World War II,* BAE Agricultural Monograph 1 (Washington, D.C.: Bureau of Agricultural Economics, 1950).

33. Scruggs, "Bracero Program," pp. 161–163.

34. Holmaas, *Agricultural Wage Stabilization,* pp. 3–4. For a discussion of Claude Wickard and the controversies surrounding his administration, see Dean Albertson, *Roosevelt's Farmer: Claude Wickard in the New Deal* (New York: Columbia University Press, 1961).

35. P. F. Williams and Harris Barnes to L. I. Jones, August 4, 1943, RG 224, Office of Labor, General Correspondence, box 59.

36. Holmaas, *Agricultural Wage Stabilization,* p. 23; Scruggs, "Bracero Program," pp. 161–162; Edward L. Schapsmeier, "Farm Policy from FDR to Eisenhower: Southern Democrats and the Politics of Agriculture," *Agricultural History* 53 (January 1979): 361–362. Chester Davis lasted only three months and was replaced by Marvin Jones.

37. For an overview of the farm labor program, see Wayne D. Rasmussen, *A History of the Emergency Farm Labor Supply Program, 1943–47* (Washington, D.C.: Bureau of Agricultural Economics, 1951); Schapsmeier, "Farm Policy from FDR to Eisenhower"; Scruggs, "Bracero Program"; Hahamovitch, *Fruits of Their Labor.* Roosevelt vetoed the Bankhead Bill, which included farm labor costs in parity rates.

38. *Memphis Commercial Appeal,* March 21, 1943; I. F. Stone, "The Farm Bloc

Goes to War," *Nation,* March 27, 1943, pp. 440–441, in Sillers Papers, box 29; Drew Pearson in *Memphis Commercial Appeal,* September 5, 1943.

39. For letters of opposition to the farm bill, see Luigi Antonio to Franklin D. Roosevelt, April 21, 1943; James G. Patterson to Roosevelt, April 21, 1943; H. A. Freeman to Roosevelt, May 3, 1943; and H. L. Mitchell to Roosevelt, April 17, 1943, all in RG 224, Office of Labor, General Correspondence, box 22. See also Mitchell to Phillip Murray, March 15, 1943, and F. R. Betton to Mr. Chairman and Members of the Committee, March 1943, STFU Papers, box 44.

40. T. G. Standing to Conrad Taeuber, October 5, 1942, RG 83, Bureau of Agricultural Economics (BAE), General Correspondence, Farm Labor, box 241; *Delta Farm Press,* March 30, 1944; Frank McCallister to Victor Rotnem, August 12, 1943; H. L. Mitchell to Rotnem, July 7, 1943, STFU Papers, box 45. Rotnem was in the Civil Rights Division of the Justice Department. See also W. C. Banks to Mitchell, April 3, 1943, STFU Papers, box 44; Says A to NAACP, June 17, 1942, NAACP Papers, group 2, Legal Files, box 71.

41. J. R. Hatchell to H. L. Mitchell, May 11, 1943, STFU Papers, box 44. Twenty-four of those responding said they could not leave until they had finished their sharecrops or their jobs as part-time workers. Legal Case of R. Booker, n.d., STFU Papers, box 52. For Mississippi planters' complaints regarding the union's activities in the Delta, see Governor Paul Johnson to Claude Wickard, April 24, 1943, Office of Labor, General Correspondence, box 16.

42. Arkansas Annual Narrative Report, Farm Labor Program, 1944, RG 33, Records of the Federal Extension Service, Farm Labor Program, National Archives, College Park, Md., (hereafter cited as Federal Extension Service Records), box 11; *Osecola (Ark.) Times,* March 10, 1944; H. L. Mitchell, Conversation with Director Patterson, November 25, 1942, STFU Papers, box 41; Statement of H. L. Mitchell, "The Farm Labor Supply Bill," January 1944, STFU Papers, box 52.

43. Minutes of the Delta Council Special Labor Committee, November 23, 1942, box 14; Walter Sillers, Jr., to Governor Thomas Bailey, January 7, 1945, box 9, both in Sillers Papers.

44. Unsigned and undated petition in Oscar Johnston Papers, General Correspondence; Walter Sillers, Jr., to Governor Thomas Bailey, April 4, 1944, Sillers Papers, box 9.

45. E. P. Leftwich to Oscar Johnston, October 1, 1940; Johnston to Leftwich, October 5, 1940; Johnston to James R. Leavell, September 15 and 24, 1942, Oscar Johnston Papers, General Correspondence.

46. Delta Council Labor Group Meeting, August 5, 1942, Sillers Papers, box 14.

47. W. P. Ketschmar to Walter Sillers, Jr., July 1, 1942; Will Whittington to Sillers, July 2, 1942; W. H. Mounger, Jr., to Will Whittington, June 29, 1942; and "Delta Council Accepts Japanese Evacuees," n.d., all in Sillers

Papers, box 15. On local USES offices, see "Report of Activities, USES, in Cooperation with the Delta Council," 1942, and H. L. Mitchell, "A Plan to Utilize the Agricultural Labor of the South," October 6, 1942, both in STFU Papers, box 41.

48. "Arkansas Annual Narrative Report, Farm Labor Program," 1944, RG 33, Federal Extension Service Records, box 11; "Mississippi, Farm Labor Supervisor's Annual Report," 1943, RG 33, Federal Extension Service Records, box 26.

49. Aubrey D. Gates to Paul McNutt, September 11, 1944, RG 224, Office of Labor, General Correspondence, 4-WP-WZ (Wages); *Delta Farm Press,* June 15, 1944, March 30, 1945; "Mississippi Farm Labor Supervisor's Annual Report."

50. Petition to President Franklin D. Roosevelt from the Wage Labor Conference, September 7, 1942, STFU Papers, box 40.

51. STFU Press Release, n.d. (1943); George W. Hill to Brigadier General Phillip G. Bruton, October 4, 1944; Paul McNutt to Marvin Jones, September 29, 1944, all in STFU Papers, box 46.

52. STFU Press Release, August 23, 1945, STFU Papers, box 55; Oscar Johnston to Tom Linder, February 13, 1945, Sillers Papers, box 27; *Delta Farm Press,* February 13, February 15, February 22, March 1, May 22, June 28, and August 16, 1945.

53. Greenville Wage Hearings, August 23, 1945, p. 108; and Greenwood Wage Hearings, August 27, 1945, p. 7.

54. Delta Council Board of Directors Meeting, July 12, 1945, Sillers Papers, box 29.

55. *Delta Farm Press,* July 19, 1945; H. L. Mitchell to Dorothea Kahn, July 31, 1945, STFU Papers, box 55; Wage Hearings, Tunica, August 24, 1946, p. 28.

56. Wage Hearings, Belzoni, Mississippi, August 21, 1946, p. 61; Greenwood Wage Hearings, August 22, 1945, p. 85; Wage Hearings, Osceola, Arkansas, August 29, 1945, p. 23; Greenwood Wage Hearings, August 23, 1946, pp. 28–29.

57. Wage Hearings, Clarksdale, Mississippi, August 24, 1945, p. 83.

58. Greenville Wage Hearings, August 23, 1945, pp. 71, 78, 79, 91; Belzoni Wage Hearings, August 21, 1946, pp. 11–14, 17, 20, 48; Clarksdale Wage Hearings, August 24, 1946, p. 24; Cleveland Wage Hearings, August 23, 1946, pp. 51–58; STFU Press Release, January 4, 1945, STFU Papers, box 53; *McGehee (Ark.) Times,* November 16, 1944; *Osceola (Ark.) Times,* June 2, 1944.

59. Greenville Wage Hearings, August 23, 1945, p. 116.

60. Greenwood Wage Hearings, August 22, 1945, pp. 127–129.

61. Greenville Wage Hearings, August 23, 1946, p. 67.

62. Wage Hearings, Forrest City, Arkansas, August 30, 1945, pp. 99–102, and Osceola Wage Hearings, August 29, 1945, pp. 101–116; Divisional Farm

Labor Conference, Office of Labor and Extension Service, January 18–20, 1945, RG 224 Office of Labor, General Correspondence, Wage Stabilization Board, Cotton, Mississippi; *Delta Farm Press,* August 22, 1945.

63. STFU Press Release, August 23, 1945, box 55; H. L. Mitchell to K. T. Sutton, September 1945, box 56, both in STFU Papers. For the role of the AAA, see the *Delta Democratic Times,* August 16, 1945; for the role of the extension agents, see the *Delta Farm Press,* August 22, 1945. On voting statistics, see H. L. Mitchell to K. T. Sutton, box 56, STFU Papers, and Wilson R. Buie to Charles F. Brannen, September 19, 1946, RG 224, Office of Labor, General Correspondence, Wage Stabilization Board. For the injunction, see Willard F. Shackleford, James Dantzler, Lee Jones, Leonard Moran, Fred Hampton, and others versus U.S. Department of Agriculture and C. S. Dupree, Chairman, Arkansas, U.S.D.A. Wage Board, STFU Papers, box 56. For reference of elections in commissaries, see Greenwood Wage Hearings, August 22, 1945, p. 34.

64. "An Annual Wage for Farm Labor," September 1946, STFU Papers, box 56. In June of 1945, the USDA reported the average picking wage in Mississippi as $2.50 per hundred pounds, while in many cases workers received higher rates. The average picker gathered 150 pounds daily for five days a week in eight weeks, earning approximately $4.50 per day, $22.50 per week, and $180 for the season. With the $2.10 ceiling, this income was reduced to $3.15, $15.75, and $126, respectively. See H. L. Mitchell to Chester Bowles, February 23, 1946, RG 224, Office of Labor, General Correspondence, Wage Stabilization Board; H. L. Mitchell to Editor of the *Memphis Press Scimitar,* November 7 and November 24, 1945, both in STFU Papers, box 56; *Delta Farm Press,* December 1945–February 1946.

65. Mississippi produced the same ten-year average of bales with one-half million acres less than the 1943–1944 average. See *Delta Farm Press,* January 10, 1946; STFU Press Release, STFU Papers, box 58; Wilson R. Buie to Charles F. Brannen, September 19, 1946, RG 224, Office of Labor, General Correspondence, Wage Stabilization Board; and *Delta Farm Press,* November 28, 1946.

66. Education Policy Meeting, Delta Council, November 11, 1941, Sillers Papers, box 29.

67. Arthur Raper Field Notes, Survey of Coahoma County, Arthur Raper Papers, Southern Historical Collection, University of North Carolina, Chapel Hill.

68. Ibid.

69. Ibid.

70. Ibid.

71. Ibid.

72. Frank Alexander, "Cultural Reconnaissance Survey of Coahoma County, Mississippi," December 1944, RG 83, BAE, General Correspondence, 1941–1946, Farm Population and Rural Welfare, Single County Reconnaissance Surveys, Southeast, box 251.

73. John Kirk, "He Founded a Movement: W. H. Flowers, the Committee on Negro Organizations and the Origins of Black Activism in Arkansas, 1940–1957," in Brian Ward and Tony Badger, eds., *The Making of Martin Luther King and the Civil Rights Movement* (New York: New York University Press, 1996), pp. 31–33.

74. Ibid., pp. 35, 38–39.

75. A number of scholars have stressed the importance of returning veterans in the postwar freedom struggle. See John Dittmer, *Local People: The Struggle for Civil Rights in Mississippi* (Urbana: University of Illinois Press, 1994); Charles M. Payne, *I've Got the Light of Freedom: The Organizing Tradition and the Mississippi Freedom Struggle* (Berkeley: University of California Press, 1995); and Timothy B. Tyson, *Radio Free Dixie: Robert F. Williams and the Roots of Black Power* (Chapel Hill: University of North Carolina Press, 2002).

76. Annie Mae Bankhead, interview with Len Day, December 13, 1974, p. 105. Interview is located in the University of Arkansas at Little Rock Archives.

77. Ibid., p. 106.

78. Ibid., pp. 107–108, 112.

79. *Atlanta Daily World,* December 24, 1940, TCF, 69:0273.

80. *Louisville (Ky.) Courier Journal,* July 29, 1942, TCF, 79:0794.

81. *Chicago Defender,* November 29, 1947, NAACP Papers, group 2, box C10.

82. The account of this election is taken from Dittmer, *Local People,* pp. 1–9, and Steven F. Lawson, *Black Ballots: Voting Rights in the South, 1944–1969* (New York: Columbia University Press, 1976), pp. 100–115.

83. Dittmer, *Local People,* p. 2.

84. *Pittsburgh Courier,* July 13, 1946, TCF, 97:0042.

85. Dittmer, *Local People,* pp. 3–9.

86. *Kansas City (Mo.) Call,* September 10, 1941, TCF, 71:0764.

87. Leonah C. Williams to Ella J. Baker, August 7, 1944; Reverend E. C. Sevier, Dee Gillespie, and Reverend E. C. Jackson to NAACP, April 1946, both in NAACP Papers, group 2, box C10.

88. Untitled clipping, June 12, 1943, TCF, 82:0506.

89. *Kansas City (Mo.) Call,* November 27, 1942, TCF: 77:0978.

90. *Atlanta Daily World,* October 1, 1942, TCF, 77:0143.

91. *Chicago Bee,* January 25, 1942, TCF, 77:0103.

92. *Memphis World,* October 7, 1949, TCF, 108:1011.

93. *Chicago Defender,* October 4, 1947, TCF, 99:0746; *Baltimore (Md.) Afro-American,* March 8, 1949, TCF, 99:0615; *Atlanta Daily World,* September 17, 1942, TCF, 77:0143.

94. *Chicago Defender,* April 13, 1940, TCF, 65:0947.

95. Ibid., March 30, 1940, TCF, 67:0521.

96. W. B. Harper to Hodding Carter, April 10, 1947, Hodding Carter, Jr., Papers, Correspondence, box 2, p. 4, Mitchell Memorial Library, Mississippi State University, Starkville.

97. Pfc. Reuben C. Smith to Theodore Bilbo, September 10, 1945, Bilbo Pa-

pers, M2, Negro Matters, folder 9, box 1066, McCain Archives and Library, University of Southern Mississippi, Hattiesburg.

98. The Voice of the Colored Workers of the Navy Department to Bilbo, n.d., Bilbo Papers, M2, Race Issue, Correspondence, folder 10, box 1085.

99. Private A. Burns to Bilbo, n.d., Bilbo Papers, M2, Negro Matters, folder 11, box 1067.

100. Dittmer, *Local People,* p. 17.

101. John W. Martyn to Bilbo, November 9, 1945, Bilbo Papers, M2, Negro Matters, folder 11, box 1067.

102. Education and Policy Committee, Delta Council, November 11, 1941, box 29; J. W. Bradford to Delta Council, April 2, 1942; J. W. Bradford to Walter Sillers, Jr., April 2, 1943, box 11; and John B. Brunini to Dorothy Lee Black, October 14, 1942, box 29, all in Sillers Papers.

103. Charles W. Wade to Bilbo, June 5, 1943, Bilbo Papers, M2, Race Issue, Correspondence, folder 4, box 1084.

104. Betty Carter to Hodding Carter, August 14, 1944, Carter Papers, box 1.

105. *New York Times,* November 13, 1947, TCF, 99:0906.

106. Rev. A. Reed to NAACP, December 7, 1942; Reed to NAACP, October 25, 1949; Reed to Representative Oren Harris, January 25, 1950; and Reed to Senator John McClellan, January 25, 1950, all in NAACP Papers, group 2, box C8.

107. Walter Sillers, Jr., to James Eastland, November 6, 1950, Sillers Papers, box 24, folder 19. For a fine discussion of the increasing global awareness among southern African Americans, see Tyson, *Radio Free Dixie.*

108. Clipping in Bilbo Papers, Negro Matters, folder 4, box 1066.

109. Oscar Johnston to Lamar Fleming, Jr., May 31, 1943, Oscar Johnston, General Correspondence.

110. Pete Daniel, *Breaking the Land: The Transformation of Cotton, Tobacco, and Race Cultures since 1880* (Urbana: University of Illinois Press, 1985), p. 248.

111. The Youth of the Rural Organizing and Cultural Center, *Minds Stayed on Freedom: The Civil Rights Struggle in the Rural South* (Boulder, Colo.: Westview Press, 1991); For a discussion of Mrs. Hamer's trip to West Africa and its effect on her political consciousness, see Chana Kai Lee, *For Freedom's Sake: The Life of Fannie Lou Hamer* (Urbana: University of Illinois Press, 1999), pp. 103–107.

Acknowledgments

The list of acknowledgments for a book that took this long to write resembles that of an Oscar winner. I am grateful that my expressions of gratitude are not limited to two or three minutes. This endeavor was made possible by a number of superb archivists and librarians. James Rush of the National Archives provided important guidance in the early stages of this project. I also greatly benefited from the warm support of Bobby Roberts, former director of the University of Arkansas at Little Rock Archives; Tom Dillard and Cary Cox of the Butler Center for Arkansas Studies; Michael Dabrishus of the University of Arkansas Special Collections, Fayetteville; Anne S. Wells and Michael Barnes of the Mitchell Memorial Library, Mississippi State University; the late Sammy Crawford of the Delta State University Archives; the staff of the McCain Library and Archives, the University of Southern Mississippi; and David Moltke-Hansen, former director of the Southern Historical Collection at the University of North Carolina, Chapel Hill. I am also grateful to the staffs of the Mississippi Department of Archives and History, the Arkansas History Commission, and the interlibrary loan staff of the University of Pennsylvania.

Several foundations have supported this project. I received fellowships from the American Council for Learned Societies, the American Philosophical Society, and the Smithsonian Postdoctoral Fellowship Program. Other funding came from a Southern Region Education Fund Grant, an American Historical Association Albert Beveridge Grant, a Winthrop Rockefeller Grant, and Penn State's Graduate Research and Development Office.

I was privileged to work for five years with the Delta Teachers' Academy of the former National Faculty. I worked with public school teachers in the several states that make up the Mississippi Delta, an experience that shaped in numerous ways my understanding of the region's history. I wish to thank especially Veronia and Thelma McGee and Dorothy Tillman of Yazoo City, Mississippi; Stella Seals, Olivia Nash, Elea Robertson, and Gloria Phillips of Wilson, Arkansas; Flossie Ware of Memphis, Tennessee; and Mary Herndon of Jackson, Missouri. They kindly shared their memories and understandings of the complex history of the Mississippi Delta. With their help, I interviewed various people in the region. I especially thank Stella Seals for introducing me to the late Mrs. Lucy Oliver. I enjoyed team teaching with Kathi Kern, Dell Upton, Jean Billingsley Brown, Karl Raitz, Ruel Tyson, Michael Friedland, and Martha Vail. I shall always remember the wonderful summer teaching institutes that we shared in the Delta.

I was fortunate to work with Nasheed Madyun, formerly of the Delta Cultural Center in Helena, Arkansas. Nasheed and Arthur Washington kindly introduced me to a number of people in the Elaine region, including the Reverend C. B. Bingham, who took time from his own work to drive me around southern Phillips County and introduce me to descendants of people who had been involved in the Elaine Massacre. Mrs. Ruth Jackson, Mr. Mose Jackson, and Mrs. Gladys Hammond shared their memories of life in the Delta. I wish to also thank Dr. Robert Miller, mayor of Helena, for helping me to identify people with knowledge of the Elaine Massacre and for providing me with a copy of his grandfather's memoir.

I had the privilege during the course of this study of working with two documentary film projects that related to my own work in the Delta. The late Henry Hampton of Blackside Films provided an amazing venue for scholars and activists to meet and work together on important historical and social issues. I shall always value my time spent with Henry and his staff. I was also fortunate to have worked with Richard Wormser as he was developing his four-hour documentary series on African American life in the Jim Crow South. We spent several days in southern Phillips County searching for people knowledgeable of the Elaine Massacre and of African American life in the region. Richard kindly shared the material he had uncovered.

Several friends and colleagues read this work at different stages and offered great personal support. Pete Daniel has continued to serve as the ideal mentor and friend, offering a warm place to stay in Washington and sharing his passionate interest in southern history. Jack Temple Kirby, Harold D. Woodman, and Eugene Genovese have not only read and critiqued this work at different stages, but have also provided encouragement and a generous spirit for which I shall always be grateful. Barbara Fields, Sylvia Frey, Thavolia Glymph, John Higginson, Joseph P. Reidy, and Julie Saville have provided enduring friendship over the years, and they have been my teachers in spite of themselves. My special thanks to Barbara for inviting me to travel with her up the Mississippi River on the Delta Queen. Winston James engaged me in many conversations on twentieth-century African American history and the Red Summer, and Peter Gran shared his broad knowledge of world history and Gramsci. Drew Gilpin Faust kindly provided me with an affiliation at the University of Pennsylvania during an important stage of this project, and Steven Reich shared his work on the timber mill workers of East Texas. I wish also to thank both outside readers of the manuscript for Harvard University Press: Steven Hahn, who identified himself, and the second, anonymous reader, for their strong and helpful critiques of the book.

My colleagues at the Pennsylvania State University have been an amazing community of collegiality and support. My various department heads, Gary W. Gallagher, Sally McMurry, and Gregg Roeber, provided me with the space and time to finish this project on my own terms—an amazing feat given the Taylorite methods of production and management that guide the contemporary university. Mrinalini Sinha kindly read the entire manuscript, helping me to see the global implications of my work. Daniel Letwin also read and critiqued the manuscript. William Blair not only read various drafts of the manuscript, but also generously provided his keen editorial skills. His friendship, along with that of Kum Kum Chatterjee, Alan Derickson, Gary Gallagher, Lori Ginzberg, Thavolia Glymph, Isabel Knight, Joan B. Landes, and Sally McMurry, carried me through some of the most difficult stages of this work and I am deeply indebted to them. I also wish to thank Dan Beaver, Cary Fraser, Amy Greenberg, Paul Harvey, On-Cho Ng, Susan O'Brien, William Pencak, Adam Rome, Guido Ruggiero, Janina Safran, James Sweeney, and the staff members of my department: Ed Dumond, Karen Ebeling, Darla Franks, Lynn Moyer, Linda Neihart, Judy Shawley, and Karen Weaver, for their good-natured support. Gene Foreman, a member of the journalism department at Penn State, read the manuscript and shared with me his vast knowledge of Arkansas history, as well as many other topics. Finally, I wish to thank Joyce Seltzer and David Lobenstine for their encouragement and hard work on this book. Many thanks also to Julie Carlson for her fine copy-editing. It is far better because of their efforts.

I have been fortunate to work with many fine graduate students, some of whom now have their own careers in the field. They have aided me as research assistants and have inspired me with their own fine work. I wish to thank especially Peter Carmichael, Greta deJong, Charles Holden, Arthur Jarvis, Charles Lumpkins, Meredith Lair, Sarah Lawrence, Susan Shirk, Lynn Vacca, and Susan DeWeese. Craig Williams in the Geography Department created the maps for the book.

A number of friends have provided support and escape from the isolation that often defines the world of writing. I wish to thank Sandra Barney, Robin Becker, Mary Ann Blair, Joy Bowman, Clement Hawes, Lisa Henderson, Millie Learn, Joe and Jeanne McGinn, Theodore Norton, Marie Sears, Margaret Spears, Kermit and Hazel Stephenson, and Ann Marie Turnage. I especially thank Nina, Tatayana, Nadia, and Vera Gersenko, and their families, for enriching my life.

My family has endured many absences from important events and holidays. I wish to thank them all for their love and support: my mother, Virginia Parks Woodruff, and father, the late Wallace Green Woodruff; my sister, Angela, and my brothers, Woody, George, and Sam, as well as Kent Lewis, Becky Woodruff, and Julie Woodruff. My niece Caroline Elizabeth, and my nephews—Bowdy, Mercer, Woody, and Zachary—have not been so forgiving, and I look forward to spending more time with them. Melissa Webb Wright has lived with the final stages of this book. She read the entire manuscript, bringing her perspective as a feminist, a geographer, and a fine writer. I am deeply grateful for her understanding, support, and companionship. Finally, I wish to thank Hilda and the late Salvin Silverblatt,

Helene Silverblatt, and Robert Buser, for providing me with their kindness and generosity throughout this project. Irene Silverblatt took time away from her own important work to accompany me on various trips to the Delta. Her keen analytical mind and her insights as an anthropologist broadened my understanding of the South, and her good humor and patience made ordinary travels for research into pleasant excursions. I dedicate this book to her with gratitude and admiration.

Index